ACES OF THE LUFTWAFFE

ACES OF THE LUFTWAFFE

The Jagdflieger in the Second World War

PETER JACOBS

Frontline Books
London

Aces of the Luftwaffe
This edition published in 2014 by Frontline Books,
an imprint of Pen & Sword Books Ltd,
47 Church Street, Barnsley, S. Yorkshire, S70 2AS
www.pen-and-sword.co.uk

Copyright © Peter Jacobs, 2014

The right of Peter Jacobs to be identified as the author of this work
has been asserted by him in accordance with the
Copyright, Designs and Patents Act 1988.

ISBN: 978-1-84832-689-7

CIP data records for this title are available from the British Library

For more information on our books, please visit
www.pen-and-sword.co.uk, email info@frontline-books.com
or write to us at the above address.

Printed and bound by CPI Group (UK) Ltd, Croydon CR0 4YY

Typeset in 10.5/15 pt ITC Slimbach

Contents

Plates

Acknowledgements

Having spent a full career in the Royal Air Force, and having served on a number of the RAF's finest fighter squadrons, I was personally delighted when Michael Leventhal gave me the opportunity to write this book. While I have written many books and articles about the RAF during the Second World War, this gave me an exciting opportunity to take another look at many of those same air campaigns but this time from the opposite end of the telescope and to look at them from the Luftwaffe's perspective. How fascinating it proved to be.

The subject is hardly new to military historians as it has been covered in various formats many times before but I was keen to set each air battle into context so that the reader understands why the Luftwaffe was involved in a specific campaign and why a particular individual was fighting in combat at that time.

Mike Spick covered the topic superbly well in his book *Luftwaffe Fighter Aces*, which he wrote for Greenhill Books nearly twenty years ago, and this proved to be an excellent place to start. I am particularly grateful to Mike for taking the time to go through my work and for providing me with extremely helpful advice on a subject that he has studied for many years.

As my research continued, I was keen to look deeper behind the scenes so that I could understand why the air battles were being fought and also to understand the views and beliefs of some of the Luftwaffe's leaders that were shaping the air war over the many fronts that it fought.

While an increasing amount of information has come into the public domain through being made available online, institutions such as the Bundesarchiv-Militärarchiv at Freiburg and the National Archives at Kew will always remain the repositories of information and illustrations. As a military historian and author, I am so grateful to both organizations for the use of material and illustrations over the years. I am also extremely fortunate to have been allowed privileged access to the Air Historical Branch at RAF Northolt and have spent the last nine years of my service career at the RAF College Cranwell, which boasts one of the finest libraries in the country, and so I am always pleased to be able to offer my thanks to the staff of both the AHB and the RAF College in this way.

Away from the more formal institutions, there are no end of excellent books and publications on the Luftwaffe. Whether the reader is a novice or is someone who has studied the subject in great depth over many years, there are plenty of publications to choose from. Unsurprisingly, many have come from Germany, for example from the highly acclaimed author Jochen Prien, but there are also many others published outside of Germany that have been written by extremely knowledgeable authors who have been fortunate to have access to veterans and archives over many years. These include books written by Theo Boiten, Martin Bowman, Robert Forsyth, Tony Holmes, Eric Mombeek, Simon Parry and Dr Alfred Price to name just a few, but I would like to thank three authors, in particular, who took the time to help me. First of all I would like to thank my colleague Chris Goss, another former RAF officer, who somehow seems to have found the time to write numerous titles on the Luftwaffe over the years. My thanks also go to Donald Caldwell in the United States, another Frontline author who is specifically knowledge-able on JG 26, one of the finest fighter wings, and to John Weal who has written a number of superbly illustrated titles for Osprey Publishing. I consider all three to be experts in their fields and I am extremely grateful to them all for their time, their willingness to help and for providing me with the superb illustrations included in this book. I could not have managed without them. I would also like to thank the reviewers at Frontline for their advice and comments; I have learned so much from them as well.

Finally, I would like to thank Michael, once again, and his team at Frontline Books for the finished product you see today.

Introduction

Conflict has been around for thousands of years but war in the air is just a hundred years old. The Luftwaffe, at the forefront of Hitler's war machine during the Second World War, was in existence for just ten of those years yet it produced some of the greatest names in the history of air combat and produced the highest scoring fighter pilots of all time.

During the Second World War, an Allied fighter pilot was considered to be exceptional if he was credited with thirty or forty victories. Even the top scoring Allied fighter pilot, the Soviet ace Ivan Kozhedub, credited with sixty-two victories, was completely over-shadowed by well over a hundred Luftwaffe pilots, called *Jagdflieger*, who all exceeded his score. If using the generally accepted definition of an ace as being a pilot who achieved five aerial victories, then the Luftwaffe produced aces in the thousands but rather than use the term 'ace', the Luftwaffe used the term '*Experte*' as recognition of proficiency in the air as well as acknowledging the number of victories achieved.

How the Luftwaffe managed to produce so many high-scoring fighter pilots compared to the Allies is often the subject of great debate. Those sceptical about the figures will believe the claims to be highly exaggerated but a fighter pilot may genuinely have believed that he had achieved success, even though it may not have always been possible to confirm the success with evidence. For example, an enemy aircraft may have last been seen descending into cloud emitting smoke and flames or may have crashed into the sea but was unobserved by anyone else, and at night it would often prove impossible to observe the outcome of a quick aerial engagement when attacking large numbers of enemy bombers; the fighter pilot rarely had time to observe the result of his encounter.

The Luftwaffe High Command went to great lengths to verify the success of its pilots, probably more so than any other air force during the Second World War. There was a strict requirement for written confirmation of the kill by the claimant and by at least one other aerial witness plus, if possible, a witness on the ground. As can be imagined, this system created a lot of paperwork, particularly from claimants on the Eastern Front, and in the latter half of the war it was not unusual for a claim to take more than a year to be officially confirmed. When taking all this into account, and even if the historian accepts these high figures to at least be in the right 'ball-park', then the achievements of many Jagdflieger are clearly quite extraordinary.

Unlike many of his Western counterparts, who often received lengthy breaks between stressful front-line operational tours, there was usually no end in sight; he simply carried on throughout the war and either survived, if he was lucky, or was killed or taken as a prisoner of war. There was also a chasm between success on the Eastern Front compared to in the West and other theatres such as the Mediterranean or North Africa. Against the Western Allies only a handful achieved a century of victories whereas in the east more than seventy achieved this feat, with eight going on to surpass 200 and two claiming more than 300 victories.

While these facts could suggest the Red Air Force was less capable than its western Allies, which may well have been true when Germany first invaded the Soviet Union in 1941, this was certainly not the case as the war progressed and the high totals are more a reflection of the vast scale of the air war in the east. The figures do, however, support the fact that the Jagdflieger was better trained than his Russian adversary, certainly up until the later stages of the war, and reflects just how good the *Jagdwaffe* (the fighter arm's) tactics had become. Those who became combat leaders were masters of aerial combat and they also benefitted from having a more capable aircraft. Both the Messerschmitt Bf 109 and the Focke-Wulf FW 190 were far better fighters than anything the Russians initially produced, although it is fair to say that by the end of the war the Soviet fighters were every bit as good as the late-war versions of the Bf 109 and FW 190, but in the end there was little the Jagdwaffe could do to counter the sheer numbers of Red aircraft that he came across over the Eastern Front.

The highest accolade was the award of the Knight's Cross, or Ritterkreuz des Eisernen Kreuzes (Knight's Cross of the Iron Cross) to give it the full and correct name, and 500 Experten received such recognition. Its award was generally based on the number of victories achieved, although the qualifying number varied enormously as the war progressed and often differed between operational theatres. In the early months of the war, twenty victories would usually merit the award whereas towards the end of the war, for example on the Eastern Front, a hundred victories may have been required to receive the same recognition. For those achieving further success there was the award of the Oak Leaves (Eichenlaub) to the Knight's Cross and even greater success was rewarded by the Swords (Schwertern) with the ultimate award of the Diamonds (Brillanten) being reserved only for the very best. Only nine ever received the highest recognition and it can be no coincidence that of the twenty-seven members of the German forces to receive this ultimate recognition, the first five recipients of the Diamonds were all Jagdflieger.

For the convenience of the reader, I have used the English term of Knight's Cross with the associated Oak Leaves, Swords and Diamonds where applicable rather than using the German Ritterkreuz mit Eichenlaub, Schwertern und Brillanten. I have, however, kept to German terminology in a number of areas, such as for Luftwaffe organization – where I have used Geschwader, Gruppe and Staffel rather than their English-language equivalents – and used the appropriate ranks throughout. A glossary at the end of the book and the appropriate appendices, which cover the English equivalents of ranks and unit organizations, will assist the reader. I have also used the accepted abbreviated term of 'Bf' (short for Bayerische Flugzeugwerke) when referring to the earlier Messerschmitt fighters – like the Bf 109 and Bf 110 – and have only changed to 'Me' for later designs – for example the Me 163 and Me 262 – to be consistent with German terminology used at the time.

The story of the Jagdflieger is a quite staggering one. When considering the number of air battles fought across all the operational theatres during the Second World War, particularly on the Eastern Front where the sheer scale of the air fighting was immense, it makes it all but impossible to capture the story under one cover. A book of this size and covering such a vast subject can only ever be just the tip of the iceberg and it has simply not been possible to dwell too long in any one particular area or on any one specific unit or individual. Anyone wishing to study a particular campaign, unit or individual in more depth may well find that other authors have already covered those specific areas of interest in far more detail. But a book on this subject would clearly be lacking if it failed to mention the exploits of some of the finest, such as Erich Hartmann, the highest scoring fighter pilot of all time, Hans-Joachim Marseille, the 'Star of Africa', Werner Mölders, the first recipient of the coveted Diamonds, and Adolf Galland, perhaps the most famous of them all. Otherwise, given the vast subject, deciding what to include or not include was down to personal preference but I was keen to ensure that all the major campaigns were covered to some extent to provide an understanding of the air war being fought.

Because there is so much that could have been written, I have resisted the temptation simply to repeat a number of exploits that may have appeared somewhat similar and, therefore, rather repetitive to the reader but have chosen instead to give examples of some of the aerial actions that took place and, where it helps to better inform the reader, have provided a simple background behind the air battles that were being fought. When appropriate, I have also described some of the tactics adopted by a number of the high-scoring Jagdflieger to achieve their great success.

There were many other challenges to overcome when writing this book and these included having to smooth out the inevitable variations between sources, as well as deciding which of two different spellings of names to use and having to translate German words into English. Ultimately, though, I had to choose the spelling of one word over another variation, which will be equally correct, in order to be consistent but if I have made any errors through my failure to grasp the German language then I can only apologize in advance. Other significant challenges included trying to piece together the movements of fighter units and individuals between the operational theatres as the war progressed. For this reason, I have chosen to tell the story by operational theatre but keeping within the chronology of the Second World War as much as possible to make it easier for the reader to follow and to put the air campaign of each operational theatre into the overall context of the war.

Unfortunately, there is not the space to cover the personal lives of these men other than brief mentions here and there. While some were die-hard Nazis, others were far from it. Some came from noble families with a long tradition of military service, whereas others were sons of humble farmers or coal miners who rose to prominence through their own natural abilities. Some clearly hunted for glory whereas others did not. Individually they were quite different but collectively they formed a most potent fighting force.

Finally, while the highest-scoring Experten have rightly earned their place in this book, I have also included many others who did not survive the last days of the Reich or score highly enough to become household names but were no less courageous. Only space prevents me from writing more. I hope you enjoy the book.

Peter Jacobs

Chapter 1

Fledgling Days

In time of war a nation needs its heroes and the fighter pilot has always held a fascination that has captured the imagination of his public at home. The first fighter aces appeared over the Western Front during the First World War and, ever since, history has tended to judge the fighter pilot by the number of victories achieved in the air rather than by flying skills or leadership in combat. But these qualities often go hand-in-hand. A pilot with few flying skills was unlikely to survive for very long, let alone become an ace, and those who led in combat were often best placed to influence an aerial encounter and to achieve success in the air.

Those destined to be successful in air combat soon learned that it was not all about dashing around the sky as fast as possible taking on anyone and everyone – those who elected to choose this method were destined not to survive – but they did require a unique combination of flying and personal qualities to succeed: excellent aircraft-handling skills; a good understanding of his own aircraft's performance and that of his opponent; quick reactions; good eyesight; anticipation; patience; courage and self-control to name but a few and, of course, they needed to be good shots.

The air campaigns fought by the Luftwaffe on all fronts during the Second World War, and specifically those fought by the fighter pilot, the Jagdflieger, were amongst the most intense in the history of air warfare but what stands out most is the number of aerial victories achieved by the high-scoring fighter pilots, the *Experten*, who totally eclipsed their Allied counterparts.

The successes of German air power did not come overnight and while it could be argued that its origins lie with its infancy during the First World War, the Luftwaffe was born following Adolf Hitler's rise to power. Although the Treaty of Versailles was still in effect, and had restricted Germany's construction of new aircraft types, the treaty had never been meticulously observed and Germany's interest in aviation had gone from strength to strength with various clandestine methods of training aviators in Russia and a number of undercover air squadrons being set up in Germany. While the strength and capabilities of these squadrons did not amount to much, their existence, particularly as far as trained pilots was concerned, provided a nucleus for the creation of a new and powerful air force.

On achieving power Hitler appointed Hermann Göring, a highly respected fighter pilot of the First World War, as deputy leader of his Nationalsozialistische Deutsche Arbeiter Partei (the Nazi Party) and Reichskommissariat für die Luftfahrt (Reich Commissioner of Aviation). The official formation of the Luftwaffe was still two years away but Göring, as Hitler's deputy, had many responsibilities and so had little time for building a new air force. The task, therefore, was left to Erhard Milch, the former Commercial Director of Germany's national airline Lufthansa and now Göring's own deputy as the Nazis' first State Secretary for Aviation.

More so than Göring, Milch deserves the credit for the initial formation of the Luftwaffe, although he never held any great respect for Göring. Milch set about his task by dividing the Reich Aviation Ministry, the Reichsluftfahrtministerium (RLM), into a number of offices. The most important sub-division was the Air Command Office, as this would effectively become the General Staff, and he also set about expanding the German aviation industry and building new facilities for the training of aircrew, albeit secretly, to create a new air force.[1]

The Luftwaffe officially came into existence on 1 March 1935 with some 20,000 personnel and nearly 2,000 aircraft. It was never going to be possible to keep the build-up of an air force secret and so the following week Hitler announced its existence to the world and a week later he renounced the military clauses of the Treaty of Versailles. Selected to be its first Chief of the General Staff was Walter Wever, an infantry officer by background but a man of great vision and a great strategist. Aware of Hitler's intentions, Wever was led to conclude that Germany's main enemy in any future conflict would be the Soviet Union. His thinking, therefore, was to produce an air force to take on the might of Russia while concurrently waging a war of revenge against France and possibly Britain. He was also astute enough to know that air superiority would probably be an elusive goal and so he believed it would be easier to defeat an air force on the ground at its sources, by attacking aircraft factories and industrial plants, rather than to try and defeat it in the air. His desire was for a bomber force capable of reaching the heart of Russia's industrial cities and beyond, and so his concept of a four-engine strategic aircraft, known as the Ural Bomber, led to the design and construction of two prototypes.

Amongst Wever's other strengths was his ability to work with and manage the expectations of difficult men such as Göring and Milch. He found them both, at times, equally difficult. Göring seemingly had little time for the new Luftwaffe while Milch had risen to the top very quickly, with Wever believing that his military rank of General der Flieger had been given rather than earned.

Wever's limited experience as a pilot cost him his life in June 1936 when he crashed his Heinkel He 70 during take-off. He was replaced by Albert Kesselring, a strong supporter of Hitler and the Nazi regime but another high-ranking officer without any aviation combat experience. Crucially, Kesselring decided to cancel development of the Ural Bomber because of its cost in raw materials to build[2] and because of its high fuel consumption, which he felt Germany could ill afford given its lack of oil resource. While Kesselring cannot solely be held to blame for this decision, the Luftwaffe would now never have an effective long-range strategic bomber during the Second World War.

The loss of Wever had created a further problem as Kesselring and Milch seemed unable to get on. Göring could have dealt with the matter but chose not to and the internal wrangling would never really go away. Kesselring would later resign to be replaced by the extremely bright Hans-Jürgen Stumpff as Göring continued to make further changes to the hierarchy, seemingly not for the better, as aircraft and armament production fell behind. Hitler now made the Luftwaffe's expansion programme a priority as it transitioned towards a new generation of aircraft with the emphasis being on large numbers to impress Hitler who, in turn, wanted to impress the world.

Despite the continuing wrangles at the higher levels, the Jagdflieger prepared for hostilities that would inevitably come. The teaching was based on perfecting basic fighter manoeuvres, consisting of various turns and rolls, to position the fighter pilot behind his opponent. One of the earliest manoeuvres taught was the barrel roll in which an aircraft makes a complete rotation on its longitudinal axis while following a helical path and maintaining its general direction and height.

While pure flying skills would help a pilot learn how to master his aircraft in the sky, it was not the only important factor in learning how to become a good fighter pilot. Additional factors such as his aircraft's design, specifically its speed and ability to turn hard, were vital. The faster the aircraft then the greater the radius of turn and the less its rate of turn became in degrees per second. The ability to turn hard in combat also depended on the aircraft's wing loading and where all other factors were equal, the pilot flying the aircraft with the lower wing loading would be able to out-turn his opponent. However, hard manoeuvring would reduce the aircraft's speed. Speed could be maintained by losing height but height was also important because an aircraft with height advantage could be hard to see and height could always be turned into speed, either to reduce the range to the target or to help make an escape.

The easiest way to shoot down an opponent was to get line astern of the target, where there would be little or no deflection, and where a pilot could manage his closing speed to give him the maximum time possible to shoot an opponent down. The closer he could get then the easier it would be to hit his opponent whereas firing at excessive range meant the bullets were subject to the effects of ballistics, such as gravity drop, and a heavily manoeuvring target would be harder to hit because of the amount of lead required in the aim.

As far as a defending pilot was concerned, it was all a matter of whether he could see his attacker; if not, he could not react and often stood little chance. Once seen by his opponent, the attacking pilot could then have the problem of having too much speed, particularly if attacking from a higher position. If too fast, the attacker could not maintain a position inside a turn and would overshoot to the outside, and once the attacker was forced to overshoot then the defender had the opportunity to reverse his direction of turn back towards his opponent. This would often lead to a series of turn-reversals, known as scissors, with each pilot trying to get on to the tail of his opponent. A pilot could elect to keep his speed higher than his opponent so that he could change direction during a reversal by rolling more quickly. However, it was not advisable for a pilot in an aircraft with lesser performance than his opponent to generate a scissors manoeuvre in combat because his opponent would eventually force him out ahead, thereby gaining the opportunity to bring his guns to bear. Any speed advantage over an opponent also gave a pilot the option to pull up and convert his excess speed into height, then use aileron to turn in the desired direction and then to pull out and roll the aircraft upright in a manoeuvre known as the Immelmann Turn (named after the First World War pilot, Max Immelmann, who had created the manoeuvre), so that he could reposition himself without too much horizontal displacement or dive away and disengage from the fight.

There was much to learn but the low engine power of aircraft during the 1930s and the design techniques at the time restricted the number of offensive manoeuvres that could be carried out. There was also the fact that the fighter tactics being taught were still based on those adopted during the First World War as many instructors were often quick to exert authority based on their own experiences many years before. These included men like Theo Osterkamp with thirty-two victories from the First World War who would become the first commander of Jagdfliegerschule 1, one of seven fighter pilot schools eventually established, although the Luftwaffe was not alone in this ideology as many European air forces were doing the same.

The Luftwaffe was given the opportunity to test its capabilities in a combat arena when the Spanish Civil War broke out in 1936. The war between the Nationalists and the Republicans had started when dissatisfied Spanish generals, led by the pro-Fascist General Francisco Franco, launched a coup against the Spanish government in Madrid. The attempt only achieved limited success and so Franco appealed to Hitler and the Italian leader, Benito Mussolini, for help.[3]

Luftwaffe fighter units were asked for volunteers to join an expeditionary force and the first batch included a cadre of six fighter pilots to fly the Heinkel He 51 biplanes sent to Spain.[4] The volunteers were not authorized to enter combat and so the pilots took on a training role but as Soviet support to the Republican cause increased, Milch and, to a lesser extent, Göring were in favour of providing Franco with more support. Hitler agreed and so activated the Legion Condor, led by Hugo Sperrle. More He 51s bearing Spanish Nationalist insignia followed and by the end of the year thousands of men and tons of equipment had been shipped to Spain with a fighter group, Jagdgruppe 88 (J./88), being established under the command of Hauptmann Hubertus Merhardt von Bernegg.

Those who volunteered for Spain were very capable pilots but they soon found they were up against a stronger force, both technically and numerically, with the He 51 biplane proving inferior to the Soviet Polikarpov fighters; the I-16, in particular, as a monoplane design was arguably the most modern and most capable fighter in the world at that time. The Jagdflieger quickly learned that he could not afford to become fixated on his own target but instead had to observe the overall situation and assess the risks, while maintaining a three-dimensional awareness of what was going on around him, and all while flying in a highly dynamic and changing environment.

Although the He 51 was technically inferior to the Soviet fighters, Sperrle did have the better quality pilots who quickly developed new tactics. One of those pilots was Oberleutnant Adolf Galland who arrived in Spain during the early summer of 1937. Galland was twenty-five years old and already an experienced pilot having gained previous flying experience prior to joining the Luftwaffe. Now leading the third Staffel of J./88 based at the Valencia-Ebro front, Galland displayed a unique style of leadership. He quickly proved to be an inspirational leader and a great analyst by paying particular attention to the tactics being employed and then analysing the results of each mission before adapting his tactics for future missions.

As far as countering the Soviet fighters was concerned, one of the most successful tactics employed by the Legion's pilots was to ensure they had superior numbers. This not only offered tactical advantage but also caused the Russian fighter pilots to increase their fuel consumption and eventually forced them to land. Then, once they were back on the ground, the Legion's bombers, which would be airborne in the vicinity, would attack the Russian fighters on the ground. While this tactic offered some success, the fact remained that the Luftwaffe's fighter force, the Jagdwaffe, was equipped with biplanes that were little better than the fighters of the First World War.

The ongoing conflict in Spain provided the ideal opportunity to introduce the new fighter, the Messerschmitt Bf 109, into combat. The 109 had first flown in 1935 but design had begun in secrecy the year before to meet a future requirement for a single-seat daytime fighter armed with machine guns that was capable of reaching an operational ceiling of 33,000 feet, with an endurance of an hour, and was also capable of maintaining a speed of 250 mph for up to twenty minutes at 20,000 feet. The new aircraft-design techniques included a semi-monocoque fuselage with an enclosed cockpit and cantilever wings with a retractable undercarriage. The aircraft initially produced by Messer-schmitt was designated the Bf 108, a quite different aircraft, but many of its design features were included in the prototype for the Bf 109. Its advanced wing, with slots and trailing edge flaps, gave it an unmatched manoeuvrability.

The Bf 109 was introduced into service in 1937 and soon started to equip J./88 in Spain. Powered by a Junkers Jumo 210 engine, the Bf 109B represented the cutting edge of aircraft technology. Armed with two MG 17 7.9 mm machine guns its introduction proved to be an immediate success and the Bf 109B quickly proved to be a better fighter than the I-16. However, the build-up of numbers of 109s in Spain was slow and so the pilots of J./88 had to improvise. Instead of adopting a formation of three aircraft, called a Kette, the 109 pilots chose to base their tactics on a two-aircraft formation, called a Rotte, to give more flexibility.

The balance of air power in Spain soon tipped in favour of the Legion. The campaign also taught valuable lessons about other aircraft, such as discovering that the Ju 52 was unsuitable as a bomber. To be fair, the Ju 52 was never intended to be used as bomber, and was only ever considered as a stopgap, but its lack of performance in the role simply emphasised the urgency of replacing it with the new Heinkel He 111 twin-engine medium bomber and the single-engine Junkers Ju 87 Stuka dive bomber. The Legion also learned the value of close air support for ground forces as the capabilities of the Ju 87 won over some of its hardest critics, although its vulnerability to modern fighters would become evident later. The Heinkel He 46 and He 70 were also found to be unsuitable as reconnaissance aircraft and this led to the Dornier Do 17, which also had the capability to operate as a long range bomber.

With the successful introduction of the Bf 109, the He 51 was gradually withdrawn as a fighter but it did continue for the time being in the ground-attack role. By the end of 1937, J./88 had established air superiority over the battlefield. Since April the first Staffel had been commanded by Oberleutnant Harro Harder and by the time he returned to Germany in December, to be replaced by Wolfgang Schellmann, he had scored eleven victories during the year, for which he would later be awarded the Spanish Cross in Gold with Swords and Diamonds, the highest award for the campaign. Schellmann, too, would do well, outscoring his predecessor by one victory during his nine months in Spain, for which he would receive the same recognition. During the same period the second Staffel had been led by Oberleutnant Günther Lützow, who achieved five victories during the year, including the first recorded by a Bf 109, before he was replaced in September by Joachim Schlichting who would also go on to achieve five victories during his nine months in Spain. Both Lützow and Schlichting would later receive the highest recognition.

Small numbers of Messerschmitts were now able to roam over the front line and pounce on any enemy bombers before they could even reach their targets. The early Bf 109B did suffer from limited capability when escorting bombers, and so lessons identified in Spain led to the improved Bf 109C and Bf 109D with improved performance and armament, although these variants would not arrive in Spain until the following year.

Techniques continued to evolve in Spain but one young pilot, more than any other, helped to shape the tactics that would later bring the Jagdwaffe so much success during the opening months of the Second World War. Although he did not arrive in Spain until the spring of 1938, Werner Mölders would go on to become the Legion's leading fighter ace of the Spanish Civil War with fourteen victories. When he arrived in Spain he was twenty-five years old and already an experienced pilot. Mölders was assigned to the third Staffel under the command of Adolf Galland at a time when the ageing He 51s were being replaced by the new Bf 109. Galland did manage to get ten flights in the new 109 before his tour in Spain came to an end and it impressed him to the point of persuading him that from now on he wanted to fly fighters rather than ground-attack aircraft.

With the departure of Galland, Mölders was given command of the third Staffel and he quickly set about re-shaping some of the Luftwaffe's fighter tactics for the 109 that he believed would work well in Spain. These included development of the classic Schwarm of four fighters, a formation in the shape of the extended fingers of a hand, comprising of a pair of Rotten with the lead aircraft of each Rotte flying ahead of his wingman, known as his Katschmarek, who was positioned about 200 yards behind the leader with the task of protecting his tail. Each Rotte could either work independently or they could work together depending on the mission and threat. This not only gave the formation complete freedom to manoeuvre but it also meant that the pilots were able to concentrate on looking out for the enemy rather than the Katschmarek having to concentrate on maintaining close formation with his leader.

When operating as a Schwarm, the pair of Rotten would often be staggered in height with the second Rotte taking up a position higher and on the opposite side to the sun to increase the chances of spotting an aggressor by using the sun to their own advantage. The next step was soon adopted by using one large formation of three Schwärme; either in line abreast, stepped up in line astern or in a swept formation. But even operating as a Schwarm was not without its problems, mainly caused by the large frontage of the formation that could easily be in excess of 500 yards, as the task of manoeuvring was not always easy. Any sizeable heading change would cause the outermost aircraft to lag considerably behind its leader, even when allowing for changes in throttle settings between the leader, who would have to throttle back, and the outside man at full throttle. The solution was the cross-turn, a manoeuvre first used by the Royal Air Force at the end of the First World War, when the outside man pulled up and crossed over his leader onto the new heading and was then followed by his colleagues in sequence from the outside inwards; this ended with the Schwarm on its new heading and its formation intact with the members of the formation on the opposite side to that previously held.

Mölders claimed his first victory in Spain, an I-15, on 15 July 1938. Within four days he had taken his score to three, having added another I-15 and an I-16, and by October his total was thirteen. His tactics had worked well and had enabled other young pilots, such as Horst Tietzen and Wolfgang Lippert, to develop under his command; both achieved success during the same period with seven and five victories respectively. Mölders was promoted to Hauptmann in October, after which he claimed his fourteenth and final victory of the campaign – an I-16 near Molar on 3 November – before he returned to Germany the following month to develop fighter tactics within the RLM in Berlin.

The Spanish Civil War ended in March 1939 when Republican resistance collapsed and the government finally surrendered to Franco. The Legion Condor, nearly 20,000 strong, had made a significant contribution towards Franco's success in Spain and had demonstrated the vital importance of air power in supporting any land campaign. It had unleashed the Luftwaffe in a combat arena for three years and the war had proved invaluable for the development of new fighter tactics and formations.

The visionary tactician, Werner Mölders, and the inspirational combat leader, Adolf Galland, were two of just twenty-eight members of the Legion to receive the Spanish Cross in Gold with Swords and Diamonds, the highest recognition for the campaign; eleven of them had served with J./88, including two men who would go on to achieve greater success during the Second World War – Leutnant Walter Oesau, who flew with the Stab of J./88 and scored nine victories, and Oberfeldwebel Reinhard Seiler who flew with the 2. Staffel and also scored nine victories.

In addition to those receiving the highest recognition, the campaign in Spain helped some 200 Jagdflieger receive their baptism of fire. By the end of the Spanish Civil War the Legion had accounted for nearly 400 aerial victories for the loss of seventy-two of its own aircraft. More importantly though, personnel had gained valuable experience of operating in conflict, particularly at night, and much had been learned about the technical aspects of the new Bf 109, He 111, Do 17 and Ju 87. The Legion also found that well-armed bombers could defend themselves against enemy fighters during daylight operations and most within the Luftwaffe's senior ranks believed that close air support was the key to success; this led to further development of the role after Spain, although it would be at the expense of adopting a strategic role for air power and this would ultimately contribute to Germany's defeat in the Second World War. But for now, the campaign in Spain had enabled the Luftwaffe to gain a significant advantage over its potential foes in Europe.

The Luftwaffe was now expanding rapidly. There were already more than 600 Bf 109s in service – a mix of B, C and D variants. However, the new He 111 bombers entering service had priority on the supply of Daimler-Benz engines, rather than them going to the fighters, and this delayed the introduction of the latest fighter variant, the Bf 109E 'Emil', until early 1939 when it arrived for the final days in Spain.

The Emil was the first major re-design of the Bf 109 and would become the first mass-produced variant. It quickly proved to be an excellent fighter with unmatched performance in the climb with its engine, the improved DB 601A, featuring variable-speed supercharging and the introduction of fuel-injection rather than using a carburettor. This would give the 109 pilot a huge advantage during air-to-air combat as fuel could still be fed to the engine during manoeuvres of 'negative-g' by being injected; under the previous design of using a carburettor the fuel flow was often starved and could cause the engine to cut out.

The Bf 109E was an excellent aircraft to fly in terms of its handling qualities at slow and medium speeds, where it was responsive and lacked any tendency to spin, but it did take some getting used to when manoeuvring at higher speeds; this was due to the heaviness of the controls and the lack of a rudder trimmer, which meant the pilot was constantly required to apply rudder when flying straight at high speed. However, when operating on and near the ground, the 109E was described by many of its pilots as rather unforgiving. It could be a difficult aircraft to manage during take-off and landing because of its narrow track and less than robust undercarriage design, and because of the torque produced by the power of its engine.

Although the Luftwaffe had continued to struggle to sort out its higher levels of command, it did sort out its combat units at the tactical level and the structure put in place would remain essentially unchanged throughout the Second World War. The largest fighting unit, the Geschwader, consisted of a hundred or more aircraft. These were effectively wings with aircraft of the same type and role, and were designated accordingly; a Jagdgeschwader was a fighter wing and a Kampfgeschwader a bomber wing, with each given a number, for example Jagdgeschwader 1 (abbreviated to JG 1) and Kampfgeschwader 51 (KG 51).

The commander of each Geschwader, the Geschwaderkommodore, varied in rank from Major to Oberst. The Geschwader was sub-divided into three or four Gruppen (groups), with each Gruppe consisting of approximately thirty aircraft and commanded by a Gruppenkommandeur typically at one rank lower than the Kommodore, with an additional staff flight called a Stab. Gruppen were allocated roman numerals, for example the third Gruppe of JG 1 was designated III./JG 1, and each Gruppe was further sub-divided into typically three Staffeln (similar to squadrons) with each given an arabic designation; for example, the second Staffel of JG 26 was designated 2./JG 26.

Notwithstanding the lack of a strategic bomber, which, incidentally, no air force in Europe possessed in 1939, the Luftwaffe would enter the Second World War with an impressive array of aircraft, both in terms of capability and numbers, with some 3,000 aircraft, of which two-thirds were allocated to the Eastern Front. The He 111 would remain at the centre of the bombing campaign throughout the war but while it had been considered virtually invincible when it first rolled off the production line in 1937 the reality would soon prove different. The other mainstream medium bomber, the Do 17, could also be used as a long-range reconnaissance aircraft and a newer aircraft, the twin-engine Junkers Ju 88, was now appearing. The Ju 88 had originally been intended to be a long-range bomber but changes to its design, brought about because of the desire also to employ the aircraft as a dive bomber, led to an increase in its weight and this, in turn, would impact on its range, speed and handling. Completing the bomber force were the Ju 87 dive bombers that had performed so well in Spain.

As for the fighters, twenty-eight Jagdgruppen were equipped with the Bf 109, ranging from the earliest B variant to the most advanced Emil. The 109 would prove to be the Luftwaffe's most important fighter during the early years of the war but if it had a weakness at all it was its limited endurance, which meant it lacked the ability to escort bombers over long distances. As the concept had been for medium bombers to defend themselves, this gap in capability would have to be managed by the twin-engine Messerschmitt Bf 110 Zerstörer, which had been designed for long-range escort and was now available in considerable numbers.

Powered by two DB 600 engines, the Bf 110 was a heavily armed aircraft with a battery of two MG FF 20 mm cannon plus four MG 17 7.9 mm machine guns mounted in the nose. A second crew member managed the radio communications and acted as the rear gunner, although all the aircraft had to protect its rear was a single MG 15 7.9 mm machine gun. As more DB 601s became available this engine was preferred for later variants, making the 110 capable of 330 mph at 20,000 feet and giving the aircraft a ceiling in excess of 32,000 feet but its size and weight meant it was far less manoeuvrable and slower to accelerate than the 109.

While new aircraft appeared in large numbers, the previously territorial nature of the Luftwaffe's organization meant that its structure was not suitable for highly mobile operations in the future and so it re-organized into four Luftflotten, each consisting of a mix of fighters and bombers, with the emphasis being on a lightning war of speed, rather than a war of attrition. There were further high-level changes as the Luftwaffe was re-organized yet again during 1939. Hans Jeschonnek succeeded Stumpff as Chief of the General Staff, but Jeschonnek was arrogant and short-sighted and did not get on well with Milch. Jeschonnek also struggled to get on with many of Göring's closest associates, none of whom seemed to like either Jeschonnek or Milch, and so Jeschonnek's appointment only added to the fragmentation that had been a long time coming in the highest levels of command.

As Germany approached war in Europe, Göring seemingly did not have the ability to lead the enormously expanded Luftwaffe and Milch had become isolated from the centre of power while other key leaders, such as Jeschonnek and Kesselring, did not have the strategic insight of Wever.[5] The Luftwaffe was simply reacting to the day-to-day political pressures from Hitler but Jeschonnek, as a strong supporter of the

Führer, believed that Hitler could achieve his political and military objectives in Europe without waging war against Britain. Jeschonnek had not particularly planned for a war against Britain, because few believed that Britain would be as bold as to declare war on Germany, but he was preparing for war on a large scale as Germany had already annexed and occupied both Austria and Czechoslovakia.

The fragmentation that had developed between the most senior commanders may well have resulted in Hitler entering the Second World War unaware that the Luftwaffe had any weakness at all. How much Jeschonnek consulted with Göring and how much Göring chose to share with Hitler is unclear. If Göring did perceive there to be any concerns, and if he did share those with his Führer, then Hitler clearly decided to ignore them. Equally, it may well be that all three saw the Luftwaffe as a war machine of the greatest military strength and none saw any weaknesses at all but the fact remains that it entered the Second World War ready to commit its resources to a tactical conflict rather than a strategic one.

Chapter 2

Blitzkrieg

To Hitler's senior military commanders, the true gravity of the situation in Europe did not become apparent until a matter of days before Germany's planned invasion of Poland, which finally took place during the early hours of 1 September 1939. Hitler had categorically forbidden any action in the west because he knew that the French Army would outnumber Germany's forces on that front while he concentrated on the east and the invasion of Poland. The plan for the attack on Poland, essentially a pincer movement involving Army Group North and Army Group South, was to see an invasion on a huge scale with more than a million soldiers on the ground supported by 1,300 aircraft, nearly 70 per cent of which were bombers.

The Luftwaffe was initially tasked with destroying the three opposing Polish air divisions on the ground, by a series of attacks against airfields, after which it would support the Army; Luftflotte 1, commanded by Albert Kesselring, was to support Army Group North, while Alexander Löhr's Luftflotte 4 would support Army Group South.[6]

The Polish Air Force consisted of less than a thousand aircraft with a large number being obsolete types. The Poles lacked any centralized command and control for their air assets, and the wide dispersal of the 150 or so fighters available meant that Poland's major cities and key industrial areas were poorly defended with only fifty fighters available to defend Warsaw.

Not only did the Polish Air Force lack quantity but it also lacked quality. Its main fighter aircraft, the PZL P.11, was outdated and would prove no match for the Bf 109, of which more than 150 would be used by Luftflotten 1 and 4 during the campaign. The Poles had, however, seen war coming and their precautionary aircraft dispersal plan, while not ideal, meant that their assets were not located at the main airfields but were instead tactically dispersed around a hundred temporary locations. This in itself led to communications issues, which in turn would cause the Poles huge command and control problems but, contrary to popular belief, the Luftwaffe would be unable to destroy the Polish air divisions in just a matter of hours.

Early morning fog on the opening day of the invasion disrupted the German plan considerably, particularly in the northern part of Poland where most of the Luftwaffe's air power was concentrated. Few of Kesselring's combat units could get airborne at the right time and so the large-scale and synchronized all-out air assault could not take place, and it would not be until the weather improved during the afternoon that Luftflotte 1 could commit more forces. The weather was slightly better in the south, allowing Löhr's units to operate much as planned and there were many successful raids against Polish airfields and ground installations.

The first air-to-air combat occurred when some thirty P.7 and P.11 fighters of the Polish Pursuit Brigade intercepted a force of nearly a hundred He 111s of Luftflotte 1 attacking an airfield at Okęcie near Warsaw. The He 111s were being escorted by Bf 110s of I(Z)./LG I, led by Major Walter Grabmann, which were slow to react but eventually the Zerstörer pilots accounted for at least two of the Polish fighters.[7] The Bf 110s were in action again later in the day but this time performed considerably better against the same opposition and accounted for five Polish fighters, although Grabmann was wounded during the encounter when his aircraft was hit by a P.11.

The lack of a cohesive defence by the Poles had meant that only half of the Luftwaffe's combat missions on the first day had encountered the Polish Air Force. The rest had been flown in direct support of the Army on the ground and so the most noticeable successes of the first day of fighting belonged to the close air support units.

The following day the Bf 110 pilots learnt the harsh lesson of why not to stay and enter combat with the more agile P.11. Even though the Zerstörer pilots had a numerical advantage of some three to one, six P.11 pilots were able to put up a most credible performance and shoot down three of the Bf 110s, although two of the P.11s were also destroyed.

After the second day of fighting, Kesselring was left to conclude that the Polish Air Force had been only partially neutralized. Nonetheless, he was satisfied that the Poles had effectively been paralysed as a result of the speed of the campaign.[8] From now on operational sorties in support of the ground forces would be given his highest priority with most of the bomber-escort missions being flown by the Bf 110s, leaving the Bf 109s to operate at shorter range. Kesselring was now able to transfer some of his units to Löhr's air fleet in the south to support the main advance on Warsaw, after which Luftflotte 1 would gradually phase out of the battle.

Hitler had clearly not reckoned with Britain and France fulfilling their guarantee of Poland's sovereignty, and on 3 September Britain and France declared war on Germany. A British Expeditionary Force was sent to France along with a token force of RAF aircraft, including army co-operation Blenheim and Battle light bombers, and four Hurricane fighter squadrons.

Although there was little in the way of action undertaken by Allied forces on the ground, there were early aerial clashes over France and Germany. Göring now became increasingly anxious about Germany's western borders and within days transferred more fighter units to the protection of its interior. Meanwhile, in Poland, the land battle was starting to reach its climax as the Polish capital came increasingly under attack with Warsaw eventually falling; Poland's last sporadic resistance ended on 6 October. The campaign had lasted just thirty-six days during which the Polish Army of more than a million men had been annihilated.

The close air support tactics that had been perfected in Spain had now been vindicated on a much larger scale. Furthermore, the Luftwaffe had lost fewer than 300 aircraft during the Polish campaign and had emerged from it in total glory, justifiably so as this was the first time in the history of air warfare that an independent air force had played such a decisive role in a land campaign. The speed of the campaign had meant that Britain and France were unable to provide any military assistance to Poland, leaving the Polish fighter pilots, in their inadequate aircraft, to face the might of the Luftwaffe, although many Poles had performed well. They had proved skilful in aircraft handling, often making them difficult to shoot down, and their aircraft's dark camouflage scheme made them difficult to see when at low level where they blended in with the natural terrain and woodland of Poland.

The skill and courage of the Polish pilots provided an early reminder there were harsh battles to be won. Furthermore, many Polish airmen would manage to escape their homeland and make their way across Europe to continue their fight against the Nazis. Ultimately, though, while the Polish P.11 pilots did enjoy some successes in the air, accounting for more than half of the losses suffered by the Luftwaffe, they were no match against the overwhelming superiority faced.

The brief campaign in Poland had seen the two latest variants of the Bf 109 perform very well. The Bf 109D, with a maximum speed of more than 320 mph and a greater rate of climb and higher ceiling than previous models, retained the armament of four MG 17 machine guns (two mounted in the nose and one in each wing) as an attempt to fit a 20 mm cannon that was capable of firing through the propeller hub had, at that time, proved unsuccessful. The Bf 109E, with the improved DB 601 engine, had an even greater performance and was capable of 350 mph at 12,000 feet and boasted an initial rate of climb of more than 3,000 feet per minute and a service ceiling of over 34,000 feet. It had retained the two nose-mounted machine guns but the wing-mounted machine guns were replaced by an MG FF 20 mm cannon in each wing to give the aircraft a great increase in firepower.

The tactics used by the Luftwaffe in Poland had proved most successful. They were often based on either the dive and zoom tactic or high-speed slashing attacks. The idea of staying and entering combat with the opposition was resisted and the campaign also saw the decoy tactic being successfully employed. The idea was that one aircraft would fly alone and look vulnerable to the opposition but this lone aircraft was protected from above. Any attempt by the opposition to get on to the tail of the decoy was acted upon immediately by the rest of the formation who would quickly swoop on the attacker.

The top scoring fighter pilot of the campaign was Hauptmann Hannes Gentzen, the Kommandeur of Jagdgruppe 102 equipped with Bf 109Ds. Gentzen was the only pilot to achieve more than five victories during the campaign, eventually being credited with seven (five bombers and two fighters), but many other 109 pilots scored their first successes during the campaign, including Leutnant Gustav Rödel of 2./JG 21, Leutnant Hans Philipp of I./JG 76, Feldwebel Erwin Clausen and Feldwebel Friedrich Geisshardt, both of I(J)./LG 2. A number of Bf 110 pilots also achieved success in Poland including Oberleutnant Gordon Gollob of 3./ZG 76 and Hauptmann Wolfgang Falck who led 2./ZG 76. But despite the successes in Poland, the Bf 109 had only played a peripheral part in the campaign as it had essentially been held back by the High Command in case British and French bombers carried out retaliatory attacks against German cities.

While the Luftwaffe's leadership basked in the glory of their overwhelming victory, there remained deficiencies in their strategies and in the training methodologies, which had all come about because of the rapid build-up for war when the emphasis had been on quantity rather than quality. Full of confidence from his success against Poland, Hitler now turned his attention to the west and by November the aerial clashes on the Western Front had intensified.

With more than a thousand combat aircraft, the French Armée de l'Air looked impressive in terms of numbers but its force was unbalanced in terms of capability with fewer than 500 modern single-engine fighters available. The French had two main fighter types. One was the Morane Saulnier MS.406, a fairly agile fighter and capable of speeds of up to 300 mph. Although its speed and rate of climb were inferior to the Bf 109, its wing loading was comparable and in the hands of the right pilot the MS.406 would prove to be a very capable adversary for the Bf 109D or even the Bf 109E. The other French fighter, the American-built Curtiss Hawk 75, would perform even better against the Bf 109 because its rate of climb and overall handling qualities were better than the MS.406 and its wing loading was lower than the Bf 109. Again, in the hands of a good pilot, the Hawk 75 would prove to be far more capable than some of the Luftwaffe pilots had been led to believe.

An example of how hard the French pilots resisted occurred on 9 November when Bf 109Ds of JGr 102, led by Hannes Gentzen, attacked a French reconnaissance aircraft being escorted by nine Hawk 75s over the Maginot and Siegfried Lines. Despite everything being in Gentzen's favour as he led the 109s into attack, including height and numerical advantage, the French pilots had spotted their attackers and fought back fiercely with four Bf 109s being shot down and another four forced to land; only one Hawk 75 was damaged.

Not all encounters would turn out this way but it did teach some harsh lessons. Although the 109s had entered the fight with a clear advantage, there may have been a degree of arrogance amongst the pilots and rather than taking on their French opponents in a turning fight they may have been better off sticking to the less risky dive and zoom tactic.

The Luftwaffe's first fighter-to-fighter encounter with the Royal Air Force is believed to have taken place on 22 December when Bf 109s of III./JG 53 encountered a number of Hurricanes. Two Hurricanes were shot down, one of which was claimed by Werner Mölders. Again the 109 pilots had been happy to enter a turning fight against their opponents rather than adopting the dive and zoom tactic, which would more likely have resulted in greater success.

The performance of the Hurricane made it a match for the Bf 109, but the RAF's tactics during the early days of the Second World War had been based on engaging large numbers of unescorted German bombers flying in close formation, rather than being based on how best to counter a formation of modern fighters. The British assumption had always been that any attack would be made from bases in Germany and that the enemy fighters would not have the range to provide any escort. The likelihood of Germany acquiring bases closer to Britain had not been seriously considered and this concept had led to the RAF developing just three main fighter tactics, all of which involved a number of fighters attacking a single bomber; either from line astern or line abreast, or for three fighters to attack a single bomber simultaneously from the rear and beam. All three tactics relied on the bomber not carrying out any evading manoeuvres, which had been presumed most likely given there was little difference between the top speed of the bombers and fighters at the time, but these somewhat rigid tactics meant that the RAF fighter pilots had to spend more time worrying about their own positioning and formation, rather than looking out for the Luftwaffe.

With poor weather during much of the winter of 1939–40, the air war on the Western Front had produced little more than a few skirmishes with both sides now locked into what became known as the Phoney War, or *Sitzkrieg* (sitting down war). There were, however, encounters over north-west Europe during this period, particularly over the northern corner of the Franco-German border where Allied reconnaissance aircraft often ventured, and a number of future *Experten* opened their accounts during the winter months. These included Rolf Pingel, Hans von Hahn, Heinz Bär, Anton Hackl, Max Stotz, Wolf-Dietrich Wilcke, Joachim Müncheberg and Erich Leie; all would later go on to exceed a century of victories during the war.

Keen to make a further move in Europe, Hitler launched his offensive against Norway and Denmark, called Operation Weserübung, during the early hours of 9 April 1940 under the pretence of protecting Denmark's and Norway's neutrality against Franco-British aggression. Denmark was overrun in just a matter of hours, although the invasion of Norway proved far more difficult. Britain and French forces intervened but the Luftwaffe's X. Fliegerkorps – which specialized in coastal operations and consisted of more than 250 bombers and a hundred fighters under the command Hans Ferdinand Geisler – played a decisive role in the occupation of Norway, which was completed in early June when the British evacuated their forces at Narvik.

The extended period of inactivity on the Western Front had given France valuable time to prepare for war and two new fighter types entered service during the early months of 1940. The better of the two was the Dewoitine D.520 with a top speed of 330 mph and an operational ceiling of 33,000 feet, and the second was the Bloch MB.152 with similar performance. Most of the fighters were based in the northern and eastern parts of France but the French air-defence system was generally ineffective. It relied on a series of observer posts using telephone to communicate to the command centres; there were only a handful of mobile radio direction-finding sets, later known as radar, located in France during early 1940.

Rumours in France of a German invasion were now rife while in Germany Göring and his senior commanders had every reason to be full of confidence. The Luftwaffe now possessed more than 5,000 aircraft (a thousand more than at the outbreak of the war), including more than 1,700 bombers and 1,600 fighters. Kesselring, now in command of Luftflotte 2, had just over 800 fighters; 630 Bf 109Es (serving with JG 1, 2, 3, 20, 21, 26, 27, 51, TrGr 186 and LG 2), thirty Bf 109Ds of JG 2 and 145 Bf 110C/Ds of ZG 1 and 26. Of similar strength was Luftflotte 3, led by Hugo Sperrle, with 775 fighters; 600 Bf 109Es (JG 2, 51, 52, 53, 54, 76 and 77) and 175 Bf 110C/Ds (ZG 2, 26, 52, 76 and LG 1).[9]

With more than 3,000 modern combat aircraft available to Luftflotten 2 and 3, and with Germany's proven successes in Spain and Poland, only modest resistance from Allied fighters, the majority of which were considered inferior to the Bf 109, was expected over north-west Europe. Nonetheless, almost all of the Luftwaffe's fighters were brought together for Hitler's new offensive against France and the Low Countries with twenty-seven Jagdgruppen moving forward to airfields along Germany's western border.

The plan was based on speed and simultaneous assaults on Germany's neighbouring countries in the west. In the north, Army Group B would invade the Netherlands and Belgium to draw the Allies into believing that this was the main attack, while Army Group A would deliver the main blow through the Ardennes and Luxembourg to by-pass the Maginot Line, France's most valuable line of defence. The plan would open up the whole of northern France to the advancing German Army but it clearly violated the neutrality of Belgium and the Nether-lands with neither country having a modern air force. The Aeronautique Militaire Belge, the air component of the Belgian military, was equipped with fewer than 200 aircraft, of which the vast majority were obsolete biplanes, and the Nederlandse Militaire Luchtvaart, the air division of the Royal Netherlands Army, was a small indigenous force of less than a hundred aircraft of various types, none of which could be considered very capable.

Just as in Poland, the Luftwaffe would support the Army. Kesselring and Sperrle were assured that the British, French, Belgian and Dutch air forces could amass little more than a thousand fighters and a thousand bombers between them. Even allowing for the British providing another thousand aircraft from their bases in southern England, the High Command was extremely confident and would focus fighter operations on preventing the Allied air forces from hindering the offensive by destroying key targets such as bridges over the various rivers to slow down the rapid advance by the German Panzers.

The calm and uncertainty of the Phoney War came to a sudden end during the early hours of 10 May 1940 when Germany invaded France and the Low Countries. More than 300 He 111s and Do 17s of Luftflotte 2 carried out a series of devastating attacks against twenty enemy airfields, while German airborne forces and fast-moving armoured columns advanced into Holland and Belgium. The opening day was all about the speed of the German advance and the success of the Luftwaffe's bombers against Allied airfields and major lines of communication such as roads and rail centres. By the end of the first day the Dutch and Belgian air forces had effectively been eliminated and the French and British forces had suffered considerably. Aerial activity had mainly involved Allied fighters intercepting German bombers, with many claims being made on both sides, but there had been no air-to-air combat of note between fighters on the opening day.

The following day saw more attacks against airfields in northern France as the RAF committed more fighters from southern England. The Luftwaffe now commenced a more tactical campaign, for which it was best trained and equipped, with the first significant air-to-air combat with Allied fighters as the Messerschmitts entered the fray. Over Belgium and northern France the Bf 109s of III./JG 1 and Bf 110s of II./ZG 1 were patrolling the Albert Canal and Maastricht area at first light and gained an early success when they spotted RAF Blenheims carrying out a reconnaissance patrol of the area; four Blenheims were shot down. There were further successes for the Bf 109s of I./JG 1 and I./JG 27 while engaging nine Belgian Battles tasked with attacking the bridges over the Albert Canal. The Battles were escorted by six Gladiators but they were no match for the 109s; six Battles and four Gladiators were shot down.

The second day had started well for the Luftwaffe as its Messerschmitts carried out numerous strafing attacks against Allied airfields in Belgium and northern France, achievinging the destruction of many Allied aircraft on the ground. But there were already ominous signs for the Bf 110 when pitched against a very capable opponent such as the Hurricane. One example was during a mid-afternoon encounter over Mourmelon when RAF Hurricanes intercepted a force of thirty He 111s escorted by Bf 110s of I./ZG 2. The initial interception was carried out by three Hurricanes but they were soon joined by seven more, and then even more Hurricanes joined in having been patrolling in the area; four of the Bf 110s were shot down, as were two of the He 111s, for the loss of just one Hurricane.

Later that afternoon, Bf 109s of I./JG 51 were patrolling the area from The Hague to Rotterdam when they spotted twelve Hurricanes. Having gained the early advantage, the 109s attacked the Hurricanes from high and line astern but once they had been spotted one of the Hurricane sections was able to react. The fight lasted several minutes and resulted in five Hurricanes being shot down for the loss of three 109s. Two of the Hurricanes were claimed by Leutnant Ernst Terry, two by Oberleutnant Heinrich Krafft and the other by Unteroffizier Franz Schild.

In the early evening the French Armée de l'Air carried out its first bombing mission of the war against strategically important bridges. The raid was carried out by twelve LeO 451 medium bombers that were being escorted by eighteen MS.406s but the formation was intercepted by Bf 109s of I./JG 1. During the fierce fighting that followed, the French fighter pilots fought bravely and the encounter ended up even, with a handful of victories claimed on both sides.

It had been a hard day of aerial fighting with the Bf 109s generally causing havoc amongst the Allies. Until that day very few Allied pilots had experienced air combat and persisted in flying around in formations that proved unwieldy in combat with there being several cases where the 109s managed to carry out attacks unseen. The Jagdflieger had an excellent aircraft, he had been well trained and his tactics were fluid and flexible enough to react to the dynamism of aerial combat.

While the Allied fighter pilots suffered against the Bf 109s, they continued to enjoy success against the bombers and Bf 110s. The Bf 110 Zerstörer pilots were now fully aware of their vulnerability to the Allied single-seat fighters and had to adopt more defensive tactics, the main one being to form a defensive circle so that the rear of each aircraft was protected by the guns from the aircraft behind it.[10] The large circle, often more than a mile in diameter, gave the 110 a commanding position in the sky and made it difficult for the Allied pilots to attack while it retained the option for the Zerstörer pilot to counter-attack should the opportunity arise. Even if the 110s chose to remain in a defensive circle during any lengthy engagement, the Allied pilots could never take their eyes off the Zerstörers for one moment and so the Bf 110s were often able to influence an aerial exchange indirectly.

While this tactic did offer some protection, particularly if the circle was kept from becoming too large, it did not prevent an attack from above or from the beam but this in itself caused the Allied pilots some difficulty because they were now presented with higher deflection angles that required a greater degree of accuracy on the part of the attacker. The key moment would come when the Zerstörers had to break from their defensive circle and this would often provide the Allied fighter pilot with an opportunity to pick off any stragglers. The Zerstörer pilot had also learned to zoom into a near vertical climb to enable his gunner to shoot at a pursuing fighter. Although this technique made it extremely hard for the gunner to try and hit an attacking fighter, it also gave the attacker a problem; any return fire from the Bf 110 would occupy the attacking pilot's mind and give the Zerstörer a chance to make its escape, particularly if there was any cloud cover above.

The speed and strength of the German advance on the ground resulted in the capture of the main bridges over the River Maas and the Albert Canal, allowing two Panzer divisions to cross into Belgium. The Germans were determined to hold the bridges and allocated Bf 109Es of JG 27 to protect them. In one encounter over Maastricht on 12 May, nine Blenheims were intercepted by two Gruppen of 109s from JG 1, led by Hauptmann Joachim Schlichting, Kommandeur of I./JG 1 and a veteran of the Legion Condor. Six Blenheims were shot down and the third Gruppe of JG 1, which had been patrolling over Liége, accounted for two more as the Blenheims attempted to make an escape.

An indication of the achievements enjoyed by the Messerschmitts that day was that of JG 27, which had flown nearly 350 sorties and claimed twenty-eight victories for the loss of just four of its own Bf 109Es. One pilot to enjoy success that day was Hauptmann Adolf Galland. After serving with the Legion Condor, Galland had returned to Germany in 1938 where he was employed in the RLM writing technical manuals and devising doctrine based on his experience as a ground-attack pilot in Spain; these ideas were later developed for dive-bomber tactics used by the Ju 87 Stuka. During the early days of the Second World War he flew the Henschel Hs 123 biplane but having briefly flown the Bf 109 in Spain he had remained determined to become a fighter pilot and had now been given his chance as the operations staff officer of JG 27.

While serving with JG 27, Galland had been able to meet up again with Werner Mölders, now Kommandeur of III./JG 53, and Mölders offered him the opportunity to fly with his unit to gain experience of the Bf 109E. These sorties proved invaluable for Galland and he quickly learned new tactics such as giving a Staffel the freedom to operate as an effective unit so that it could seize the initiative by using a single spotter aircraft to mark the position of an enemy formation; a visual type of early warning system. On occasions Galland was given the opportunity to act as Gruppenkommandeur and he quickly gained even further experience as a combat leader. He was even able to pass on new tactics to his own Kommodore of JG 27, Max Ibel, who agreed to adopt Galland's ideas.

During the morning of 12 May, Galland was flying with his wingman, Leutnant Gustav Rödel. While patrolling to the west of Liége at just over 12,000 feet Galland spotted eight Hurricanes about 3,000 feet below. The Hurricanes were escorting Blenheim bombers tasked with attacking bridges in Holland. As the Bf 109s had not been spotted, Galland immediately attacked from an advantageous position of high and astern. As he pressed home his attack he found himself willing his opponent to defend himself, almost hoping that someone would warn him, but the Hurricane took no evasive action. Galland's first burst was fired from too great a range but at last the Hurricane pilot reacted, although his avoiding action only succeeded in taking the Hurricane towards Rödel who now made his attack. With the other Hurricanes making off in all directions, Galland pressed home a second attack and the Hurricane was seen spinning down with its rudder missing and parts of the wing breaking off. Galland knew that the Hurricane was finished and decided against wasting any more ammunition and went off instead to look for another. One tried to escape by diving but Galland was soon on its tail and closing at a distance of just a hundred yards. The Hurricane was seen entering a half-roll into some cloud as Galland attacked again from very close quarters at a height of 1,500 feet. The Hurricane zoomed for a second, then stalled and dived vertically into the ground.

Both Hurricanes had crashed to the north of Liége and had there have been more Bf 109s on the scene at the time then the outcome could have been even worse for the Hurricanes. It had been a classic attack by Galland and Rödel, who had used height and the sun to gain their advantage, enabling them to carry out their attack unseen. Galland claimed his third victory later that day and would go on to achieve twelve victories during the battle for France.

One young pilot to score his first success of the war during the opening days of the French campaign was 22-year-old Leutnant Günther Rall of 8./JG 52. The son of a businessman, Rall had been raised in the Black Forest region of Germany and joined the Army in 1936. Having been persuaded by a friend to transfer to the Luftwaffe, Rall qualified as a pilot in 1938 and joined JG 52. On 12 May 1940 he was amongst a number of Bf 109s escorting a reconnaissance aircraft when it was attacked by three French Hawk 75s that had failed to notice the escorting 109s. Rall was quick to pounce and claimed one of the Hawks. He was understandably delighted to have joined the exclusive list of those who had shot down an enemy aircraft. The first victory could often prove elusive for any fighter pilot and many would never achieve a single victory but Rall would never look back and would go on to become the Luftwaffe's third highest-ranking *Experte* of the war.

Two days later, 14 May, turned out to be a day of heavy air fighting as the Allies fought hard to prevent a German breakthrough of the French defences at Sedan. The Jagdwaffe flew more than 800 sorties during the day and claimed to have shot down ninety British and French aircraft. It had been a good day for the Luftwaffe and would later prove to be its best day of the French campaign, becoming known as *Tag der Jagdflieger* ('Day of the Fighter Pilots').

Amongst the highest achievements that day was five victories by Oberleutnant Hans-Karl Mayer of I./JG 53. Mayer had already experienced air combat during his time with the Legion Condor and was now serving with 1./JG 53. His Staffel had been circling near Sedan during the afternoon at a height of 15,000 feet while waiting for Ju 87 Stukas tasked with bombing French positions around the town when the Bf 109s were attacked from above by six Hurricanes. Followed by his wingman, Leutnant Hans Ohly, Mayer dropped down to protect the Stukas and quickly claimed one of the Hurricanes. Mayer could now see more enemy aircraft and quickly shot down a Fairey Battle, followed by two Blenheims before claiming another Battle just a few minutes later. The day had undoubtedly belonged to the Messerschmitts and had been a disastrous one for the Allies. However, amongst I./JG 53's losses that day was Oberfeldwebel Walter Grimmling who had been credited with JG 53's first victory of the war.

As German forces advanced on the ground, the Jagdgruppen moved forwards and started to occupy Allied airfields in Belgium and northern France. These included some quite austere operating sites that were barely anything more than a farmer's field and the Luftwaffe soon learned the importance of having a good supply line. The advance on the ground had proved so quick that fuel and aircraft supplies could not keep up and this often meant the Messerschmitts were operating on their limits as far as endurance was concerned, and often without sufficient spares.

Nonetheless, the Jagdwaffe was on top as the German advance gathered pace but the fact remained that the Bf 110 Zerstörer, despite its success as a long-range fighter during the campaign in Poland, fared badly at the hands of better fighter opposition. Even with a rear gunner to protect the aircraft from behind, the two main areas where the Bf 110 suffered were in its lack of ability to turn hard and its roll rate; this would put the Zerstörer crew at a disadvantage when encountering single-seat fighters, such as the Hurricane.

To counter the Bf 110's disadvantage against the Hurricane, it usually enjoyed the advantage of numbers and so if a Staffel was engaged by enemy fighters then other Staffeln were often in the vicinity to provide support to the unit under attack. This often involved a tactic of using layers of Bf 110s, with a handful of formations each consisting of ten or twelve aircraft, with each formation separated in height by about 1,000 feet to provide protection from above. But even with a large formation of up to fifty or sixty Bf 110s, there were still losses amongst the Zerstörer units as the 110 continued to prove inadequate against the Hurricane.

Some of those who had enjoyed early successes in Poland and France now became victims themselves. One was Oberleutnant Werner

Methfessel of V.(Z)/LG 1 who had been credited with four victories during the campaign in Poland and had added four more to his total over France. On 17 May, Methfessel and his radio operator, Unteroffizier Heinz Resener, were amongst a number of Bf 110s escorting He 111s when they were shot down by Hurricanes. Methfessel and Resener's aircraft crashed to the west of Reims and was one of three Bf 110s shot down during the action, and one of eight successes claimed by the Allies that day. Even though the Bf 110s of V.(Z)/LG 1 had both numerical and height advantage against what appears to have been just one flight of Hurricanes, the Zerstörers were only able to account for one Hurricane shot down and could not prevent the loss of three aircraft.

The following day there were similar losses, including the loss of four Bf 110s from 5./ZG 26 near Cambrai during the afternoon. Led by the Staffelkapitän, Hauptmann Eberhard Trützschler d'Elsa, the Bf 110s were escorting He 111s at medium altitude. The weather was scattered cloud and as there was no activity at medium level d'Elsa decided to look beneath the clouds. The Staffel descended but unfortunately for the Zerstörer crews they came out of cloud in the middle of a formation of Hurricanes.

The aerial combat that followed turned out to be one of the most extensive experienced by pilots on either side with the outcome being the loss of the four Bf 110s, including that of d'Elsa. A number of Bf 110s of 6./ZG 26, led by Hauptmann Theodor Rossiwall, had been in the vicinity and had seen d'Elsa take his formation below cloud but Rossiwall's formation had then become involved in heavy fighting above the clouds. Now back at their airfield at As in Belgium, they waited; their colleagues now overdue. Eventually an aircraft of the fifth Staffel landed. It was Oberfeldwebel Kurt Rochel, a veteran of the Legion Condor, who had to force-land as a result of damage to his aircraft. His plane had been hit but both he and his radio operator, Unteroffizier Willi Schöffler, were unhurt. A little later the damaged Bf 110 of Oberleutnant Artur Niebuhr and Unteroffizier Klaus Theissen also returned. Then there was another and then another, and slowly the survivors of 5./ZG 26 returned. But aircraft were still missing. As darkness came, and without word from other airfields, the Staffel crews feared the worst.

D'Elsa had trained and led the unit for a long time and his loss would be felt hard by his men.

In fact, although wounded, d'Elsa had managed to crash-land between Douai and Cambrai. Both he and his radio operator, Unteroffizier Hermann Rossler, were captured by the French and became prisoners of war, although they would later return from captivity, but such were d'Elsa's injuries that he would not return to flying duties. Theodor Rossiwall was now given command of the Staffel but initially he had just three serviceable aircraft available to him.

Despite some successes, the fact that thirty-five Bf 110s had already been shot down by the RAF alone, in just the first week of the campaign, did not go unnoticed on either side. These losses were 50 per cent higher than those suffered by the Bf 109s during the opening week of the campaign, a statistic made worse by the fact that the vast majority of sorties were being flown by the 109s. A total of ninety Bf 110s would be lost to enemy action by the end of the campaign (24 per cent of the Bf 110 strength) and although 169 Bf 109s were lost during the same period this figure represented just 12 per cent of the Bf 109 force.

Few losses had a greater impact than that of the Gruppenkommandeur of II./JG 26, Herwig Knüppel, another veteran of the Legion Condor and commander of the Gruppe for the past year. He was shot down by Hurricanes on 19 May. His 109 was one of three aircraft lost by the Gruppe during the combat and crashed to the north-west of Lille, killing Knüppel.

Despite such losses, victory in France was soon in sight. The Germans had flooded through the gap between the Allied armies in the northern and southern parts of the region and the main German advance had now reached a line between Cambrai and St-Quentin; Cambrai had fallen and Amiens was soon to follow. The Germans had also reached Péronne, leaving no Allied forces between them and the sea as more Allied airfields were evacuated. The following day the Germans successfully opened up a corridor between Arras and the Somme as advanced Panzer units reached the coast. As the Panzers closed in on Dunkirk, Göring was guilty of letting the euphoria of success cloud his military judgement. He believed that the Luftwaffe alone was capable of defeating the Allies and he managed to convince

Hitler to rest the Panzers should they be needed to advance on Paris. The rest of the hierarchy, including Milch, Jeschonnek and Kesselring, did not agree.

Göring would prove to be wrong and in the context of the Second World War it was a crucial error on his part, though his units were already tired and resources were stretched after two hectic weeks of air fighting. The RAF started to withdraw across the Channel as the British evacuation of Allied soldiers at Dunkirk commenced on 26 May. Amongst his many reassurances, Göring had convinced Hitler that the Luftwaffe could prevent any evacuation but the Allies had built sufficient defences to the approaches of Dunkirk. Although the Luftwaffe did its best, the Allied evacuation could not be stopped.

It was in the vicinity of the evacuation beaches where Bf 109 pilots encountered the RAF's Spitfire for the first time. The date of the first known aerial engagement between the two types was 23 May when Bf 109Es of I./JG 27 encountered Spitfires to the south of Calais. The similarities between these two great fighters, not only in their design but in their performance, were uncanny, almost identical.

The similarities between the Bf 109E and the Spitfire I become most evident when comparing the technical specifications of each design. The engine of each fighter – the DB 601A of the Bf 109E and the Merlin III of the Spitfire IA – produced almost identical power with each engine producing over 1,000 hp. This gave the two fighters almost identical performance when climbing to a height of 20,000 feet, which both types could reach in just under eight minutes. Although the Bf 109E had a greater ceiling than the Spitfire's 30,000 feet, at medium level each fighter was capable of 350 mph at 15,000 feet.

There were, however, some differences in the engine design for each fighter. The fuel-injection of the Bf 109E's DB 601 engine meant it was able to cope when unloading at zero-g – a manoeuvre used to gain maximum acceleration – and so was able to dive better than the Spitfire. If a Spitfire tried to follow then its Merlin engine, with a normal float type carburettor, would be unable to deliver fuel and so it would splutter or even stop during the manoeuvre. This meant the Spitfire pilot had to perform a half-roll before pulling towards his evading opponent by which time the Bf 109E would usually have made its escape.

There were also some design differences as well. As far as size was concerned the Bf 109E was slightly smaller than the Spitfire, although its weight was marginally greater. It was a little shorter than the Spitfire's 30 feet and its wingspan of just over 32 feet was less than the Spitfire's 37 feet. This gave the Spitfire a wing area of more than 240 square feet, some 40 per cent greater than the Bf 109E, meaning the Spitfire's wing loading (and the Hurricane's for that matter), was less than that of the Bf 109E.

Because of the Spitfire's good rate of roll, its pilot could shake off a Bf 109E by using a flick half-roll manoeuvre and then quickly pulling out of the subsequent dive. The 109 pilot would find this defensive manoeuvre difficult to counter because of his own rapid build-up of speed in the dive, making the elevators too heavy to effect a quick pull out of a dive.[11] But the relatively high wing loading of the Bf 109E was offset by its shorter and square-tipped wing design that incorporated leading edge slots, which would project forward of the wing at slow speed to increase lift and to improve its ability to turn hard. However, these were reported to operate asymmetrically at times; this would affect the lateral stability of the aircraft as well as giving the occasional problem when closing in for a kill during combat. An experienced 109 pilot would invariably get the better of an inexperienced Spitfire pilot who could be afraid to pull too hard in a turn for fear of stalling his aircraft. But on balance, and with every other parameter being the same, including the skill level of the pilots, the Spitfire was capable of turning slightly tighter than the Bf 109 at medium altitude.

Where the two fighters did differ was in their armament. The Spitfire was armed with eight wing-mounted 0.303 inch Browning machine guns whereas the Bf 109E was armed with a mix of cannon and machine guns, with two 7.9 mm machine guns immediately above its engine, slightly staggered in their location, and two wing-mounted 20 mm cannon. Although the Spitfire's Brownings proved reliable, they lacked the punch of the Bf 109E's cannon, the shells of which inflicted more damage than a rifle-calibre machine-gun round.

The differing armament of the two designs meant that the Bf 109E had a 25 per cent greater weight of firepower than the Spitfire and Hurricane but had a lesser rate of fire than the RAF fighters. The Spitfire and Hurricane could put more rounds in the air in any half-second or one-second burst and so the probability of a hit was greater for the Spitfire and Hurricane although their destructive power hit-for-hit was less than that of the Bf 109E.

There were other factors that came into play during air-to-air combat. The Bf 109 canopy, with its side-hinge design and heavy metal frame, meant there were areas of visual obstruction for the pilot when compared to the sliding canopy design of the RAF fighters, and the rearward view from the 109 was poor. Also, the cockpit of the 109 was more cramped than the British designs and the seat was also lower in the Bf 109, which meant the pilot's legs were more stretched, although this was not always a bad thing, particularly when manoeuvring hard, as the body position was more favourable for resisting g-forces.

But even when taking all of these subtle design differences between the Spitfire I and the Bf 109E into account, the fighters were essentially evenly matched and so the outcome of any duel often came down to the skill and experience of the pilots involved and the tactics used. In the right hands either aircraft was capable of outmanoeuvring the other, and victory would often be achieved by the pilot with the initial tactical advantage or with the greater knowledge of his opponent's strengths and weaknesses in combat.

These early exchanges over the beaches at Dunkirk gave both sides a valuable insight into the capability and tactics of their main adversary, and these lessons would be taken forward into the opening exchanges of the Battle of Britain that was soon to follow. The fact that the Spitfire proved such a capable adversary had initially come as a shock to the Luftwaffe but the Bf 109 pilots usually enjoyed numerical superiority. The RAF fighters generally operated as a squadron, or even as a flight, with typically no more than a dozen or so aircraft, whereas the Messerschmitts were operating at Gruppe strength with some thirty or more aircraft, and the RAF pilots faced the additional problem of operating at considerable ranges from their home base.

During the heavy aerial fighting at the end of May and early June 1940, the Jagdwaffe flew some 2,000 sorties[12] of which 80 per cent were flown by the Bf 109s. The British evacuation of Dunkirk ended on 3 June but fighting continued until the French surrender some three weeks later, by which time many of the Bf 109 units had returned to Germany for a rest and to re-equip in preparation for the planned invasion of England.

The battle for France was over. It had been a resounding victory for the Luftwaffe with the Jagdwaffe achieving success on a quite staggering scale; more than fifty pilots were credited with five victories or more. The most successful was 26-year-old Wilhelm Balthasar, Kapitän of 1./JG 1, with twenty-three victories during the campaign, including five in one day on 5 June followed by four more the next, to add to his seven victories in Spain. The second most successful was Werner Mölders of III./JG 53 who was credited with sixteen victories during the campaign to add to his fourteen successes in Spain and a further nine achieved during the opening months of the Second World War. Mölders was now the highest scoring *Experte* with a total of thirty-nine victories and, on 29 May, became the first Jagdflieger to be awarded the Knight's Cross of the Iron Cross; two weeks later, Wilhelm Balthasar became the second.

During the later weeks of the campaign in France, Mölders had been averaging one victory for every three missions flown but even he was not invincible, despite having flown more than 130 combat missions since the outbreak of the war. During the late afternoon of 5 June he spotted six Moranes near Compiègne being attacked by other Messerschmitts before Mölders eventually got his chance. As Mölders curved towards line astern of a Morane, a favoured position for an attacker and one that allowed him to keep the nose of his aircraft on his victim, the Frenchman turned hard, resulting in Mölders briefly losing sight of his opponent. The Morane now made its escape at low level while evading further attacks by two more Messerschmitts. Mölders, at a height of 3,000 feet, suddenly heard a bang. He had been hit and quickly realized that his engine has been shot to pieces as his control column lurched forward. Mölders had no option but to bail out of his aircraft and was taken prisoner, but he was fortunate as just three weeks later, after the surrender of France, he was released. Even though he was as experienced in air combat as anyone else at the time, Mölders had been shot down by an aircraft he had not seen.

The two other top scorers of the campaign were Adolf Galland, now

Kommandeur of III./JG 26, with fourteen victories during a one-month period between May and June, and 24-year-old Leutnant Helmut Wick of 3./JG 2 who achieved twelve victories over France. Galland had gone from strength to strength during the battle of France. Considering he had made the transition from ground-attack pilot to fighter pilot just a few months before, Galland had quickly become one of the most capable and highly respected pilots in the Jagdwaffe. Wick, who had joined the Luftwaffe in 1936 and was only ever considered an average pilot during training, had been fortunate to blossom under the tutelage of Werner Mölders during his time with JG 53. At the outbreak of the Second World War he was transferred to JG 2 and claimed his first victory in November 1939 flying only his sixth combat mission. During the campaign in France he had quickly added to his total and on 6 June was the first pilot of his Gruppe to complete a hundred combat missions, claiming his tenth victim on the same day. Others to achieve double figures in victories over France were Oberleutnant Lothar Keller of 1./JG 3 and Oberfeldwebel Werner Machold of 1./JG 2; both were credited with ten victories during the campaign.

The campaign against France had seen the Luftwaffe control the sky and had enabled German forces to dominate the battlefield. The Bf 109 had proved to be better than most of its Allied adversaries and its superior tactics, developed from the experiences gained during the earlier campaigns in Spain and Poland, meant the Jagdflieger now proved supreme.

Chapter 3
Battle for Britain

The French armistice brought a period of celebration for Germany as Hitler still believed that Britain would want to negotiate for peace that he would so gladly have granted. This was not unrealistic given the British attitude towards Hitler during the late 1930s but by June 1940 Britain was led by a new and tougher Prime Minister, Winston Churchill, and clearly there would be no peace.

The euphoria following the defeat of France seemed to have removed any doubts that might have existed in the German High Command about its ability to defeat the RAF. Göring had convinced Hitler that his Luftwaffe would ensure the sky over the Channel and southern England would be secure for an invasion to take place. Furthermore, there was a strong belief within some quarters that an invasion of southern England should not be delayed. Milch, for one, believed that any delay would allow the British to regroup across the Channel and by the time Hitler was ready to commence operations against Britain it would be too late.

Not all shared this opinion. Jeschonnek was revelling in the victory over France but, while the Luftwaffe seemingly idled its time away, Britain was preparing for a full-scale war. Aircraft production in Britain increased, particularly of fighters, and the quantitative advantage enjoyed by the Luftwaffe at the start of the war was quickly eroding away. Nonetheless, it remained an impressive air armada. Between them Kesselring and Sperrle had more than 1,200 bombers, 400 dive bombers and 1,100 fighters (800 Bf 109s and 300 Bf 110s). They would be at the forefront of the onslaught with the fighter elements coming under the control of the Jagdfliegerführer for each air fleet, their task being to achieve aerial supremacy over the English Channel so that the bombers could pave the way for the German invasion of southern England.

Opposing the Luftwaffe across the Channel was RAF Fighter Command consisting of nearly fifty squadrons of Spitfires and Hurricanes, totalling just over 750 aircraft, under the command of Air Chief Marshal Sir Hugh Dowding. Fighter Command was organized into three, and very soon four, operational groups covering large geographical areas. Each group had the responsibility of protecting its own area with its own centralized command and control system, although the overall system was sufficiently flexible to allow mutual support between groups.

The RAF also enjoyed the benefit of early warning provided by a chain of radar stations along the southern and eastern coasts of Britain, meaning it would not have to waste vital resources by having to provide air patrols over southern England. The Hurricane and Spitfire pilots would also be operating close to home, allowing them to maximize best use of their fuel, and any aircraft damaged during air combat stood a realistic chance of either force-landing or making it back to its own base. Furthermore, any pilot shot down who survived uninjured could return to flying in a short period of time. Fighter Command also benefitted from an established network of communications links between its headquarters and the various group and sector operations rooms around southern England.

For the Jagdwaffe the brief period of rest was soon over and from the beginning of July the Jagdgeschwader moved forward to their new airfields in France. Although Hitler would not yet allow a full-scale aerial offensive over southern England he did allow attacks against British shipping in the Channel, and the *Kanalkampf* (Channel Battle), which commenced on 10 July 1940, marked the opening phase of what would later become known as the Battle of Britain.

With a number of Jagdgeschwader still settling at their new bases in northern France, it was mostly the Bf 109s of JG 51, and then JG 26 and JG 53 that took part in the opening exchanges. There was a cloudy start to the day but the weather gradually improved and one of the first exchanges on the opening day involved twenty Bf 109s of III./JG 51, led by Hannes Trautloft, accompanied by thirty Bf 110s of I./ZG 26 escorting twenty Do 17s tasked with attacking a large convoy off Folkestone. The formation was intercepted by thirty RAF fighters patrolling the area and so the attack achieved little success with only one ship sunk. One of the Bf 110s was shot down but the Bf 109s claimed six aircraft destroyed, three of which were claimed by Walter Oesau, the Kapitän of 7./JG 51; his three victims were all Spitfires.

It was cloudy again the following day but there were sufficient gaps to allow further attacks against shipping off the east coast of England as well as attacks against Portland and Portsmouth. The pattern was much the same during the following days with the cloudy weather, light rain and occasional fog preventing any activity of note but there were further attacks against British shipping off Dover and the south coast of England. The Bf 109s had been allowed to carry out *freier Jagd* ('free fighter') sorties, which gave them relative freedom to roam.

With its build-up complete, the Luftwaffe was now ready to commence its major offensive against Britain. Kesselring's Luftflotte 2 consisted of I. Fliegerkorps in north-east France, commanded by Ulrich Grauert, II. Fliegerkorps in Belgium (Bruno Loerzer) and IX. Flieger-korps in Holland and north-west Germany (Joachim Coeler). Sperrle's Luftflotte 3 consisted of IV. Fliegerkorps in Brittany (Alfred Keller) and V. Fliegerkorps in the Seine area (Robert Ritter von Greim). Also available was X. Fliegerkorps of Luftflotte 5 in Norway under the command of Hans Geisler.

The vast area now under German occupation meant that the Luft-waffe was able to spread its resources far and wide, with bombers based as far west as Brittany and as far north as Norway from where they could reach most of Britain. But the limited combat radius of the Bf 109E meant it was effectively restricted to operations over south-east England and would only be able to reach as far as London if deployed forward to airfields in the Pas de Calais region, and could only operate over the south-west of England if operating from bases in and around the Cher-bourg Peninsula. Therefore, the Bf 109s were based at airfields in two main areas. The majority of Jagdgeschwader – JG 3, 26, 51, 52 and 54 – were allocated to Luftflotte 2 and spread across twenty airfields in the Pas de Calais. Those allocated to Luftflotte 3 – JG 2, 27 and 53 – were spread across a number of airfields further west in Normandy, Brittany and the Channel Islands. At each airfield there was typically one Gruppe, with its three Staffeln and Stab flight, led by a Hauptmann or Major.

The aerial exchanges during the opening ten days of the campaign against Britain had been relatively small-scale with losses on either side amounting to a handful a day. The Bf 109Es of Trautloft's III./JG 51 continued to enjoy success against the RAF and during one encounter with twelve Boulton-Paul Defiants, a rather cumbersome single-engine fighter with no forward-firing guns but armed instead with a powered rear turret, near Dover on 19 July, Trautloft's unit shot down six without loss and it was only the intervention of Hurricanes that prevented the destruction of the entire Defiant squadron.

Both Galland and Mölders experienced their first action of the campaign over the Channel during July. Galland, leading III./JG 26 and now promoted to Major, was impressed by the Spitfire during his early exchanges with the type over the Channel, particularly in a slow-speed dogfight when he found the Spitfire was capable of out-manoeuvring the Bf 109E. During one encounter, an inferior number of Spitfires successfully forced Galland's Gruppe into a hard manoeuvring fight that resulted in the 109s becoming short of fuel. Galland was fortunate to make his escape but did so only by executing a long curving dive that the Spitfire behind him was unable to match, and so Galland got away at low level across the Channel and back to his base in the Pas de Calais.

Galland shot down his first Spitfires at the end of July, and was subsequently awarded the Knight's Cross for his seventeen victories, but the Spitfire had already demonstrated to him that it was an extremely capable aircraft. He felt the Bf 109 was the better aircraft when making an attack but it was not so capable when having to defend against a Spitfire, which, although he found it to be a little slower than the Bf 109, was much more manoeuvrable in combat.

It was still early days in its operational life but the Spitfire was now appearing in increasing numbers and its pilots were learning quickly. Even those amongst the Jagdwaffe with plenty of combat experience were discovering that victory over Britain was far from certain. Mölders, having also been promoted to Major and now leading JG 51, was also impressed by the Spitfire. He, too, had been fortunate to escape with his life when his first action in command ended in near tragedy. While escorting a formation of bombers he was wounded in the leg during a clash with Spitfires and had to crash-land back at base, although one of his young pilots, Oberleutnant Richard Leppla, Kapitän of 3./JG 51, scored the first of his eventual sixty-eight successes during the action that day.

These early exchanges across the Channel often showed that the Jagdwaffe had the better tactics and usually, but not always, the Jagdflieger came out on top. The RAF was still using rigid tactics based on a typical squadron-size formation of aircraft whereas the Jagdgruppen flew in fluid and flexible formations with breadth, depth and variations in altitude. Even when the RAF chose to adopt a single aircraft as a weaver, which flew above and astern of the formation to act as lookout and to guard the main formation from attack from high and behind, the pilots of Fighter Command soon learned the weaver proved too vulnerable and eventually abandoned the idea.

The Luftwaffe's basic fighter formation remained based on the Staffel, led by the Staffelkapitän with his Rottenflieger as his number two, swept above and to one side of the leader. The distance and height between the two aircraft varied according to many factors such as cloud conditions, sun position and the threat direction at the time. The rest of the Staffel flew echeloned behind the leader and above him with part of the formation swept to the left of the Kapitän and the other to his right. The size of each element would depend on the number of aircraft the Staffel had available on the day but, typically, one element would operate as a Schwarm, with the Schwarmführer leading the four aircraft and his wingman, the Rottenflieger, flying above him and swept on the outside of the overall formation. The other pair, led by a Rottenführer, would also be swept above and on the outside of the formation. On the other side there would be either another Schwarm of four or a number of pairs depending on the size of the Staffel, and they would fly at a height and position depending on all the factors the Staffelkapitän needed to take into account.

The Jagdflieger would usually have two main advantages: numbers and height. He also had the advantage of only having one responsibility: to engage the RAF fighters or, at least, to prevent them from engaging the bombers. However, he did not have all the advantages. It was unnerving to cross the Channel in a single-engine fighter and any technical malfunction could soon result in disastrous consequences. It was also important continuously to maintain awareness of how much fuel he had, which was never easy during combat, and so he had to fly around with his eyes continuously scanning the fuel gauge in his cockpit to see when the low-fuel warning light started to flash.

The Bf 109's limited endurance would prove critical throughout the Battle of Britain. The Jagdgruppen were not helped by having first to join up in a large formation and it could take up to thirty minutes after take off before the 109s had crossed the Channel, even at the narrowest point, which would then give only about twenty minutes of combat time before it was necessary to head back home. Even the units based in the Pas de Calais could spend little time over southern England as the 109's combat radius of approximately 125 miles proved to be a limiting factor, and anything beyond London was certainly out of reach.

Aircraft recognition was also proving a problem. In the air the Bf 109 looked remarkably similar to the Spitfire and Hurricane, and when taking into consideration the large number of fighters that were involved in the aerial exchanges, and the speed of decision-making for the fighter pilot during air combat, it became increasingly important on both sides to prevent firing on a friendly aircraft. Some Bf 109 units began to apply large areas of yellow paint to aircraft engine cowlings, rudders and wing tips to make recognition in the air easier.

The Jagdwaffe was now involved in a quite different air war to what it had encountered before, where it had flown in support of a ground offensive. It was now about gaining air superiority and the RAF had to be defeated, or at least reduced to a level where it could not mount any great opposition to the planned invasion of Britain.

Operations across the Channel during July and early August saw the Luftwaffe's bombers sink some 70,000 tons of British shipping while its fighters carried out a number of *freier Jagd* sorties over the Channel and south-east England to probe the RAF's defences. It had already become apparent to the Jagdwaffe that the RAF fighters always seemed to be in the right place at the right time, and gradually the exchanges swung in favour of the RAF as the pilots of Fighter Command became more familiar with the Bf 109E and its tactics.

Hitler had already ordered the preparation of a seaborne invasion of Britain and his Directive 17 issued on 1 August called for the Luftwaffe to use all available resources to defeat the RAF. The Bf 109 units were now at their peak strength and the air battle intensified on 8 August when fierce attacks were carried out on a Channel convoy off Dover and the Isle of Wight. The day produced the heaviest air fighting to date, involving more than 150 aircraft, and resulted in the Jagdwaffe claiming twenty RAF fighters shot down.[13]

The second phase of the offensive, *Adlerangriff* ('Eagle Attack'), began on 13 August and was intended to annihilate Fighter Command with the Luftwaffe's bombers attacking the RAF's ground organization; specifically the airfields, the radar sites and Britain's aircraft industry. The opening day, known as *Adler Tag* ('Eagle Day'), was hampered by poor weather during the early morning and meant the day started badly with Kesselring having to cancel Luftflotte 2's involvement in the morning operations, although Sperrle was able to commit Luftflotte 3. Improvement in the weather during the afternoon meant that Luftflotte 2 was able to participate but, despite flying nearly 1,500 sorties during the day, the Luftwaffe failed to target the Spitfires and Hurricanes of Fighter Command and only thirteen RAF fighters were destroyed; the Jagdwaffe lost twenty-seven fighters, eighteen of which were Bf 110s and nine were Bf 109s. It had been far from one of the greatest days in the Luftwaffe's short history as had been so eagerly anticipated at its start.

Two days later the weather had turned fine and the most intense day of fighting so far followed, including raids against targets in the north of England by bombers of Luftflotte 5 operating from Norway. Many RAF airfields were damaged and more than thirty RAF fighters were claimed, although the Jagdwaffe had suffered heavily with more than seventy aircraft claimed by Fighter Command.

The weather stayed good for the following three days and 18 August proved to be the hardest day of fighting to date when the Luftwaffe launched three major raids against targets in southern England. German intelligence had assessed that nearly 600 of Fighter Command's aircraft had been destroyed since the beginning of July and estimated that the RAF's fighter strength was now just 300 fighters, of which 200 were in the south-east of England. The reality was somewhat different as the RAF still had 800 single-engine fighters available, with more than 300 fighters in the south-east alone. However, the Luftwaffe still boasted a large and capable force with nearly 800 bombers, 280 dive bombers,

700 Bf 109s and more than 150 Bf 110s. The Bf 109s of Luftflotte 2 now occupied fourteen airfields in the Pas de Calais with nearly 450 aircraft available from JG 3, 26, 51, 52 and 54, while the Bf 109s of Luftflotte 3 remained further west with JG 2 in the vicinity of Le Havre, JG 27 occupying airfields along the Cherbourg Peninsula and JG 53 centred round Rennes.[14]

Fine weather meant that a full day of operations could be planned but a layer of haze over southern England prevented the first raid from carrying out its attack until mid-day. The bombers of Luftflotte 2, escorted by Bf 109s, were tasked with carrying out strikes against the RAF sector airfields of Biggin Hill and Kenley. The Bf 109s of III./JG 26, led by Gerhard Schöpfel, were more than twenty miles ahead of the main bomber force in an attempt to bring the RAF fighters into the sky.

Schöpfel was quick to spot a squadron of Hurricanes beneath him and decided to gain the early initiative. Leaving his formation intact above, so as not to give away the element of surprise, Schöpfel pounced alone. He knew the larger formation was likely to be seen but the Hurricane pilots were unlikely to spot a lone fighter coming out of the sun. The tactic worked. The tightness of the Hurricane formation allowed Schöpfel to create havoc amongst its ranks. In no time at all he claimed two Hurricanes flying as weavers above the squadron and he then attacked the main formation, succeeding in shooting down two more. Schöpfel had claimed four Hurricanes in just a few minutes, bringing his total to twelve.

While Schöpfel had managed to enjoy success, the story was not the same elsewhere as the RAF's reaction to the three major raids during the day had been much stronger than expected. Fighter Command had matched the Luftwaffe's sortie rate of nearly a thousand during the day and by nightfall seventy German aircraft had either been shot down or severely damaged; half of these had come down in southern England. The RAF losses in the air were half that but many more aircraft had been destroyed or damaged on the ground as the day ended as the most costly single day of the campaign so far for both sides.

A deterioration in the weather over southern England prevented much air activity during the following few days but on 24 August it all changed. Again the RAF airfields took a pounding with raids extending as far as the Midlands and South Wales. The pattern was much the same just two days later, and then again on 28 August when the Luftwaffe also flew 600 sorties at night. Fighter Command was now under real strain but poor German intelligence was proving frustrating for those escorting bombers to carry out attacks against airfields that later proved to be inactive. Furthermore, the advantages of the Bf 109E over the Spitfire and Hurricane were rarely exploited as the German bombers were operating at medium altitude where most of the strengths of the 109 were lost.

Göring was far from satisfied as losses mounted. The Luftwaffe's bomber crews also complained, citing a lack of fighter protection as the reason for their own high losses. The Bf 110, in particular, had proved a disappointment and had been unable to protect either the bombers or itself from the marauding Spitfires and Hurricanes. Göring refused to agree to the plea from his commanders to remove the Bf 110 from the battle, choosing instead to task the Bf 109 units to escort the 110s, thus creating the quite bizarre tactical situation of a fighter having to protect another fighter escorting a bomber. The Bf 110 was not the only aircraft causing concern as the Ju 87 Stuka, which had promised so much during the early months of the war, had also suffered badly against the RAF fighters and now had to be withdrawn from the battle.

Göring decided to reprimand his commanders for a lack of aggression and replaced some of his pre-war leaders with pilots with proven combat experience. Many Luftwaffe officers thought that this decision was interfering and almost amateurish; they believed that Göring should have been offering motivation rather than criticism. However, the decision now provided the opportunity for some of the younger pilots to lead in air combat. Adolf Galland was to be given command of JG 26 and his appointment meant that Gerhard Schöpfel, who had served as Staffelkapitän of 9./JG 26 since the outbreak of war, would become Kommandeur of III./JG 26. Other new appointments included promotion to Major for Günther Lützow who was given command of JG 3; Hanns Trübenbach was given command of JG 52; Günther Freiherr von Maltzahn, Kommandeur of II./JG 53, replaced Hans-Jürgen von Cramon-Taubadel as Kommodore of JG 53; and Hannes Trautloft was appointed Kommodore of JG 54 with Walter Oesau replacing Trautloft as Kommandeur of III./JG 51.

Göring also decided to use the Bf 109s as close escorts for the German bombers, another decision hugely disliked and one that met severe opposition from men like Galland and Mölders who now felt robbed of their freedom to roam and to engage the enemy on their own terms. This would now place the Bf 109 pilot in severe difficulties as he was used to having height advantage, which he could convert into increased speed so that he could swoop down on his opponent. He had also learned that many RAF pilots seemed to find it harder to spot an attacker over their right shoulders, and so having attacked from a position high and astern, he would then pull up in his opponent's blind spot from below and astern to achieve his kill.

As close-escort fighters the 109s were now tied to the route of the bombers as well as their heights and timings. They were already operating at the limit of their combat radius over southern England and the difference in speed between the Bf 109s and the bombers meant the 109s were required to zig-zag across the Channel to maintain formation with the slower bombers but not give up too much speed. The Jagd-flieger often found that he was poorly positioned and now had to look up for the Spitfires and Hurricanes as they picked their moment to make their attack. Even when engaging the RAF fighters his speed was often too low and this meant he could only make one turn and fire a short burst, after which he was unable to continue his attack. He would often be left to watch the Spitfires and Hurricanes freely engage the bombers that he was there to protect. Furthermore, the lack of any fighter–bomber affiliation training between the different Geschwader, either before the war or since its start, had now become most evident.

These changes in tactics did have some success as German bomber losses reduced over the following two weeks. Göring also believed the RAF was on its last legs and was now reduced to less than 200 fighters. Whether this was due to poor intelligence or because he simply wanted to believe that victory was in sight is unclear but he now turned on the RAF, its infrastructure and its command and control. By early September the Luftwaffe was mounting raids of up to 1,500 aircraft a day against Fighter Command bases in the south-east of England and during the two weeks of air fighting leading up to 6 September losses were around 300 aircraft on each side.

As far as the fighter-to-fighter battle was concerned, the Luftwaffe had lost about 150 Bf 109s with the RAF losing around 200 Spitfires and Hurricanes. The British aircraft industry was working hard to replace losses and was able to maintain the RAF's front-line fighter strength consistently at around 650 aircraft throughout the summer of 1940 but it was the loss of pilots that had become the key factor. In just one week Fighter Command lost 230 pilots killed, wounded or missing and it was not only the number of pilots that was cause for concern, it was also that the quality and experience levels of the pilots were being diluted, with Fighter Command having lost about a quarter of its squadron commanders and half of its flight commanders.

The intensity of the air activity over the Channel and southern England meant that the personal scores of some had increased noticeably. Once again, the most successful included Werner Mölders, who scored his twenty-seventh victory of the war on 26 August, bringing his overall total to forty-one, and Adolf Galland, who recorded his twenty-second victory on 15 August having claimed three Spitfires during the day. Another to achieve considerable success was Helmut Wick, the Kapitän of 3./JG 2. During the late afternoon of 26 August Wick claimed two Hurricanes over Portsmouth in the space of just a few minutes to bring his total to twenty-two, earning him the Knight's Cross, awarded to him personally by Göring, after which Wick was appointed as Kommandeur with promotion to Hauptmann.

Inevitably, though, there were also losses and one to fall during this period was Oberleutnant Horst Tietzen, the Kapitän of 5./JG 51. Tietzen had been the fourth to achieve twenty victories during the war but on 18 August, with his overall score on twenty-seven (including the seven he had achieved in Spain), he was shot down by a Hurricane over the Thames Estuary; his body was eventually washed ashore at Calais in northern France.

While Dowding considered withdrawing his fighters north of London he knew that to do so would effectively hand control of the sky over the Channel and southern England to Göring. Dowding knew that the RAF needed a change of fortune, a miracle even, if Britain was to survive but he could not have imagined that Hitler's fury following a relatively small-scale attack by Bomber Command against Berlin would lead to a sudden change in the Luftwaffe's tactics that would give Fighter Command valuable time to recover.

Hitler had publicly expressed his outrage at the attack on Berlin and pledged to erase British cities in return and now ordered daylight attacks on London. It would be the turning point of the battle. Even Göring could see this change of tack was a mistake as it would divert attention from gaining the air superiority that he so clearly desired.

The bombing campaign against London began during the afternoon of 7 September, marking the third phase of the offensive. The Luftwaffe had managed to replace most of its losses with new aircraft and the total number of aircraft now available was nearly 2,000; only 15 per cent less than at the start of the campaign. The first day saw 600 bombers carry out attacks against the docks with the heavy raids continuing into the night. It was the start of the Blitz and targets would soon include other major British cities.

On 15 September the plan was to mount the largest formations to date with two main raids against London during the day. The first was to take place around mid-day and was to centre on the rail network on the southern edge of the city, and the second, a much larger raid during the mid-afternoon, was to centre on the docks and warehouses in the east of London and to the south of the River Thames.

At their airfields in the Pas de Calais, the experienced Bf 109 pilots were familiar with the routine. On this day there was a leisurely start to the morning, with breakfast for those that could stomach it, and then the briefing; their task, once again, to provide close escort for the bombers attacking London. When it was time to prepare for take-off they climbed into their cockpits. It would take several minutes for each Gruppe to get all its aircraft off the ground but by 11.00 they were airborne and climbing above 15,000 feet to orbit above the coastline to wait for their formation of bombers to arrive; there were twenty Do 17s. Timing was important. London was nearly a hundred miles away and on the limit of their operational radius. They had to make sure they were in position and ready to join up to head north across the Channel but they did not have fuel to waste in lengthy holds or overly complicated manoeuvres to join up in formation. Looking northwards they could already see that the weather was not quite as good as forecast, which might cause a problem for the bombers but could always offer the fighters protection if necessary. It would be no easy ride. The RAF had remained undefeated and those that had crossed the Channel many times before were used to counting the losses on return.

The first Bf 109s crossed the English coastline at 11.30. These 109s were the lucky ones as they were ahead of the main force and were given the freedom to roam as their task was to get at the RAF fighters first and to disrupt their formations before the Spitfires and Hurricanes could reach the bombers.

As the first 109s arrived over southern England a small formation of twenty more Bf 109Es of LG 2, all carrying bombs, were getting airborne from their airfield at Calais. Their task was to get ahead of the main bomber formation and to carry out nuisance raids on London just minutes before the main attack. Even when laden with bombs, the fighter-bombers could transit nearly 100 mph faster than the main bombers and so would have no trouble in passing them en route. They even enjoyed the luxury of being escorted by more Bf 109s to provide them with their own fighter protection.

The air armada began to cross the English coastline to the south-east of London but the formation had already been detected by radar stations along the English coast and the first RAF squadrons were already airborne. There was a further problem as the cloud was much thicker than expected and a strong headwind had slowed the whole formation down, which reduced the time the Bf 109s could spend over southern England. While the RAF and Luftwaffe locked horns, the first bombs fell on London as the clocks in the city struck mid-day. The fighter-bombers of LG 2 had been fortunate. They had arrived over London unchallenged and now started their attack, the pilots carefully selecting their targets from 20,000 feet. One by one they entered a 45-degree dive before finally releasing their bombs from a height of 3,000 feet. Just forty minutes later it was all over and the last of the raiders were back over the Channel and on their way home.

Several claims were made by both sides but one to enjoy success during the mid-day encounter was Oberleutnant Hermann-Friedrich

Hauptmann Hannes Trautloft (*far right*), Kommandeur of III./JG 51, pictured at St-Omer Clairmarais in July 1940. Trautloft served with the Legion Condor in Spain and commanded 2./JG 77 during the invasion of Poland and then I./JG 20 during the campaign in France, adding three more victories (one in Poland and two in France) to the five he achieved in Spain. Trautloft is pictured with other Jagdflieger of the Stab, *L to R*: Oberleutnant Otto Kath; Leutnant Werner Pichon-Kalau; and Leutnant Herbert Wehnelt. (*Chris Goss collection*)

Hauptmann Hans-Karl Mayer, Staffelkapitän of 1./JG 53, pictured at Cherbourg during August 1940 after a lucky escape. Mayer was a veteran of the Legion Condor, claiming eight victories in Spain, and had served during the French campaign before the Battle of Britain. (*Chris Goss collection*)

Recently appointed Kommandeur of I./JG 53, Hans-Karl Mayer (*2nd left*) became one of the earliest recipients of the Knight's Cross in September 1940 before he was killed over the English Channel the following month having been credited with thirty victories. (*Chris Goss collection*)

Above: Debriefing during August 1940 – III./JG 26 Kommandeur Major Adolf Galland with his officers: (*left, outer*) medical doctor; (*L to R*) Hauptmann Gerhard Schöpfel, Oberleutnant Franz Beyer, Leutnant Gerhard Müller-Dühe, Leutnant Josef Bürschgens, Leutnant Walter Blume, Leutnant Gustav Sprick, Leutnant Joachim Müncheberg; (*outer right*) Hauptmann Dr Schroedter, III./JG 26 Technical Officer (with glasses). (*Bürschgens via Caldwell*)

Right: Pilots of the exceptionally successful III./JG 26 in October 1940. On the left is Leutnant Gustav Sprick (wearing the Knight's Cross awarded earlier in the month for his twenty victories), in the centre is Leutnant Klaus Mietusch and on the right is Leutnant Heinz Ebeling. (*Payne via Caldwell*)

Two of the Luftwaffe's finest Jagdflieger relaxing together during the autumn of 1940. On the left is Major Werner Mölders, Geschwaderkommodore of JG 51, and on the right is Major Adolf Galland, Gruppenkommandeur of III./JG 26. They would soon become respectively the second and third recipients of the Oak Leaves to the Knight's Cross. (*Glunz via Caldwell*)

Reichsmarschall Hermann Göring (*centre*) listening to two of his most distinguished air-combat leaders – Major Werner Mölders (*left*) and Major Adolf Galland – at the height of the Battle of Britain. (*Cranston via Caldwell*)

The rudder section of Hauptmann Wilhelm Balthasar's Bf 109, showing his impressive array of victories, taken during the later days of the Battle of Britain. Balthasar was then Kommandeur of III./JG 3, having been only the second Jagdflieger to be decorated with the Knight's Cross. (*Chris Goss collection*)

The second major re-design of the Messerschmitt Bf 109 during 1940 was the Bf 109F, with an improved engine, re-designed wings and better overall aero-dynamic performance. A handful of Friedrichs appeared during the later stages of the Battle of Britain but it would be mid-1941 before the variant came into wider use. The Friedrichs shown here belong to JG 2, which maintained a number of Bf 109Es and Fs in north-west Europe to counter the increasing number of fighter sweeps by RAF Spitfires across the Channel during 1941–2. (*Chris Goss collection*)

Major Walter Oesau (*2nd from left*) assumed command of JG 2 'Richthofen' in July 1941 having become only the third Jagdflieger to reach eighty victories and was only the third recipient of the Swords to the Knight's Cross. He is pictured with three key Jagdflieger of JG 2: Oberleutnant Erich Leie (*far left*) of the Stab of I./JG 2; Oberleutnant Rudolf Pflanz of the 1. Staffel (soon to become Staffelkapitän of 11./JG 2), and Oberfeldwebel Günther Seeger also of the Stab. (*Chris Goss collection*)

Oberleutnant Joachim Müncheberg, Staffelkapitän of 7./JG 26, prepares to leave his aircraft at Gela in Sicily on 28 March 1941 following his 200th combat sortie. He has a flare pistol in his hand and the metal Staffel command pennant on his radio mast is clearly visible. Müncheberg was still only twenty-two years old but he led his Staffel with distinction during a most successful tour in the Mediterranean when his small detachment claimed more than fifty victories without loss, twenty of which were credited to Müncheberg, earning him the Oak Leaves to his Knight's Cross. (*Bundesarchiv-Bildarchiv 427-408-19*)

The Commander of Luftflotte 2, Feldmarschall Albert Kesselring (*2nd from left*), pictured with three recent Knight's Cross winners of JG 53 in front of Kesselring's aircraft during his visit to Sarush airfield on 9 August 1941. It was the early days of Barbarossa and confidence is clearly high. *L to R*: Leutnant Herbert Schramm (Flugzeugführer of III./JG 53), Kesselring, Hauptmann Wolf-Dietrich Wilcke (Kommandeur of III./JG 53) and Leutnant Erich Schmidt. Both Schramm and Wilcke had been awarded the Knight's Cross just three days earlier while Schmidt had received his the month before. (*John Weal*)

Pilots of 7./JG 26 at Ligescourt in northern France after their return from Libya in 1941 having provided valuable support to Rommel's Afrika Korps. *L to R*: Feldwebel Karl-Heinz Ehlen; Feldwebel Edmund Wagner; Oberleutnant Klaus Mietusch; Hauptmann Gerhard Schöpfel (III./JG 26 Kommandeur); Oberleutnant Joachim Müncheberg; Leutnant Theo Lindemann; unknown; Oberfeldwebel Karl Kühdorf; unknown. (*Schöpfel via Caldwell*)

Leutnant Hans-Joachim Marseille (*facing the camera*) of 3./JG 27. Quick to develop his abilities as a fighter pilot in the desert war of North Africa, Marseille reached the zenith of his career during 1942 when he was awarded the Knight's Cross, Oak Leaves, Swords and Diamonds within a period of just seven months. (*John Weal*)

Above: Oberleutnant Erich Rudorffer (*right*), Staffelkapitän of 6./JG 2, pictured with his Geschwaderkommodore, Oberstleutnant Walter Oesau, in early 1943. Rudorffer led his unit during the Tunisian campaign, scoring twenty-seven victories and ended the war with a total of 224. (*Chris Goss collection*)

Left: Successful pilots of JG 26 in late 1941 or early 1942. *L to R*: Leutnant Theo Lindemann; Hauptmann Joachim Müncheberg; Oberleutnant 'Wutz' Galland; Oberleutnant Kurt Ebersberger. (*Glunz via Caldwell*)

Hans-Joachim Marseille, the 'Star of Africa'. Marseille flew the Bf 109 for his entire combat career before his death on 30 September 1942 and achieved all but seven of his 158 victories against the RAF's Desert Air Force over North Africa, more than any other *Experte* claimed against the Western Allies. (*John Weal*)

Oberleutnant Fritz Holzapfel of 13./SKG 10 pictured at Gerbini in Sicily in front of his heavily camouflaged FW 190 during July 1943, just days before the airfield was captured by the Allies. The unit had been used in a variety of ground-attack roles in Tunisia during the final days of the North Africa campaign, attacking targets such as airfields, harbours, vehicles and troop concentrations. (*Chris Goss collection*)

Joppien, the Kapitän of 1./JG 51. The two Spitfires he claimed brought his total to twenty-one for which he was awarded the Knight's Cross. Joppien would emerge from the battle against Britain as the fifth-highest scorer with twenty-six victories during the campaign and was appointed as the Gruppenkommandeur. There was also a brace of victories for Leutnant Erich Schmidt of 9./JG 53. Schmidt had scored his first success only just a month before, a Spitfire over the Isle of Wight on 12 August, but he was quick to learn and the two Spitfires he shot down to the south of London brought his total to six.

There was a brief lull in the early afternoon before the second raid, a large bomber force of more than a hundred He 111s and Do 17s, crossed over south-east England soon after 14.00. The three lead bomber formations, totalling seventy aircraft, were spread over a large front stretching six miles with each bomber formation protected by a Gruppe of Bf 109s. The second wave of two bomber formations, totalling fifty more bombers, and each protected by a Gruppe of Bf 109s, were just three miles behind.[15] The aerial action soon intensified once more as the first bombs fell on east London at 14.45. The cloud had thickened since the morning raid and now covered much of the sky with a cloud base of just 2,000 feet that extended vertically in places to more than 10,000 feet and prevented many of the bombers from identifying their main targets.

For the next fifteen minutes German bombs rained on the east and south-east of London. The fighter-to-fighter exchanges were fast and furious as the 109s did not have the fuel to be drawn into long manoeuvring dogfights with the RAF. The most successful form of air combat was to get in quick and hit hard and then quickly disengage. Some of those with plenty of combat experience were already masters at such tactics. Adolf Galland, for example, leading JG 26, gave a masterful display of such a tactic during an engagement with Hurricanes over the Thames Estuary when he carried out a swift surprise attack from the blind spot, and quickly dispatched into the ground his thirty-third victim of the war.

There were other successes too, with the young Erich Schmidt, airborne again having only just returned from the mid-day raid, adding another Spitfire to his total. Another to gain success was Hans 'Assi'

Hahn, Kapitän of 4./JG 2, who claimed his eighteenth victory, a Spitfire over London, during the afternoon. Hahn would be awarded the Knight's Cross and appointed as Kommandeur of III./JG 2 the following week after taking his tally to twenty victories.

At the end of the afternoon raid, the Luftwaffe had claimed nearly twenty RAF fighters shot down and damaged many more but in return had lost a dozen fighters and more than twenty bombers. As the 109s landed back at their airfields in France, it was clearly evident that the RAF was far from defeated.

Activity over the following days was relatively minimal but on 27 September there were more heavily escorted daylight raids against London and Bristol followed up at night with further attacks against London. Again the Luftwaffe suffered badly, particularly amongst the Ju 88 crews, and three days later saw the last of the mass daylight raids against England; these raids resulted in further heavy losses for relatively negligible damage.

A new bombing phase commenced on 1 October, mainly under the cover of darkness with few daylight raids. When daylight raids did take place, they were usually made by small numbers of Ju 88s, escorted by Bf 109s carrying bombs at high altitude, protected by more Bf 109s flying above. While these swift raids suffered few losses, they had no strategic impact at all.

The nightly raids against London and other targets would continue until May 1941 during which London would be bombed more than seventy times. Targets included fifteen more cities across Britain but the Blitz never achieved success for many reasons, not least because Germany had no possibility of mounting an effective bombing campaign against Britain's war industries due to its lack of a strategic bomber.

In the six weeks since the opening day of the offensive against London, the Luftwaffe lost one-third of its bomber strength and one-quarter of its fighters – which resulted in Hitler cancelling the invasion of Britain indefinitely. Fighter Command was far from defeated and Göring was again quick to blame his fighters, saying they had let the Luftwaffe down. But his pilots had not let him down. As far as the tactical battle was concerned, several had distinguished themselves with forty achieving ten victories or more during the battle against Britain.

Adolf Galland was credited with thirty-five victories during the campaign with the other highest scorers being Walter Oesau (thirty-four), Helmut Wick (thirty-one) and Werner Mölders (twenty-nine). This brought the overall total for Mölders to sixty-eight and Galland's to forty-nine, for which both were awarded the Oak Leaves to the Knight's Cross. Oesau and Wick would both be promoted: Oesau as Kommandeur of III./JG 3 and Wick, also awarded the Oak Leaves, promoted to Major and appointed Kommodore of JG 2 at the age of just twenty-five, making Wick the Luftwaffe's youngest Major and Kommodore at the time.

Many others achieved great success, including Oberleutnant Herbert Ihlefeld of I./JG 77 with twenty-four victories, Oberleutnant Hermann-Friedrich Joppien, Kapitän of 1./JG 51, with nineteen victories during the Battle of Britain (twenty-three overall), and Hauptmann Gerhard Schöpfel, Kommandeur of III./JG 26 with seventeen victories during the campaign (twenty-one overall); all three were awarded the Knight's Cross in September 1940.

Despite the vulnerability of the Bf 110, the most successful Zerstörer pilots during the Battle of Britain were Major Erich Groth of III./ZG 76, credited with thirteen victories, and Oberleutnant Hans-Joachim Jabs of 2./ZG 76 who was credited with twelve victories (eight Spitfires and four Hurricanes) for which he was awarded the Knight's Cross in October. Other Bf 110 pilots to have achieved double figures during the campaign, all with ten victories, were Leutnant Rolf Kaldrack of III./ZG 76, Feldwebel Walter Scherer of III./ZG 26 and Leutnant Eduard Tratt of I./EprGr 210. Tratt would go on to achieve a total of thirty-eight victories before he was killed in February 1944, making him the top-scoring Zerstörerflieger of the war.

Perhaps rather surprisingly there was one pilot who flew during the Battle of Britain without gaining an aerial victory. Leutnant Gerhard Barkhorn flew more than twenty combat missions with 6./JG 52 and was actually shot down during the last days of the battle but survived the ordeal and would go on to become the second-highest-scoring fighter pilot in history. The fact that Barkhorn did not gain an aerial success during the summer of 1940 is not altogether unusual as many who would go on to fame later in the war did not claim a single victory during the Battle of Britain. This was often due to how the Jagdwaffe operated tactically and most times it was the formation leaders who would get the opportunity to score victories while others supported and protected them, and often paid the ultimate price for doing so.

While there had been numerous examples of great individual achievements amongst the Jagdwaffe, the Battle of Britain was strategically a defeat for Germany and had cost some of the Luftwaffe's finest their lives. One was Helmut Wick whose war came to an end on 28 November. Flying with Erich Leie as his wingman, Wick took off from the airfield at Cherbourg-Querqueville shortly after 16.00. He had only just landed from his previous sortie during which he had claimed a Spitfire in the vicinity of the Isle of Wight. Now, with his 109 re-armed and re-fuelled, he was back in the air again and back in the same area near the Isle of Wight when he spotted a section of Spitfires nearby. Climbing even higher to gain an advantage, Wick then dived down on his opponent to claim his fifty-sixth victim. He was now ranking alongside Galland as the Jagdwaffe's highest scorer but moments later he was shot down, the victim of another Spitfire in the area.

Although Wick was seen to have bailed out of his aircraft over the sea, there was no further sign of him. In desperation, his wingman and Stab colleague, Oberleutnant Rudi Pflanz, held in the area as long as he could, searching for his friend, but when his fuel had got too low he reluctantly returned across the Channel; he even tried transmitting over the radio on the British fighter frequency that a Spitfire had been shot down in the hope that the British would mount a search in the area. However, despite extensive air and sea searches over the following days Wick's body was never found. Having flown nearly 170 combat missions, Wick was the first recipient of the Oak Leaves to lose his life in combat.

Another to fall during this period was Hans-Karl Mayer, Kommandeur of I./JG 53 and the Geschwader's highest scorer, who went missing on 17 October after taking off on a test flight. Mayer, holder of the Knight's Cross, had been credited with thirty victories; his body was washed ashore on the south coast of England ten days later.

Mayer's JG 53 had been amongst the Jagdwaffe's top scorers during the Battle of Britain with more than 250 enemy aircraft destroyed, although the Geschwader had lost more than fifty pilots killed, wounded or taken as prisoners of war. Another unit to claim more than 250 enemy aircraft was JG 26 but it had also lost nearly fifty pilots killed, missing or captured. There was no doubting the courage and commitment as the figures for JG 54, JG 27 and JG 52 were similar. And so it went on. Overall, the Luftwaffe lost more than 600 Bf 109s during the Battle of Britain, although the Jagdwaffe had claimed nearly 800 Spitfires and Hurricanes. This gave it a slightly better fighter-to-fighter kill ratio than the RAF but its successes were only one-quarter of what had been expected at the start of the campaign when figures of around 5 : 1 were anticipated, indeed expected, by the hierarchy.

The Jagdwaffe had suffered as a result of losing pilots but production of the Bf 109E continued to meet demands and deliveries remained in excess of 150 aircraft per month. The Emil had now been further improved with the introduction of the E-7 sub-variant, capable of carrying an auxiliary drop tank for additional fuel or bombs of different weights. The E-8 and E-9, which would be the final sub-variants of the Emil, followed but these were not new airframes, rather they were converted E-3s and E-4s with the E-9 being a reconnaissance version of the E-8. These latest sub-variants were powered by the improved DB 601E engine that generated 1,350 hp and had first appeared during the autumn of 1940. Production of the Bf 109E would cease in early 1942, by which time more than 4,000 Emils had been built.

The Bf 109E had proved to be the Luftwaffe's best fighter during 1940 by some margin but the next variant, the Bf 109F, had already come off the production line and had made its first combat appearance during the latter days of the Battle of Britain when it was flown operationally for the first time by Werner Mölders on 9 October.

Compared to the earlier Emil, the Bf 109F was much improved aerodynamically with changes including a much smoother and more streamlined front to the aircraft, a re-designed wing, which included new leading edge slats, and a completely re-designed tail section. Many experienced pilots felt the 109 Friedrich was the best handling of all the 109 series and the variant also benefitted from greater fuel efficiency, which increased its combat radius by more than a third.

As 1940 came to a close, the Luftwaffe's bombers continued the nightly raids against London. Hitler still believed there remained an outside chance of British morale collapsing and Churchill submitting to defeat but the reality was quite different; even Göring had lost interest in the campaign, returning instead to Berlin to concentrate on his collection of art and other treasures. The number of German bombing sorties against London gradually decreased from nearly 4,000 in December 1940 to below 1,500 by February 1941, and by May the last major raids had been flown against London.

Any thoughts of a renewed campaign against Britain during the spring of 1941 never materialized as Hitler turned his attention elsewhere, which is not overly surprising given that he had not considered Britain his main enemy when war had broken out nearly two years before and defeating Britain was certainly not his highest priority now. Hitler chose instead to leave the planned invasion of Britain on the sidelines, to be returned to if and when necessary.

The Jagdgeschwader in northern France soon returned to strength as the improved Bf 109F appeared in greater numbers. There was also a change in strategy by RAF Fighter Command. Having spent the first eighteen months of the war fighting a defensive air battle, the RAF fighters were now able to go on to the offensive for the first time and carried out a mix of low-level incursions across the Channel to attack Luftwaffe airfields and installations, with larger formations carrying out fighter sweeps to entice the Jagdwaffe into combat.

Great air battles raged along the Channel Front throughout the summer of 1941. The roles of the two air forces were now reversed as the Jagdflieger were fighting over their own, albeit occupied, territory and had the advantage of operating close to their own airfields. When flying as a formation of four, the pilots found that flying in line abreast offered advantages over the finger-four but as more Jagdgruppen were deployed elsewhere, it was left to JG 26 and JG 2 to become the RAF's main adversaries during their daytime excursions across the Channel, with the two Geschwader having to defend the entire Channel coast and Atlantic Wall stretching from Belgium to Spain.

Still commanding JG 26, and now an Oberstleutnant, Adolf Galland had been Germany's first recipient of the Swords to the Knight's Cross with Oak Leaves. The announcement of his Swords came on 21 June and he received the news in hospital that evening having been shot down during the late afternoon after claiming his seventieth victory, a Spitfire to the north of Etaples. Galland was instructed not to fly any more combat missions but he ignored the order and continued to lead JG 26 against the incursions and fighter sweeps, adding twelve more RAF fighters to his total before the end of August.

Galland's three Gruppen were based at Moorseele in Belgium, and at St-Omer and Abbeville in northern France. Amongst Galland's many distinguished pilots was Oberleutnant Josef Priller of 1./JG 26 who went on a run of victories in a period of six weeks between mid-June and the end of July 1941 when he claimed twenty-four RAF fighters including twenty-two Spitfires, to bring his overall total to forty-four and earn him the Oak Leaves to his Knight's Cross.

Leading JG 2 was Wilhelm Balthasar, who had been appointed Kommodore earlier in the year having previously served during the Battle of Britain as Kommandeur of III./JG 3. During the last week of June 1941, Balthasar claimed nine enemy aircraft, including five RAF Blenheim twin-engine light bombers in the St-Omer–Lille–Gravelines area, to bring his total to forty-seven victories, including the seven he had claimed during the Spanish Civil War. On 2 July came the announcement of the award of the Oak Leaves to his Knight's Cross for his fortieth victory of the war but then on the following day he was killed during combat with RAF fighters to the south-east of St-Omer. Balthasar was posthumously promoted to Major and buried alongside his father at a First World War cemetery in Flanders.

Appointed as Balthasar's replacement was the high-scoring Walter Oesau. Oesau enjoyed much success while leading JG 2 on the Channel Front. His first success, a Spitfire during the afternoon of 10 August 1941, was followed up two days later by shooting down five Spitfires during the day to take his total past a century of victories.

JG 2 took its total number of victories past 800 during the same month to make it the leading fighter wing. Amongst the most successful were: 23-year-old Oberleutnant Egon Mayer, Kapitän of 7./JG 2 based at St Pol-Brias, who was awarded the Knight's Cross in August having achieved twenty victories; Oberleutnant Siegfried Schnell, Kapitän of

9./JG 2, who claimed fifteen Spitfires during July, for which he was awarded the Oak Leaves to his Knight's Cross; and Oberfeldwebel Josef Wurmheller of II./JG 2, who claimed ten Spitfires in three weeks during August, which earned him the Knight's Cross.

It was also during August 1941 that the Luftwaffe introduced a new fighter type, the Focke-Wulf FW 190, a fighter that would become the scourge of Allied fighter pilots for the rest of the war. When the first FW 190A entered service with 6./JG 26 at Le Bourget in France, it was technically superior to its Allied adversaries. Dubbed rather emotively as the *Würger* ('Shrike'), its origins dated back to 1937 when a development contract was placed for a second German fighter to supplement the Bf 109. The contract was given to Focke-Wulf Flug-zeugbau and the design was a single-engine, low-wing monoplane fighter that could be powered by either a Daimler-Benz DB 601 twelve-cylinder engine, as fitted to the Bf 109, or a BMW 139 eighteen-cylinder radial engine. The prototype was first flown by Focke-Wulf's chief test pilot, Hans Sander, in June 1939 and early test flights witnessed speeds in excess of 370 mph. The BMW 139 was soon replaced by the BMW 801 fourteen-cylinder engine and the early production aircraft, designated the FW 190A-1 rolled off the production line in June 1941. The early aircraft were armed with two MG 17 7.9 mm machine guns in the wing roots, two fuselage-mounted MG 17s above the engine cowling, with all four machine guns synchronized to fire through the propeller arc, and two MG FF 20 mm cannon in the outer section of the wing.

The FW 190A was a superb aircraft. The general layout of the cockpit was good and on the ground the 190 offered better visibility looking forward than the 109; the 109 pilot had poor all-round visibility in comparison due to the framework design of the canopy and a large blind spot to the rear whereas the design of the FW 190's single-piece sliding canopy meant the pilot could clearly see his tail. In the air the 190 was aerodynamically beautiful. Its semi-reclined seat reduced the effect of gravitational forces on the pilot when in combat but the most impressive feature of the aircraft was its high rate of roll. Although it had a tendency to flick, the pilots soon learned how to turn this into an advantage when having to get out of a tight corner.

During the early weeks of the FW 190's combat career, the Allies were seemingly unaware of the new fighter and at times even attributed the new radial-engine fighter reports to be referring to captured French Curtiss Hawk 75As. Gradually, though, more FW 190s appeared along the Channel Front and the yellow-nosed fighters of Galland's JG 26 soon gained a fearful reputation amongst the Allied fighter pilots as their losses started to mount.

As with the introduction of any new fighter, it would take a while for the FW 190A really to shape the air war but it quickly proved to be very capable, although its performance was noted to drop off when at high altitude, in particular when operating above 25,000 feet, and every effort would be made to rectify this in later variants, particularly the A-3 which would become the first major production variant.

Focke-Wulf was soon producing 250 new aircraft every month and the FW 190A outperformed the Spitfire V, at the time the best of the RAF's fighters, in just about every aspect except its turning radius. Nonetheless, the FW 190A had considerably better firepower and straight line speed at low level, which would later lead to the British accelerating into service the more powerful Spitfire IX.[16]

Deteriorating weather towards the end of 1941 brought an end to skirmishes across the Channel and they would not resume until the following spring by which time the FW 190A was meeting the Luftwaffe's great expectations with Allied fighter losses continuing to rise. The Channel Front belonged to the Jagdflieger.

Chapter 4

The Mediterranean and the Balkans, 1941

The war against Britain had not turned out quite the way Hitler had planned but, nonetheless, he turned his attention towards a conquest in the east and war against the Soviet Union. In order to plan for such a mighty undertaking he did not want, nor could he really afford, distractions elsewhere but Hitler was more than irritated at the way his ally, Italy, had failed to achieve success in North Africa and in the Balkans. Furthermore, the strategic importance of Malta, a small island just sixty miles from the southern coast of Sicily and home to British air and naval bases, was becoming increasingly evident.

Malta was ideally situated to disrupt the Axis air and sea supply routes to the Italian colony of Libya as well as for providing vital air support to British naval units transiting through the Mediterranean. The Italian Regia Aeronautica had so far failed to neutralize the island's airfields and harbours and Hitler realized that a successful campaign in North Africa could only be possible by eliminating Malta as a British base.

Hitler was initially reluctant to assist his ally but the Italian invasion of Greece, which had commenced in October 1940, had started to struggle and British determination not to give any ground in Egypt, followed by the subsequent advance against the Italians in North Africa, now made it obvious to Hitler that the Italian position in the Balkans, Central Mediterranean and North Africa would not improve without German intervention.

The Luftwaffe committed to the Mediterranean theatre in January 1941 when Hans Geisler's X. Fliegerkorps, with more than 300 aircraft, was transferred from Norway to Sicily and Libya to support the Italians. Initially no single-seat fighters were sent to the Mediterranean as the bomber and dive bomber units were to be supported by Bf 110s of ZG 26, sent to protect the supply routes between Italy and North Africa and to conduct anti-shipping operations, as well as countering RAF reconnaissance and convoy patrols in the Mediterranean.

The first fighter unit to arrive in North Africa were the Zerstörers of III./ZG 26 under the command of Major Karl Kaschka. Arriving at Tripoli at the end of January, they were soon joined by Ju 87s and Ju 88s tasked to carry out dive bomber and air interdiction sorties in support of Erwin Rommel's new Afrika Korps, which had been dispatched to North Africa as a matter of urgency to reinforce Italian forces and prevent an Axis defeat.

While it would be some time before the Bf 109 was introduced to the desert, 7./JG 26 was sent to Sicily during early February 1941. The Staffel was led by 22-year-old Oberleutnant Joachim Müncheberg, already a combat veteran and holder of the Knight's Cross. Now with twenty-three victories and leading the only Bf 109s in the Mediterranean theatre, he faced an enormous challenge. His small unit would never exceed nine aircraft and its arrival at Gela coincided with a reduction in Luftwaffe forces in Sicily as more units were being deployed to Libya to support the Afrika Korps.

Under Müncheberg's leadership the Bf 109Es of 7./JG 26 would make a significant contribution to the air war over the Mediterranean during the next four months, flying numerous sorties against Malta and causing havoc amongst its defenders. When the 109s first appeared over the island during the late afternoon of 12 February it came as a complete shock to the defenders. One flight of Hurricanes was scrambled to intercept what the pilots believed to be a handful of Ju 88s approaching Malta at 20,000 feet but they suddenly found themselves being bounced by three 109s led by Müncheberg. In the space of just a few minutes two of the Hurricanes were shot down, one by Müncheberg, and a third returned to Malta badly damaged.

It was much the same during the days that followed. The appearance of the yellow-nosed Bf 109Es of Müncheberg's Staffel had an immediate and damaging impact on the morale of those defending Malta. The combat experience of men like Müncheberg was completely at odds with that of some of the Hurricane pilots who were experiencing air combat for the first time. The 109s were able to climb to altitude at leisure and arrive in the vicinity of the island at heights of 20,000 feet or higher where they could engage the defenders from a position of great advantage and with superior performance.

While the Hurricane had been a match for most Italian aircraft in the Mediterranean, it was outclassed when it came to countering Bf 109s. Furthermore, Malta had too few Hurricanes to mount regular patrols, the Hurricanes were of a lesser standard than those retained back in England for home defence and Malta's isolation meant it was necessary for the RAF to conserve fuel and reduce flying time as much as possible. The Hurricanes generally operated in formations of three and there were often occasions when just six aircraft were scrambled to meet an enemy raid. Radar limitations and local operating procedures exacerbated the problem, which all resulted in there being insufficient warning time for the defenders to climb to the required height to engage the raiders before they hit their target. The Hurricanes would first have to climb to 20,000 feet to the south of the island and then turn northwards to try and engage the raiders on their way home.

During the early afternoon of 26 February the Axis launched one of its biggest raids on Malta with a force of seventy aircraft – a mix of Ju 87s, Ju 88s, He 111s and Do 17s – attacking the airfield at Luqa.[17] Escorting the attacking force were Müncheberg's Staffel and Italian Macchi C.200s and while the main bomber force arrived over the airfield virtually unscathed, four of the defending Hurricanes were claimed by the Bf 109s, including two by Müncheberg. The attack proved devastating. A number of RAF Wellingtons were destroyed on the ground and there was extensive damage to hangars and other technical buildings on the airfield.

Müncheberg's Staffel was joined briefly by the Bf 109Es of I./JG 27, led by Hauptmann Eduard Neumann, which stopped off in Sicily on the way to Libya to support the Afrika Korps. During their brief stay in Sicily, Neumann's 109s twice joined Müncheberg's on operations over Malta. The first occasion was during the late afternoon of 5 March when the Bf 109Es escorted sixty bombers.[18] Once overhead the island the 109s engaged the defending Hurricanes and also carried out strafing attacks against targets of opportunity. During the raid Müncheberg added another Hurricane to his total, and another Hurricane was claimed by Leutnant Willi Kothmann of JG 27; the unit's only claim over Malta during its stay. With the Luftwaffe continuing to build up its forces in Libya, most of its units had left Sicily by the middle of March, leaving only Müncheberg's Bf 109Es to carry out nuisance raids against Malta.

Hitler's planning for the invasion of the Soviet Union was further interrupted when a change of government in Yugoslavia meant that the country abandoned proposals to side with Germany. Fearing an Allied presence in Yugoslavia or Greece would threaten his attack on the Soviet Union, Hitler decided to secure the Balkans.

Alexander Löhr's Luftflotte 4 was tasked to support the German invasion of Yugoslavia and Greece, and so VIII. Fliegerkorps, under the command of Wolfram von Richthofen, a cousin of the famous Red Baron, Manfred von Richthofen, gradually assembled in Romania and Bulgaria. As a long believer in close air support, Richthofen had much to prove as the Ju 87 Stukas had suffered badly over southern England. By early April 1941 he had under his command some 600 aircraft within 200 miles of Belgrade, the Yugoslav capital, of which over half were bombers and dive bombers located in Bulgaria. The rest, a mix of fighter and reconnaissance aircraft, were located in western Romania.

The Balkans campaign began on 6 April when a force of 150 bombers and dive bombers, mainly He 111s and Ju 87s, escorted by fighters, bombed Belgrade. Fighter units assigned to support the campaign included Bf 109Es of two Gruppen from JG 54 and a single Gruppe from each of JG 27 and JG 77. While the Yugoslav Air Force tried to intervene, its relatively modest force of 400 inferior aircraft was immediately over-whelmed. Many Yugoslav aircraft were destroyed on the ground and there was only ever brief fighter-to-fighter air combat over Yugoslavia.

With the air threat neutralized, Richthofen's units provided support to the German ground forces attacking Yugoslav defensive positions. The campaign was over within days and by 18 April the last pockets of Yugoslav resistance had disappeared. Müncheberg's 7./JG 26 was one of the fighter units involved in the brief campaign, having temporarily left Sicily on the opening day of the campaign for a new base at Taranto to operate over southern Yugoslavia.

Müncheberg had again proved to be a great leader and was inspirational to the other young men of his Staffel. Many learned from him, including one young pilot, 22-year-old Leutnant Klaus Mietusch, who had flown alongside Müncheberg as his deputy. Mietusch had joined 7./JG 26 at the outbreak of war and had served with the unit during the campaign against France. His first victory, a Hurricane over Dunkirk, came at the end of May 1940 and he added a second victory before the end of the year. While operating from Sicily he added three more to his total before claiming his sixth victory, a Hawker Fury biplane of the Royal Yugoslav Air Force over Podriga during the opening day of the campaign. Müncheberg was also credited with a Fury over Yugoslavia during the brief campaign before his Staffel returned to Sicily to resume its battle against Malta.

While the campaign in Yugoslavia had been quick and straight-forward, the campaign in Greece would prove much harder. Codenamed Operation Marita, the German invasion of Greece also started on 6 April to coincide with the attack on Yugoslavia. Greece had already been at war for some time and its mountainous terrain made close air support much harder. There was also the fact that Britain had provided support to Greece – mainly Hurricanes, Blenheims and Gladiators – and so the attacking German forces came up against a more capable opposition.

The bulk of the Greek Army was on the Albanian border in action with Italian forces and the German invasion through Bulgaria now provided a second front. The Greek Army was soon overrun and the British reinforcements retreated towards the Isthmus of Corinth as the decision was made to abandon mainland Greece. Despite some resistance by the small number of Hurricanes, the Jagdwaffe soon enjoyed air supremacy over the region. One to achieve much success during the campaign was Oberleutnant Gustav Rödel, Kapitän of 4./JG 27, who achieved six victories over Greece; three Greek fighters on 15 April and three RAF Hurricanes five days later. German forces reached the city of Athens on 27 April and by 1 May the last Allied units had evacuated the Greek mainland. Although the Luftwaffe had not had it all its own way in the Balkans, more than a hundred Yugoslav, Greek and British aircraft were destroyed, twice its own losses.

Many Jagdgruppen involved in the Balkans campaign were now transferred to the Eastern Front but III./JG 27, led by Hauptmann Max Dobislav, moved to Sicily to provide some welcome support for Müncheberg's Staffel who had now been operating alone for nearly three months without a rest. On 6 May Dobislav's 109s joined Müncheberg's in a substantial attack against Malta during which III./JG 27 made its first claim over the island. The successful pilot was 23-year-old Oberleutnant Erbo Graf von Kageneck, Kapitän of 9. Staffel, and the Hurricane he claimed over Malta was his fifteenth success of the war. Kageneck added three more victories before III./JG 27 left Sicily later in the month for the Eastern Front but he would later be killed in North Africa after sixty-seven victories for which he was awarded the Oak Leaves to his Knight's Cross.

The successful campaign in the Balkans had coincided with gains in North Africa and so the stage was now set for the invasion of Crete, which, like Malta, occupied a position of strategic importance. While an island of barren and mountainous terrain with limited lines of communication might not appear to be of any great value, the side occupying Crete could control the eastern Mediterranean by sea and from the air. As long as Crete was held by the British, the Allies were in a position to mount raids against the Balkan countries and the vitally important Romanian oilfields at Ploesti, Germany's main source of petroleum.

All Luftwaffe assets in Greece were made available for the invasion of Crete and with two air corps under his command – Richthofen's VIII. Fliegerkorps and XI. Fliegerkorps under the command of Kurt Student – Löhr had available to him an aerial force of 650 aircraft: nearly 450 bombers and dive bombers, a hundred Bf 109Es and a hundred Bf 110Cs. It was a formidable force against which the Allies on Crete could deploy fewer than thirty defensive fighters.

The German invasion of Crete, codenamed Operation Mercury, commenced on 20 May with an airborne assault consisting of gliderborne and parachute troops. Richthofen's task was to establish air supremacy over Crete as soon as possible and, although the Allied pilots enjoyed considerable success against the vulnerable Ju 52 transport aircraft, the 109s soon overwhelmed the defenders.

But on the ground the situation was quite different. The British fully intended to hold the island for as long as possible and so fighting soon developed into several small and uncoordinated actions as the Germans found the Allies well and truly dug-in. As more German reinforcements arrived, the Allies were eventually forced to fight a series of rearguard actions as they retreated south across the island from where an evacuation commenced.

While the battle on the ground raged, Richthofen turned his attention to attacking the British Mediterranean Fleet and to clearing the sea lanes to Crete. An example was on 22 May when the 109s of 7./JG 77, including Leutnant Wolf-Dietrich Huy, attacked British warships off Crete and during the course of the day inflicted serious and fatal damage to a number of ships. Huy would later be awarded the Knight's Cross, principally for his exploits during the Crete campaign, and was eventually credited with forty victories.

Crete was ultimately a lost cause for the Allies and on 1 June the remaining Allied troops on the island surrendered. While the battle for Crete did not overly delay Hitler's planned invasion of the Soviet Union, the campaign had proved costly and put an end to any idea of a similar airborne assault against Malta.

By now, most Luftwaffe units had already left Sicily for the Eastern Front and finally it was the turn of Müncheberg's 7./JG 26 to leave but unlike other units destined for the east, the Staffel moved to North Africa instead. While operating from Sicily, Müncheberg's small force had claimed nearly fifty victories, twenty of which had been credited to him to bring his overall total to forty-three, without a single loss, bringing Müncheberg a well earned Oak Leaves to his Knight's Cross.

It had been a monumental effort by the pilots of 7./JG 26, although many would not survive the war. Klaus Mietusch would be killed during the final defence of the Reich in September 1944 and others to later fall in combat included Hans Johannsen (killed in March 1942 with eight victories), Karl-Heinz Ehlen (killed in April 1942 with seven victories), Melchior Kestel (also with seven victories and killed in June 1943) and Karl Laub (seven victories and killed in December 1944).

The Luftwaffe's departure from Sicily left the Mediterranean air war temporarily in the hands of the Italian Regia Aeronautica and coincided with changes in command on the island of Malta, as well as the arrival of reinforcements. The RAF was now able to assume a more offensive campaign against Axis supply shipping operating between Europe and North Africa and by November 1941 the Allies operating from Malta were sinking three-quarters of supplies destined for Rommel's Afrika Korps.

Chapter 5

Invasion in the East: Barbarossa

While Hitler had been occupied with waging war in the west, he could do so in the knowledge that he would not have to fight a second front with the Soviet Union because of the non-aggression treaty signed with Stalin before the war. But as German forces were making advances in the west, Stalin had been busy in the east and had absorbed the three Baltic states of Latvia, Lithuania and Estonia into the Soviet Union, as well as annexing large parts of Finland and occupying part of Romania; in the first year of the Second World War, 175,000 square miles of territory and 20 million people had been brought under his rule. Stalin clearly wanted more and by the end of 1940 Hitler felt convinced that the Soviet Union posed a real threat to his own plans and so ordered an invasion of the Soviet Union. The plan, called Operation Barbarossa, was to use similar Blitzkrieg methods as before and would result in a campaign unparalleled in both scale and ferocity.

As far as the Luftwaffe's High Command was concerned, thoughts and opinions about the invasion were divided. Jeschonnek, for example, felt that Germany was at last about to embark on a proper war and was in favour of an invasion but others, of whom Göring was the most notable, were clearly against the idea. Göring felt his units had not been given a chance to rest or recuperate since the invasion of Poland. He was already fighting a war in the west and had now become increasingly involved in the Mediterranean, the Balkans and North Africa. Furthermore, neither aircraft production nor the development of new fighters was progressing as well as he had hoped. The Luftwaffe had made little progress in the year since the campaign against France and Göring was not convinced the Soviet Union could be quickly defeated. He tried several times to persuade Hitler not to continue with his plan but it was no good. In the end he simply gave up and went on leave.

Given no option but to prepare for war on the Eastern Front, the Luftwaffe made available as many assets as it could. According to Hitler, the Soviet Union would be defeated in weeks and so the Luftwaffe was expected to defeat the Soviet Air Force, both in the air and on the ground within that time, while also providing valuable support to German ground forces advancing east. These were standard Blitzkrieg tactics but in the event of a prolonged campaign in the east it was already clear that the lack of a four-engine heavy bomber would restrict operations of a strategic nature.

The Luftwaffe was able to commit three air fleets to the opening phase of the campaign, some 3,000 aircraft, of which just over two-thirds were combat aircraft, and this mass aerial force amounted to about 60 per cent of its total strength at the time. The plan was for Luftflotte 1, under the command of the energetic Alfred Keller, to support Army Group North. Its fighter component consisted of Bf 109Fs from JG 54 initially based at four airfields – Lindental, Rautenberg, Trakehnen and Blumenfeld – and a single Gruppe of JG 53 at Neusiedel, with the entire fighter force placed under the command of the very capable and popular Major Hannes Trautloft.

The strongest of the three air fleets with nearly 1,200 aircraft, of which more than 350 were Bf 109s, was Luftflotte 2, commanded by Kesselring. Luftflotte 2 was to provide air support to Army Group Centre and gain air superiority over the Eastern Front. For this task Kesselring had available to him nine Gruppen of Bf 109s: two from JG 27 and a single Gruppe of JG 52, a mix of E and F models based at Sobolevo and Berzniki, and all under the command of Major Wolfgang Schellmann; four Gruppen of JG 51 with Bf 109Fs based at Siedlce, Staravis, Halaszi and Crzevica, under the command of Oberstleutnant Werner Mölders; and two Gruppen of JG 53, also equipped with Bf 109Fs based at Crzevica and Sobolevo, led by Major Günther Freiherr von Maltzahn. Also available to Kesselring were two Gruppen of Bf 110s of ZG 26 to provide long-range fighter cover.

Alexander Löhr's Luftflotte 4 was tasked to support Army Group South. Löhr had seven Gruppen of 109s available to him: three from

JG 3 were equipped with Bf 109Fs and based at Hostynne, Dub and Modorovka, under the command of Major Günther Lützow; a single Gruppe of Bf 109Fs of JG 52, under the command of Major Gotthard Handrick, was based at Mizil/Pipera; and two Gruppen of JG 77 plus another Gruppe, I(J)./LG 2, all equipped with Bf 109Es, were based at Bacau, Roman and Janca, and were all under the command of Major Bernhard Woldenga.

The Luftwaffe had assembled a very capable force, including nearly 800 Bf 109s, but it was a smaller force than had been deployed either for the initial Blitzkrieg at the start of the war or at the height of the Battle of Britain. Hitler was about to embark on his most ambitious undertaking yet but he would do so with fewer combat aircraft than his previous campaigns in the west.

While the opposing armies on the ground might at first glance have appeared relatively evenly matched, with nearly 150 divisions available to either side, the composition of a German division compared to a Russian division was different, particularly when it came to armoured units, with the Red Army enjoying a considerable advantage in the number of tanks. As far as the air war would be concerned, German intelligence had estimated the total strength of the Soviet Air Force to be in the order of 8,000 aircraft but this would prove to be a significant underestimate. In reality the Red Air Force could muster between 12,000 and 15,000 aircraft, of which about half, including 3,500 fighters, were concentrated in the west of the Soviet Union.[19]

Soviet front-line combat aircraft were organized into air divisions, with the basic flying component of the Red Air Force being the regiment, consisting of about sixty aircraft, with each regiment being made up of squadrons along the same lines as the RAF and with numbers similar to those of a Staffel. Tactically, the Russian pilots flew in three aircraft 'vics' and, generally, the quality of Soviet pilot training had produced an inferior opponent to the Jagdwaffe. Amongst the adversaries would be the Ilyushin Il-2 Sturmovik ground-attack aircraft, which would become the single most produced aircraft in history with more than 35,000 built, and the Polikarpov I-16, the world's first low-wing cantilever monoplane fighter with a retractable undercarriage and the backbone of the Soviet Air Force.

The Red Air Force was, however, in the process of converting to new single-engine fighters to match the ability of the Bf 109E. One was the Yak-1, a fast, manoeuvrable and reasonably well armed fighter. It was aerodynamically well designed and similar in size to the Bf 109, and in terms of performance was the best of the new breed of Russian fighters, although the latest variants of the Bf 109 were quicker, particularly at heights up to 15,000 feet, and could climb slightly faster. The Yak also suffered from relatively poor firepower and the pilots lacked training in air-to-air gunnery. Nonetheless, when in a position of numerical advantage, and in the hands of a dogged and determined Russian defender, the Yak-1 would prove a very capable adversary and was the first of a series of Yak fighters that would eventually see a combined production of 37,000 aircraft. Two other Soviet fighters to enter service, both similar in size and performance to the Yak-1, were the Mikoyan and Gurevich MiG-3, designed more as a high-altitude fighter and built in increasingly large numbers during 1941, and the Lavochkin–Gorbunov–Gudkov LaGG-3. Both aircraft lacked manoeuvrability and were relatively unforgiving when in the hands of a novice pilot. The LaGG-3, in particular, suffered from poor acceleration and was hard to handle in combat, and the MiG-3, despite having the streamlined appearance of a modern fighter, proved sluggish in the air when up against a high-class opponent and its long nose reduced forward visibility when on the ground and for deflection shooting during air combat.

As far as the Soviet Air Force was concerned it was all about numbers. Quantity was considered more important than quality and it would be these four Soviet fighters – the Polikarpov I-16, the Yak-1, the MiG-3 and the LaGG-3 – that would bear the brunt of the early fighting on the Eastern Front. While individually these four fighters would prove little match for the newer Bf 109F, the Red Air Force had the benefit of large numbers. Soviet aircraft production was exceeding 1,000 aircraft per month and the Russians would soon receive large numbers of fighters from the Allies – British Hurricanes and Spitfires, and American P-39 Airacobras and P-40 Tomahawks – supplied under a Lend-Lease agreement designed to bridge the gap between the initial onslaught of Barbarossa and the Soviet's industrial machine spooling up to full capacity. By the end of the war some 10,000 fighters would be delivered to Russia under this agreement and there would be times when the Jagdflieger would find he was outnumbered by more than five to one.

The Luftwaffe went into Barbarossa knowing that the Soviet Air Force enjoyed similar numerical superiority in the air to the Soviet forces on the ground but was confident the speed of the German attack and its advance on the ground would soon outweigh any numerical disadvantage. Furthermore, the belief was that the Luftwaffe's capabilities in the air were far greater than what it would face.

Hitler eventually launched Operation Barbarossa during the early hours of 22 June 1941. The early artillery barrage signalled the start of events as the air offensive got under way with every available combat aircraft involved. It was still dark when the Luftwaffe units got airborne as any delay waiting for dawn would have given the Soviet Air Force vital time to respond to a warning of attack.

The first kill on the Eastern Front was credited to Oberleutnant Robert Olejnik, Kapitän of 1./JG 3, who was flying a reconnaissance mission along the Russian border when he spotted a pair of Russian I-16 fighters getting airborne in the semi-darkness below and promptly shot one down as the second disappeared. Whether this was the first kill on the Eastern Front is uncertain, however, as this act occurred about the same time as Leutnant Hans Witzel of 5./JG 27 was shooting down two Russian I-15 biplanes. Either way, it was still not even 04.00 and the 109s had already made their mark.

The main attacks followed, just as dawn was breaking, and caught the Soviet Air Force completely by surprise. At many airfields the Russian aircraft were lined up wing-tip to wing-tip, as if preparing for a parade, making it easy for the bombers to cause havoc, and when daylight came the attacking aircraft were able to strafe along the lines.

The plan worked well. Very few Soviet aircraft were encountered in the air and the attack took the Red Air Force completely by surprise. The first wave was then followed up by further attacks against more airfields during the day. Many Jagdgruppen were employed primarily on ground-attack missions because the Luftwaffe did not have enough bombers and dive bombers to mount large-scale raids against the high number of Russian airfields along its western border. For this role the

109s carried the SD-2 Splitterbombe, a fragmentation device weighing just 2 kg and designed to explode either on impact with the ground or just above. Each Bf 109 could carry dozens of these small devices, carried in four bulky panniers, and when dropped in sufficient numbers they could cause severe fragmentation damage to aircraft parked on the ground. Unfortunately, though, the SD-2s had to be dropped from low level where the Bf 109s were susceptible to ground fire and there were a number of occasions when the devices were known to hang up, often resulting in accidents when aircraft landed back at their airfields.

The Luftwaffe recorded just thirty-five losses on the opening day of Barbarossa but amongst those were Major Wolfgang Schellmann, Kommodore of JG 27 and holder of the Knight's Cross with twenty-five victories, and Oberleutnant Willy Strange, Kapitän of 8./JG 3. Both came down behind Russian lines and fell into the hands of Soviet troops; neither survived. Despite these losses, the opening day had overwhelmingly belonged to the Luftwaffe as it claimed 300 Russian aircraft shot down and another 1,500 destroyed on the ground.[20]

Many Jagdgruppen made claims, including JG 54 in the northern sector, led by Hannes Trautloft, which claimed forty-five aircraft on the opening day, and in the central sector two Gruppen from JG 53 accounted for more than sixty enemy aircraft with Wolf-Dietrich Wilcke, Kommandeur of III./JG 53, becoming the Jagdwaffe's first ace on the Eastern Front having claimed five Russian aircraft during the first day.

Another unit to achieve considerable success in the central sector was JG 51, which claimed nearly seventy aircraft destroyed on the opening day, with Werner Mölders personally accounting for five: four Tupolev SB twin-engine bombers and an I-153 fighter. Mölders had now become the highest-scoring fighter pilot in history having been credited with his eighty-seventh victory and surpassing the achievement of Manfred von Richthofen during the First World War. Later that day came the announcement of the Swords to his Knight's Cross with Oak Leaves, making Mölders only the second recipient of the Swords after Adolf Galland, an award which had been announced just the day before.

A technique used by Mölders against many of his victims, particularly when attacking Sturmoviks, was initially to position off to one side and at a distance from where he could carefully observe the enemy formation. He would then turn in and use his excess speed to get close very quickly, offset at an angle typically of 30 degrees, and when in range he would aim towards the central part of his target where the cockpit compartment was located. From such a close range it would prove lethal and many of his victims were shot down without having seen their attacker.

During the opening days of Barbarossa the bomber and dive-bomber crews flew up to six sorties a day as the fighters strove for air superiority from the outset. Soviet airfields were pulverized and aircraft destroyed on the ground. Kesselring's Luftflotte 2 attacked every Soviet airfield within a 200-mile radius of the front line and claimed to have destroyed 2,500 aircraft in the first week. There were similar successes all along the front and by the end of the first week German intelligence estimated that 4,000 Soviet aircraft had been destroyed for the loss of just 150 of its own; a staggering ratio of 27:1. While this very high ratio attracted some questioning within the German High Command, not least by Göring, the evidence seemed to support this success-rate and some even believed that the Jagdwaffe had under-claimed.

While German intelligence suggested that the Soviet Air Force was being wiped out in the opening days of the campaign, the fact that the Russians continued to fly thousands of sorties – more than 6,000 on the opening day alone[21] – implied otherwise. Even at the end of the first week the Soviet Air Force was still able to mount large-scale bombing raids. One example was on 30 June when waves of Russian bombers carried out heavy raids in the central sector, although this only provided JG 51 with more opportunities to add to its score. The unit promptly accounted for more than a hundred aircraft during the day to become the first Geschwader to reach 1,000 aerial victories. Mölders alone destroyed five Tupolev SB bombers in the Bobruysk area during the day, bringing his personal total to fourteen since the opening of the campaign.

The first week of Barbarossa had been a great success for the Luftwaffe. Although the Soviet Air Force had not been completely annihilated, as had perhaps been naively hoped, it had been wounded enough to allow the Luftwaffe to dominate the sky over the Eastern Front for some time. However, while thousands of Soviet aircraft had been destroyed on the ground the pilots were safe and this would make the task of forming new units much easier once aircraft had been replaced.

The Eastern Front soon stretched nearly 3,000 miles with conditions varying enormously from the cold Arctic wastes of the Barents Sea at the northern extremities to the warmer, almost sub-tropical shores, of the Black Sea in the south. With air superiority effectively in hand, the Luftwaffe was now able to turn its attention to providing air support to the advancing troops on the ground. The German army groups had made gains, although the Red Army was still occupying a vast pocket around Bialystok, which eventually fell on 1 July, and Minsk, which did not fall until 9 July. As German forces squeezed the Soviet troops within the pockets, many managed to escape but, nonetheless, some 600,000 Soviet troops were killed, missing, wounded or taken prisoner. This success was soon followed by victory at Smolensk, resulting in another 300,000 Soviet prisoners, leaving the door to Moscow, the key to victory in the east, seemingly wide open.

With little evidence of Russian resistance in the air, the 109s were able to enjoy *freier Jagd* sorties, giving them freedom to roam over the Eastern Front and to carry out attacks against targets of opportunity. When there were encounters in the air, much of the aerial combat took place at medium and lower levels where the Bf 109 enjoyed an advantage over its Soviet adversaries. The early battles had taken their toll on the Red Air Force and many Russians were thrown into the air war with barely adequate training.

The Luftwaffe also benefitted from mobile radar and a basic reporting system, which gave the Jagdgeschwader an advantage over the Soviet fighters. Confidence was understandably high as scores started to mount. By mid-July, JG 51 had destroyed 500 Soviet aircraft since the opening day of Barbarossa for the loss of just three 109s. Mölders personally passed a century of successes since the start of the war when, on 15 July, he claimed two victories during the day. Mölders had accounted for a staggering thirty-three Soviet aircraft in just over three weeks since the opening day of Barbarossa and later that day came the announcement of his award of the coveted Diamonds, the citation stating that the Führer had chosen this exemplar, the world's most successful fighter pilot, to be the first recipient of Germany's highest award.

The Eastern Front was proving to be a target-rich environment, almost a shooting gallery. In addition to Mölders, another to achieve great success was Leutnant Heinz Bär of 1./JG 51 who claimed fourteen Russian aircraft in the first two weeks of the campaign to add to his thirteen earlier in the war and earning him the Knight's Cross in early July; Bär would add thirty-three more to his total during the next month for which he would be awarded the Oak Leaves.

JG 3 had also enjoyed much success, with three of its pilots standing out. One was Major Günther Lützow, Kommodore of JG 3, who had scored his first success on the Eastern Front during the opening day of Barbarossa before he was awarded the Oak Leaves on 20 July after achieving his twenty-fourth success of the campaign and with his overall total on forty-seven. Lützow then went on to score at a high rate. Three weeks later his total was sixty-one and by early October he would become the second to pass eighty victories. The second member of JG 3 to distinguish himself was Walter Oesau, Kommandeur of III./JG 3. On 15 July Oesau became only the third recipient of the Swords to the Knight's Cross for his eightieth victory of the war, including forty-four Soviet aircraft in just five weeks, seven of which were claimed in one sortie on 12 July. The third was Gordon Gollob, Kapitän of 4./JG 3, who had also scored his first victory on the Eastern Front during the opening day of Barbarossa. Now promoted to Hauptmann and appointed as Kommandeur of II./JG 3, Gollob would add a further eighteen victories during August to bring his overall total to forty-two and earn him the Knight's Cross.

As German forces advanced on the ground, Mölders was able to move his JG 51 forward to airfields in the vicinity of the city of Bobruysk and then handed over command to Oberstleutnant Friedrich Beckh as Mölders was to be prevented from flying further combat missions for propaganda reasons. Mölders had proved to be a great leader and had earned the nickname *Vati* ('Daddy') from his men in recognition of his paternal attitude towards them and the care he had always shown towards their welfare. A devoutly religious person, he was always insistent that any Allied aviators captured by those under his command should be treated well. He was even known to have dined with some.

Göring appointed Mölders as his first General der Jagdflieger (Inspector-General of Fighters) but Mölders's life would soon come to an end, not in air combat but in a flying accident. On 22 November he was travelling to Berlin as a passenger in an He 111 when the aircraft encountered bad weather and suffered engine problems. As the pilot attempted to make an emergency landing the aircraft crashed and amongst those killed on board was Mölders; he was just twenty-eight years old. Werner Mölders was given a state funeral in Berlin the following week and buried at the Invalidenfriedhof, the traditional burial ground for distinguished Prussian military personnel, alongside Ernst Udet[22] and Manfred von Richthofen. Göring gave the eulogy and amongst the guard of honour were some of the Luftwaffe's finest, including Günther Lützow, Walter Oesau, Joachim Müncheberg and Adolf Galland, who would now succeed Mölders.

By the beginning of September 1941 the German Army was within touching distance of Kiev and was preparing for its supposed final assault on Leningrad, which commenced on 9 September. Within ten days the German forces were within a few miles of the city but progress thereafter was slow. Hitler ordered Leningrad to be placed under siege so that he could divert vital resources, particularly Panzers, to support his central push towards the strategic target of Moscow, which commenced on 2 October. The Red Army had been heavily depleted but still had 800,000 troops to defend Moscow and occupied a series of elaborate defence lines, which advancing German forces would first have to overcome.

Supporting the advancing troops on the ground had created problems in the air. Not only were the Jagdgeschwader at the end of a lengthening supply line, making it harder for the provision of fuel, ammunition and spares, but the amount of ground gained now meant the Luftwaffe had become thinly spread. There had also been an increasing number of 109s damaged or written off through accidents on the ground as a result of operating from poorly prepared airstrips or through pilot fatigue, and these losses were not always being replaced. Furthermore, resources were needed elsewhere, such as in the Mediterranean and North Africa, and this resulted in a dilution of effort for the Jagdwaffe at a time when the Red Air Force was becoming stronger by the day.

The Luftwaffe had now become overstretched and Hitler was racing against time. If his forces could not conquer the Soviet Union before the onset of winter then the Red war machine would be able to recover. It was also becoming evident how much the Luftwaffe lacked a strategic heavy bomber as its medium bombers did not have the range or capability to inflict significant damage further to the east. Soviet industry had been hit hard but it had not been destroyed. Too much time had been spent supporting the army groups on the ground instead of taking the opportunity to attack Soviet aircraft and tank factories within range of its twin-engine bombers, and so the Soviet engineers had been able to continue moving industrial machinery further east where it could be reassembled behind the safety of the Ural Mountains.

Nonetheless, the Luftwaffe had performed magnificently during Barbarossa. Many were recognized for their achievements during the campaign, including Günther Lützow, who, on 11 October, became only the fourth recipient of the Swords for his leadership of JG 3 and for his ninety-seven victories. He would become a centurion the following day with his final twenty-two victories up to that point coming in just seven days.

By December 1941 the campaign was already in its sixth month. The combination of conducting operations over a long period, often from inadequate Soviet airfields, and deteriorating weather conditions, with all the associated aircraft maintenance and logistical problems, was taking its toll. Temperatures had plummeted to −40 degrees and ground crew were having quickly to learn how to improvise cold-weather techniques, such as adding fuel to engine oil to thin the mixture so that it would not freeze and to light fires beneath aircraft engines at night to prevent them from freezing up.

Those units operating from former Soviet airfields were able to make best use of any hangar space available but, unlike the Russians, the Luftwaffe was neither equipped nor prepared for a winter campaign. The Jagdwaffe had lost 2,000 aircraft with many losses occurring as a result of the harsh operating conditions rather than due to the Soviet Air Force. While replacements were getting through in high numbers, serviceability was now proving a significant problem with less than 50 per cent of fighters being available at any one time.

As the winter weather set in, the ground offensive against Moscow slowed. The German Army was not equipped for a harsh winter campaign either and a Soviet counter-attack along the entire front during early December pushed the invaders back 200 miles. The situation was particularly desperate in the central region where the onset of winter had coincided with Kesselring's Luftflotte 2 being transferred to the Mediterranean, leaving only Wolfram von Richthofen's VIII. Fliegerkorps along the central part of the Eastern Front.

Germany's invasion of the Soviet Union in 1941 cost its Army over 200,000 killed and missing with a further 600,000 wounded. Operation Barbarossa had been the largest military operation in history in both manpower and casualties but with Germany having suffered its heaviest losses of the war, it signalled the beginning of the end of the Third Reich. For its part, the Luftwaffe had fought and won the tactical air battle but it would now be engaged in a prolonged campaign on the Eastern Front that had become increasingly more strategic in nature. The Luftwaffe was unable to fight such a campaign.

Chapter 6

North Africa and the Mediterranean, 1941–1943

The Italian entry into the war on 10 June 1940 had signalled the start of a three-year campaign in North Africa that was to be fought between the Allied and Axis powers, many of whom had colonial interests dating back to the late nineteenth century. The British reaction to Italy's declaration of war had been to cross from Egypt into Libya and this soon led to offensive and counter-offensive from either side. Hitler was concerned that a defeat of the Italian forces in the desert would risk Italy making peace with the Allies or, even worse, changing sides, and was soon convinced that only German intervention in North Africa would keep the Italians in the war. Hitler's initial plan was to send a small force to contain the situation rather than to expand it.

During the opening weeks of 1941 the Luftwaffe had built up its forces in Libya to support Rommel's Afrika Korps. The first Bf 109Es to arrive in the Western Desert were those of I./JG 27 under the command Eduard Neumann, which arrived at the small desert strip at Ain-el-Gazala in Libya on 18 April.[23] Neumann had joined the fledgling Luftwaffe at its outset and had served with the Legion Condor and was credited with two victories. A veteran of the campaign in France, Neumann had been appointed Kommandeur of I./JG 27 during the Battle of Britain. While his number of victories was relatively modest when compared to others – he only scored thirteen victories during the whole war – Eduard Neumann was nonetheless one of the finest fighter leaders.

Neumann's Gruppe was equipped with Bf 109E-7/Trops that had been fitted with ventral fuel tanks for the long transit from Germany, stopping only briefly in Sicily on the way. Neumann had become used to operating from basic airfields in Europe but conditions at Ain-el-Gazala were harsh to say the least, although the airfield would soon become the Luftwaffe's main fighter base in North Africa. Operating from Ain-el-Gazala would never be easy. The airstrip was obviously very sandy, causing conditions similar to a small sandstorm every time an aircraft taxied or took off, but there were also small rocks spread across the field, which caused damage or even injury when blown around. There was no natural protection for the aircraft and the only cover was provided by sandbagged blast pens around the site.

The 109s of I./JG 27 were in the thick of the action straight away, the pilots claiming the first four victories on the day after their arrival. All four were Hurricanes and were shot down along the coastal strip between Gazala and Tobruk. One of the Hurricanes was claimed by Oberleutnant Karl-Wolfgang Redlich, Kapitän of the 1. Staffel, and was the unit's 100th victory of the war. Another was shot down to the west of Tobruk by Leutnant Werner Schroer, the first of his many successes.[24]

Neumann was fortunate to have so many good pilots with him. Not only did he have Redlich and Schroer under his command, he had two other experienced pilots on his unit. One was Oberleutnant Ludwig Franzisket, the Gruppen-Adjutant with fourteen victories, and the other was Oberleutnant Gerhard Homuth, Kapitän of 3./JG 27, with fifteen victories. It soon proved to be a most capable unit and I./JG 27 quickly gained a strong reputation in the region; it was well-organized and well-trained, and boasted an excellent understanding of the tactics required in a desert campaign.

On the ground, the hot and dry conditions meant that sand got everywhere, causing excessive wear on engines, even with filters fitted, and the extreme heat reduced performance. However, the engine fitted to the Bf 109E, the DB 601, generally coped extremely well. Filters fitted over the air intake for the supercharger prevented ingestion of abrasive sand particles or overheating; either could cause extensive damage to the engine.

The desert war would become a war of attrition and equipment was often in short supply, not just aircraft but vehicles, clothing and food. While temperatures were constantly high, the weather conditions were not always suitable for flying as sand storms would reduce visibility to zero and even heavy rain would sometimes intervene. In the space of just an hour or two a dry sandy airfield could become a quagmire and make operations in the desert far from easy. Even when in the air, conducting operations could be difficult. Away from the coastal areas, the desert was a vast area of featureless terrain and while advancing troops on the ground were a sign of success, the great distances involved meant it was a logistical nightmare with fuel, spares and ammunition often in short supply. Furthermore, radio performance reduced over distance and often left the 109s to operate without any form of control from the ground.

However, more often than not, weather conditions were excellent for flying with clear sky and seemingly unlimited visibility, and no real obstacles by way of terrain or ground features. With few strategic targets, much of the air activity was in support of the ground forces, although the 109s of I./JG 27 were often given the freedom to operate alone and to concentrate on reducing the enemy's strength rather than be tied up in direct support of forces on the ground. The aerial fighting tended to be along the coast, often centred over the ports of Benghazi and Tripoli that were so vital to both sides, and because the position of the front line could change rapidly it was vital for the pilots to maintain an overall, and regularly updated, awareness of the situation on the ground. Having to keep a watchful eye on movements across the desert meant that most of their time was spent at medium or low level. The desert backdrop, blue sky and glaring sun often meant the 109s would typically operate at around 6,000 feet, and the high mid-day sun meant that many preferred to operate later in the day when the sun was lower and the glare less.

The types of sorties varied enormously. The Bf 109E was capable of carrying bombs or drop tanks but whenever possible flew without external stores to increase its manoeuvrability and carried out gunnery attacks against ground targets instead. In this role the 109 was given almost complete freedom to roam. The more routine missions involved escorting Ju 87s and Ju 88s but when supporting a major offensive, such as at Tobruk, the 109s were used for a variety of tasks in addition to air combat, including attacking ships or ground vehicles, armoured or otherwise; it was in the Western Desert that the fighter-bomber came into its own.

As far as air-to-air combat was concerned there were initially no surprises on either side as it was the same aircraft types operating over the desert that had fought over southern England during the Battle of Britain just a year before. The Ju 87 Stuka, for example, would perform no better in a hot and sunny climate than it had earlier done over southern England but it still remained at the forefront of the Luftwaffe's campaign in North Africa.

The Bf 109 and Hurricane would fight similar aerial battles to those they had been fighting since the outbreak of the war. As in other operational theatres, the Jagdwaffe found that the RAF tactics were outdated and, more often than not, defensive. JG 27 soon gained a reputation within the region with its use of the simple, yet effective, Schwarm formation, while maintaining the added protection of top cover. It proved a superior tactic in the desert and so mutual protection and responsibility were reinforced amongst the Gruppe's new arrivals, and the unit's discipline and preparation allowed the younger pilots to learn quickly from their more experienced colleagues.

Although JG 27 enjoyed much success, the situation on the ground had developed into something of a stalemate when Rommel was forced temporarily to abandon his attempt to take the besieged port of Tobruk until he received much-needed supplies. The 109s were often required to operate further afield, probing deeper towards Egypt, by staging through prepared airstrips near the village of Gambut, to the east of Tobruk, in order to increase their combat radius.

Despite all its success as a fighter, and to a certain extent as a ground-attack aircraft, the role of the Bf 109 would never be fully integrated into the land campaign and the Luftwaffe was never truly able to achieve the air-to-ground coordination with land forces that the Allies managed in the desert war.

The shape of the air war over the desert started to change as different types of Allied fighters appeared in the region. While the single-engine American Curtiss P-40B/C Tomahawk had not caused too much concern when it first appeared during June 1941, the more powerful and heavier-armed later variant, the P-40E Kittyhawk, with 0.5 inch machine guns replacing the 0.303 inch guns on earlier models, was a far more capable adversary; the Jagdwaffe's failure to appreciate fully the subtle differences between the sub-variants of the P-40 often proved costly.

During September the Bf 109Es of I./JG 27 were joined by II./JG 27 led by Hauptmann Wolfgang Lippert, a veteran of the campaigns in Spain, France and the Soviet Union, and a holder of the Knight's Cross with twenty-four victories. The arrival of Lippert's Gruppe enabled I./JG 27 to rotate its aircraft back to Germany and re-equip with tan-camouflaged Bf 109F-4/Trops.

A new offensive launched in November, Operation Crusader, brought the Allies quick and substantial gains. The Luftwaffe's forward airstrips around Gambut were overrun, the long siege of Tobruk was lifted and Allied forces now posed a direct threat to the German positions at Gazala. After being at Ain-el-Gazala for seven months, the 109s of I./JG 27 were forced to abandon their base, along with II./JG 27, and relocate to Martuba where they were soon to be joined by the III. Gruppe; it was the first time Bernhard Woldenga's Geschwader had been together for over a year.

The Allied offensive inevitably led to losses for the Jagdwaffe including Wolfgang Lippert, who was shot down on 23 November. Although he managed to bail out, he collided with the tail of his Bf 109F and was severely injured. He was admitted to hospital and his legs were amputated but he contracted gangrene. Lippert died of his injuries ten days after he had been shot down. Others to fall include the high-scoring Erbo Graf von Kageneck of 3./JG 27 who was mortally wounded during combat with Tomahawks and Hurricanes on 24 December. Despite his horrific wounds, Kageneck managed to get his aircraft back to base and make an emergency landing but he eventually succumbed to his wounds nearly three weeks later. Credited with sixty-seven victories and a holder of the Knight's Cross with Oak Leaves, Kageneck was just twenty-three years old.

The pendulum in North Africa now swung in favour of the Allies as the Luftwaffe could no longer operate freely over the desert. The lack of fuel and supplies also started to take effect. Fuel was being flown in by Ju 52 transport aircraft but these were susceptible to attack. Furthermore, having to abandon its airfields as the Allies advanced had cost the Jagdwaffe many aircraft that had been undergoing repairs as well as the loss of vital spares. JG 27, for example, was in a bad way, having been forced to abandon its aircraft and spares each time it was forced back across the desert and at one stage I./JG 27 was down to just four serviceable aircraft.

The combination of a prolonged campaign in North Africa and the onset of winter on the Eastern Front, which would restrict air operations over Russia for some months, saw the Luftwaffe increase its effort in the Mediterranean once more and amongst the top priorities was the conquest of Malta. Kesselring, who had commanded Luftflotte 2 on the Eastern Front, was appointed as the new Commander-in-Chief South and he now assumed command of all Wehrmacht forces operating in the Mediterranean and North Africa.

Elements previously under Kesselring's command were transferred from the Eastern Front and some of the units moving south were from Günther Freiherr von Maltzahn's JG 53. One of his units, III./JG 53 under the command of Hauptmann Wolf-Dietrich Wilcke, had briefly returned to Germany to re-equip with the Bf 109F before moving to Libya in December to be joined a few days later by the Bf 109Fs of Erhard Braune's III./JG 27. The rest of JG 53 moved to Comiso in Sicily for operations against Malta where they were joined by the Bf 109Fs of II./JG 3 led by Hauptmann Karl-Heinz Krahl.

On the island of Malta the RAF fighter defences had been reinforced and now consisted of three squadrons of Hurricanes and a Hurricane-equipped night-fighter flight. Other RAF units included detachments of Blenheim and Wellington bombers to maintain the offensive against the Axis supply lines to North Africa, as well as a reconnaissance squadron of Marylands and Hurricanes plus two Fleet Air Arm squadrons equipped with the Albacore and Swordfish.

The Luftwaffe commenced its new campaign against Malta during the morning of 20 December 1941 when Ju 88s, escorted by the newly-arrived Bf 109Fs of I./JG 53, attacked Allied shipping in the island's Grand Harbour. The attacking force of forty aircraft was met by twelve Hurricanes and a number of claims were made by both sides. One successful pilot was Oberleutnant Friedrich-Karl Müller, now Kapitän of 1./JG 53 having been promoted after ten victories while serving with the 8. Staffel on the Eastern Front. With the advantage of height and speed, the Hurricane he engaged at 20,000 feet was his twenty-second victim of the war.

The emergence of the Luftwaffe in considerable strength over Malta once more had not been a welcome sight for the defenders. Not only had the RAF suffered losses in the air but it had also suffered losses on the ground; eleven Hurricanes were destroyed during the morning. The raiders returned again the following day. This time the Hurricanes were airborne in greater numbers but the 109s still claimed four victories, one of which was credited to Maltzahn.

There were further attacks against Malta during the following days and more victories, including further success for Maltzahn. As well as negating the air threat to the Axis supply convoys, once over the island the 109s were given free range to attack whatever they could, including flying boats moored in the bays around the island, and shipping and other smaller vessels in and around Grand Harbour.

The fiercest day of action since the Luftwaffe returned to Sicily took place on 29 December and proved costly for the defenders. The first raid of the day, some forty aircraft, occurred mid-morning and was followed by a second raid of more than twenty aircraft in the early afternoon. Later in the afternoon, a third raid, including nearly twenty Bf 109s, bombed the airfields and attacked shipping around the island. By the end of the day the 109s had claimed five aircraft and destroyed a further fifteen on the ground.

The arrival of JG 53 had a devastating effect on the defenders of Malta and, despite RAF claims, only two Bf 109s were lost by the end of 1941. This, combined with the fact that no Bf 109Es had been lost in the earlier air campaign against Malta during 7./JG 26's time in Sicily, meant 1941 had proved to be particularly successful for the Jagdwaffe over the central Mediterranean. It might have been even more so had the Luftwaffe not had to divert its fighters to the Eastern Front to support Barbarossa during the year, but for the defenders of Malta it was a quite different story: nearly fifty RAF and Fleet Air Arm pilots had lost their lives.

Meanwhile in the desert, the Allied offensive, Operation Crusader, eventually ran out of steam in the early days of 1942 due to the lack of logistical support. The heart of Rommel's forces still remained and the Luftwaffe's renewed offensive against Malta had eased the supply situation as far as the Jagdwaffe was concerned. With the RAF in Malta back on the defensive once more, fewer sorties were being flown against Axis shipping and supplies were once again getting through so Rommel was able to renew his offensive in the desert. Benghazi was recaptured at the end of January 1942 and Rommel was soon pressing the British defences at Gazala.

With the pendulum swinging back in Rommel's favour once more, JG 27 moved back to its airfields around Martuba to operate as part of Nahkampfgruppe Martuba (Martuba Close-Support Group), a specialist group commanded by the Kommodore of JG 27, Oberstleutnant Bernhard Woldenga, and known locally as Gefechtsverband Woldenga (Combat Unit Woldenga).[25]

One young pilot serving with 3./JG 27 beginning to make a name in the desert war was Leutnant Hans-Joachim Marseille. At only twenty-two years old, the young Marseille was already a veteran of the earlier campaigns against Britain and in the Balkans. He was a gifted pilot and had learned his trade while flying alongside experienced pilots such as Gerhard Barkhorn, but Marseille had become a bit of a liability through his excessive lifestyle, irresponsibility and, at times, insubordination. He had joined JG 27 at the end of 1940 and it had been his new Gruppenkommandeur, Eduard Neumann, who had recognized Marseille's potential as a pilot.

Marseille was keen to learn and his methods, at times, were quite unorthodox – he regularly carried out dummy attacks against his colleagues in order to perfect his techniques. His eyesight was excellent, which enabled him to carry out an attack from a position that others might have considered unfavourable, and his marksmanship allowed him to approach the enemy at higher speed. He was also equally as happy in a slower-speed encounter when he would reduce his speed to a minimum, using flap if necessary, to give him a tighter circle against his opponent and his deflection shooting was as good as anyone around at the time. Furthermore, he was very good at aerobatics and could manoeuvre his aircraft quickly and with natural ease.

While these qualities never guaranteed success, they had enabled

Marseille to perfect a manoeuvre when engaged in combat with Allied fighters flying in a defensive circle; a standard tactic for Allied aircraft, particularly fighter-bombers, if caught at a tactical disadvantage. Marseille's technique was to dive below the horizontal plane of the defensive circle and then to pull up from underneath his opponent. He would open fire from very close range, just as his opponent was disappearing beneath the nose of his own aircraft. Marseille would then continue climbing and once above the plane of the circle he would roll inverted and dive down behind another potential victim. The whole manoeuvre was carried out in very swift movements, and his ability to judge distance and rate of closure, combined with his skill at coping with high-deflection angles, made him a great talent in air combat.

Even after making multiple claims in one sortie, Marseille often returned with ammunition to spare. Many considered him to be the best shot in the Jagdwaffe and by February 1942 his personal score had risen to forty-six victories for which he was awarded the Knight's Cross.

There were many other notable contributions in North Africa and amongst the best of the non-officer pilots was Oberfeldwebel Otto Schulz of 4./JG 27. Another veteran of the earlier campaigns against France, Britain and in the Balkans, during which he scored six victories, Schulz had arrived in North Africa in September 1941. Schulz excelled in the air war over the desert and his achievements quickly took him from a relatively modest total of nine victories to forty-four victories by the end of February 1942, surpassing the score of his own Staffelkapitän, Gustav Rödel. One of Schulz's most impressive achievements occurred on 15 February when he claimed five P-40 Kittyhawks in one mission to the south-east of the airfield at Martuba.

With Malta still under an Axis blockade, a small and extremely versatile detachment of Bf 109Fs of III./JG 27, known as the Jagd-kommando Kreta, was transferred from North Africa to Kastelli in Crete at the end of March.

The Luftwaffe had now flown well in excess of 10,000 sorties against Malta and had dropped 10,000 tons of bombs on the island. Britain's Royal Navy had effectively been forced to abandon the island and supplies continued to reinforce Rommel in North Africa. With a German victory now in sight, Kesselring wanted to launch an airborne invasion of Malta while Rommel wanted the resources instead to launch a new offensive in the desert and to push on into Egypt.

Whether to allocate vital resources to Kesselring or to Rommel would be the most important strategic decision of the Mediterranean and desert war. Hitler ruled in favour of Rommel and the situation in the Mediterranean effectively reversed overnight. Malta was again given the opportunity to recover and it would not be long before British forces were once more inflicting losses on the Axis supply lines to North Africa. Furthermore, the increasing demands of the Eastern Front meant that a number of fighter units were transferred back to Russia in the spring of 1942 to continue the offensive in the east. Amongst those units to leave Sicily for the Eastern Front were II./JG 3 and I./JG 53, while III./JG 53 moved to North Africa. This left the Bf 109s of II./JG 53 as the only fighters in Sicily, although they would later be joined by I./JG 77.

Having received Hitler's support, Rommel's new offensive in the desert commenced at the end of May and his forces captured Tobruk on 21 June. The Axis forces now made a new attempt to break through to Egypt and the ultimate goal of the Suez Canal. In the air the Ju 87 Stukas supported the Panzers on the ground as the first encounters took place between the Bf 109s and newly arrived Spitfire Vs, with the early exchanges often favouring the more experienced Jagdflieger, many of whom were now flying the more advanced Bf 109G. The 109s of JG 27, no longer required as part of Gefechtsverband Woldenga, were reinforced by the arrival of III./JG 53, under the command of Major Erich Gerlitz, that unit having moved to Gazala from Sicily to help counter the reinforcements received by the Allies. During the next six weeks these Gruppen provided much-needed air support over the desert during the battle of Gazala.

Bernhard Woldenga would soon leave the region to take up a staff appointment and his departure led to a number of changes in command including promotion to Major for Eduard Neumann and his appointment to replace Woldenga as Kommodore of JG 27, while Gustav Rödel became Kommandeur of II./JG 27 and the impressive Gerhard Homuth, holder of the Knight's Cross with thirty-nine victories, was appointed

Kommandeur of I./JG 27.

The young Hans-Joachim Marseille, now known as the 'Star of Africa', having quickly acquired something that closely resembled celebrity status in the region, continued to dominate in the air. On 3 June he enjoyed his most successful day of air combat to date, claiming six P-40 Tomahawks to the west of Bir Hacheim in just one sortie. With his personal tally at seventy-five victories, Marseille was awarded the Oak Leaves to his Knight's Cross on 6 June and appointed Staffelkapitän of 3./JG 27. Just two weeks later he would add the Swords to become only the twelfth recipient of such high recognition after his 100th victory and he was the first to reach a century of successes against the Western Allies.

Marseille's success coincided with the death of Otto Schulz who was killed on 17 June after claiming his fifty-first victory. Schulz was the third-highest scorer in the region behind Marseille and Freiherr von Maltzahn, Kommodore of JG 53.

One seemingly innocuous engagement over the desert took place during the afternoon of 7 August but it was one that would have an impact on the campaign in North Africa. By chance a Schwarm of Bf 109Fs from 5./JG 27 came across a lone Bombay transport aircraft of the RAF during a *freier Jagd* sortie behind enemy lines. The event was not unusual as Bombays were making daily flights from Heliopolis in Egypt to the Allied front line but on this occasion the Bombay was on its way back to Cairo from Burg-el-Arab having picked up Lieutenant General William Gott, the newly appointed commander of the British Eighth Army, who was on his way to Cairo for a meeting. The Bombay would normally transit at very low level, no more than 50 feet above the desert, to run the gauntlet of marauding Messerschmitts known to be operating in the area, but on this occasion was slightly higher due to an overheating engine.

Sitting higher above the desert, the Bf 109Fs, led by Oberfeldwebel Emil Clade, were looking for any target of opportunity before returning to their base at Quotaifiya to the west of El Alamein when they spotted the Bombay to the south of Alexandria. To Clade, the unescorted Bombay made an inviting and easy target, and it would have no chance against the swooping 109s. His initial attack was enough to convince the Bombay pilot to make a forced landing but, as he did so, a lethal burst of fire came from Unteroffizier Bernhard Schneider as he strafed the stricken aircraft. Amongst those killed on the Bombay was Gott.[26] General Gott would be the highest-ranking British officer to be killed by enemy fire during the Second World War and his death would lead to the appointment of Bernard Montgomery as commander of the British Eighth Army and it would be Montgomery who would face Rommel during the final decisive battles in the desert.

As Rommel's forces advanced towards Egypt, the Jagdgruppen continued to enjoy success. On 1 September Marseille made the staggering claim of seventeen enemy aircraft in three separate sorties over El Taqua, Alam Halfa and Deir El Raghat during one day. His claims were a mix of Allied aircraft. In the morning he had been escorting Ju 87s when he engaged a mix of P-40 Tomahawks and Spitfire Vs of the RAF. Then, during his second mission at mid-day, he encountered Tomahawks and Kittyhawks of the South African Air Force and finally, during his third mission in the early evening, he claimed Hurricane IIs of the RAF.

Amongst the many successes there were inevitably more losses, including Feldwebel Günther Steinhausen of 1./JG 27 who was killed on 6 September having been credited with forty victories, for which he was posthumously promoted to the rank of Leutnant and awarded the Knight's Cross. The following day came the loss of Leutnant Hans-Arnold Stahlschmidt, Kapitän of 2./JG 27 and holder of the Knight's Cross with fifty-nine victories; Stahlschmidt, a close friend of Marseille, was posted as missing in action just a week before his twenty-second birthday.

Marseille's luck also ran out soon after. On 30 September he was leading his Staffel during an escort mission for Ju 87s and his short life was to end, not in air combat but following a technical problem with his aircraft. While he was returning to base the engine of his new Bf 109G-2/Trop developed an oil leak resulting in a fire. Smoke quickly filled Marseille's cockpit, blinding him and partly asphyxiating him as he headed for home. Escorted by his wingmen, Marseille made it back over friendly territory and decided to abandon his aircraft. The standard procedure was to roll the aircraft inverted, release the harness and fall out but the smoke and fumes meant that Marseille had become disorientated. His aircraft was seen to be in a dive at the point he left the aircraft and the slipstream caused Marseille to strike the vertical stabilizer, which either killed him instantly or meant he was unable to deploy his parachute; either way, he stood no chance.

The loss of Hans-Joachim Marseille was felt by everyone in the region and his death caused the morale of the entire Geschwader to drop in a way that no other seems to have done. Promoted just days before he was killed, Marseille had been the Luftwaffe's youngest Hauptmann at the age of twenty-two, and his achievement was recognized by him being only the fourth recipient of the coveted Diamonds. Hitler had even decided to make the award personally.

Marseille's body lay in state in the back of a truck before his funeral took place at Derna on 1 October, attended by his Kommodore, Eduard Neumann, and Albert Kesselring. A portrait of this national hero was signed by Göring and sent to his mother, citing Marseille as the most outstanding fighter pilot in the world. Marseille was officially credited with 158 victories, all but seven of which were achieved during his time in North Africa, making him the highest scorer against the Western Allies.

Demoralized by their latest series of losses, I./JG 27 was withdrawn from the campaign in North Africa. The blockade of Malta could not last while the Luftwaffe continued to concentrate on supporting the Afrika Korps in the desert but there were a number of successes during the air battles over the island in 1942. Oberleutnant Gerhard Michalski, Kapitän of 4./JG 53, became the highest scorer over Malta with twenty-six victories during the campaign to surpass the earlier achievement of Joachim Müncheberg. Michalski would later become Kommandeur of II./JG 53 and be awarded the Knight's Cross with Oak Leaves before ending the war with seventy-three victories. Other high scorers over Malta included 22-year-old Oberleutnant Siegfried Freytag, Kapitän of 1./JG 77 and known as the 'Malta Lion', with twenty-five victories between July and October 1942, and Oberfeldwebel Herbert Rollwage of II./JG 53 with twenty victories between January and October.

Despite these efforts, the siege of Malta was over as the Luftwaffe's main effort went into supporting Rommel's forces in the decisive and costly battle of El Alamein, which would become the turning point of the desert campaign. The battle commenced on 23 October and one to achieve success during the opening morning was Leutnant Werner Schroer, Kapitän of 8./JG 27, who claimed two Kittyhawks, the first to the north-east of El Alamein and the second to the south-east. The following day he added two more to his total, a Kittyhawk in the morning and a Hurricane in the afternoon, and by the end of the first week of the battle, Schroer had claimed six more victories to bring his tally for October to fifteen. Two more followed in early November before Schroer left for the Mediterranean theatre with a total of sixty-one victories, all achieved in North Africa, making him the Gruppe's top marksman in theatre and the second highest scorer of the North African campaign behind the inimitable Marseille. This brought Schroer a well-earned Knight's Cross.

Having broken through the front at El Alamein on 4 November, the Allies pushed Rommel's Afrika Korps back across the desert while Operation Torch, which commenced just four days later, saw Allied forces land in Vichy-held French North Africa in an attempt to pincer the Axis forces. Hitler ordered a build-up of strength in Tunisia to fill the gap left by Vichy troops but Torch signalled the start of the end of the campaign in North Africa.

Göring was keen to abandon North Africa but Hitler, supported by the loyalty and optimism of Kesselring, wished to hold a bridgehead in Tunisia and so a new force was formed under Oberst Martin Harling-hausen, consisting of over a hundred aircraft, most of which were fighters and dive bombers, to defend the bridgehead.

The arrival in the region of large numbers of new American aircraft, including medium and light bombers such as the North American B-25 Mitchell, the Martin B-26 Marauder and the Douglas A-20 Havoc, escorted by American fighters, mainly Lockheed P-38 Lightnings and Bell P-39 Airacobras, gave the Luftwaffe a new challenge. Individually, each of these aircraft rarely provided a match for the battle-hardened Jagdwaffe but collectively they meant that the 109s were outnumbered every time they took to the sky. As the campaign entered its final phase it seemingly did not matter how good the Jagdflieger was. He was simply outnumbered. Nonetheless, although the Luftwaffe was left with modest numbers in North Africa, its fighters remained a considerable threat to the Allies and often found the edge against new pilots arriving in theatre, although the 109s could only ever enjoy partial success against such overwhelming odds and had now become reactive rather than proactive.

By now, the number of Bf 109s available in Africa had reduced to less than a hundred and so in November some reinforcements arrived, including Bf 109Gs of II./JG 51 under the command of Hauptmann Hartmann Grasser, followed soon after by the Bf 109Fs of 3./JG 1 subordinated to Grasser as 6./JG 51. While operating from Tunisia, Grasser claimed twelve victories, his last successes of the war, and took his personal total to 103. Another to achieve success was Oberleutnant Anton Hafner of 4./JG 51. Hafner, already a holder of the Knight's Cross, claimed his first victory in the region on 16 November, a Spitfire to the east of Bône, his sixty-third victim of the war. Within two weeks Hafner had taken his total in the region to seven. Seven more followed in the first week of December. Then, on 2 January 1943, Hafner was engaged with Spitfires and Hurricanes, and during the subsequent combat was shot down. Having bailed out, Hafner hit the rudder of his aircraft and would spend the next six months in hospital.

Amongst the welcome reinforcements to arrive in Tunisia during November were Focke Wulf FW 190A-4/Trops of II./JG 2 under the command of Oberleutnant Adolf Dickfeld, which were attached to I./JG 53 near Bizerta and would remain in Tunisia for the rest of the North African campaign. Already a holder of the Knight's Cross with Oak Leaves, with 128 victories, Dickfeld was a talented pilot. His success had come while serving with 7./JG 52 on the Eastern Front but he was now the newly appointed Kommandeur of II./JG 2.

Dickfeld added five more victories to his total while operating in Tunisia but was badly injured during an accident after his aircraft struck an obstacle on the airfield at Kairouan on 8 January 1943. While Dickfeld was recovering from his injuries, his Gruppe claimed more than 150 enemy aircraft destroyed during its five months in Tunisia. Two to achieve considerable success were Oberleutnant Kurt Bühligen, who claimed more than forty victories during his short period in Tunisia, and Oberleutnant Erich Rudorffer, who had assumed temporary command of II./JG 2 from Dickfeld and achieved twenty-seven victories.

The air war raged on into 1943 and one of the last aces to fall in North Africa was Joachim Müncheberg, Kommodore of JG 77. While claiming his 135th victory on 23 March, a Spitfire, his victim exploded in front of him after a close burst of cannon fire. Müncheberg's aircraft was badly damaged but he managed to bail out despite being severely wounded. Although he was soon found, Müncheberg, the nineteenth recipient of the Knight's Cross with Oak Leaves and Swords, died on his way to hospital. He was just twenty-four years old.

Having earlier been withdrawn from the North African theatre following devastating losses to his unit, Major Eduard Neumann, Kommodore of JG 27, led Stab and II./JG 27 back to Sicily to provide some amount of protection for the supply convoys desperately running the gauntlet between Sicily and Tunisia. While this helped maintain some support to the last remnants of the Afrika Korps, there were at times barely a dozen serviceable 109s for the task.

By the end of April Neumann had been replaced by Gustav Rödel after Neumann was promoted to the rank of Oberstleutnant and posted to Galland's staff in Germany. Rödel had previously led II./JG 27 and had spent much time in North Africa and knew the region well, claiming more than fifty victories in the year he had spent operating over the desert. After a short break in early 1943 he now returned to the front line and quickly brought his total to seventy-eight victories during May, for which he was awarded the Oak Leaves to his Knight's Cross.

Despite the courage of men like Gustav Rödel and others, such as 21-year-old Leutnant Willy Kientsch, the young Staffelkapitän of 6./JG 27 with sixteen victories over the desert, and who had added twelve more to his total in April and May 1943 during the last days of the North Africa campaign, it counted for little against such overwhelming Allied air superiority. As Germany faced defeat in North Africa, its fighters escaped while they could, although many ground personnel and large amounts of spares and equipment were left behind in Tunisia. By the end of April, the only Luftwaffe fighter presence in North Africa was JG 77, now under the command of Oberstleutnant Johannes Steinhoff, but by early May it was time for the last aircraft and pilots to leave for Sicily without the majority of the Geschwader ground crew or any spares.

The British advance westwards along the North African coast had reached Tunisia and the Axis forces were now caught in a pincer, out-manned and outgunned. Rommel himself left Africa in March. Nearly half of all supplies destined for his former forces in Tunisia failed to get through as the Allied offensive squeezed the Axis forces until their last resistance collapsed and they finally surrendered on 13 May.

Just weeks later, on 10 July, the Allies landed in Sicily. The 109s did what they could to deter the landings by attacking the landing beaches and countering the Allied fighters but one young pilot to lose his life over Sicily was Oberleutnant Wolf-Udo Ettel, Kapitän of 8./JG 27, just days after he had been awarded the Knight's Cross for his 120 victories. Flying from Greece with their 109s fitted with long-range fuel tanks, the pilots of 8./JG 27 carried out their first ground-support missions over eastern Sicily on 15 July. Ettel claimed three successes during two days of aerial fighting before he succumbed to ground fire on 17 July while carrying out a low-level attack against Allied positions to the south of Catania; Ettel was just twenty-two years old and was posthumously awarded the Oak Leaves to his Knight's Cross.

As the Luftwaffe abandoned its airfields in Sicily, Göring was again overly critical of his units and demanded an improvement in their fighting spirit but this only further dented morale. The Allies were able to mount 1,500 sorties a day during the opening days of the campaign, five times that of the depleted Jagdwaffe, which again faced over-whelming odds. Within a week of the Allied landings, it was down to less than fifty operational aircraft. Wolfram von Richthofen reinforced Sicily as best he could but it was too late. Days later the Luftwaffe units departed, some for mainland Italy, others for Greece to defend its approaches and the Aegean, and some returned to Germany. It was not long before Luftflotte 2 could barely mount fifty sorties a day against the sustained Allied effort. Richthofen's units based in Sardinia were also under attack and suffered further losses. Elements of JG 27, 51 and 77 were moved from Sardinia to mainland Italy to resist the Allied landings as best they could but it proved to be a token effort.

It soon became clear to the German High Command that the defence of Italy was to prove futile as more and more resources were required back in Germany for the defence of the Reich. However, small numbers of Bf 109s were left behind when Italy finally surrendered on 8 September 1943. One of the last to fall in air combat over Italy was Franz Schiess, Kapitän of 8./JG 53. Schiess had achieved much success in the Mediterranean and North Africa, becoming well known for his aggressive tactics in combat, and had been awarded the Knight's Cross after fifty-five victories. Following the Allied invasion of Sicily and southern Italy he claimed a further twelve enemy aircraft in just eleven days, seven of which were P-38 Lightnings. Promoted to Hauptmann on 1 September he was leading his Bf 109Gs the following day against B-25s attacking the rail marshalling yards at Cancello, Naples, when his unit engaged the fighter escort of P-38s. Exactly what happened to Schiess is unclear but his aircraft 'Black 1' is known to have crashed in the Tyrrhenian Sea about 25 miles to the south-west of the volcanic island of Ischia; he is believed to have been shot down by a P-38. At the time of his death Schiess was just twenty-two years old and amongst his sixty-seven victories were seventeen P-38s, making Franz Schiess the highest scoring 'Lightning-killer' of the war.

Italy's surrender left the Aegean wide open as most of the islands had been defended by Italian forces. The Allied threat to Greece and the Balkans could not be ignored and so German reinforcements were sent to the region but these were too few, too thinly spread and arrived too late to prevent Allied landings on a number of islands. Nonetheless, the Luftwaffe still managed to achieve some success over the Aegean during the later weeks of 1943 as its campaign in the Mediterranean started to draw to a close.

Two in particular made their mark. One was Hauptmann Joachim Kirschner, Kapitän of 5./JG 3 and a holder of the Knight's Cross with Oak Leaves, who took his overall total to 175 victories, and Feldwebel Heinrich Bartels of 11./JG 27, another holder of the Knight's Cross, who scored twenty-four victories in just six weeks during October and November 1943. Neither would survive the war. Kirschner was killed within days, being shot down on 17 December over Croatia. Although he had bailed out safely, 23-year-old Kirschner was captured and executed by partisans. Bartels would later be killed on 23 December 1944 while defending the Reich with his personal score on ninety-nine.

By the end of 1943 the Allied ground forces were firmly established in Italy and were progressing north towards Rome, although a series of defensive lines across the Italian peninsula meant that a breakthrough towards the Italian capital was still some months away. The Allied advance now also posed a threat to the Balkans. Increased Allied air activity over the Balkans and attacks against shipping in the Adriatic meant that the Luftwaffe's fighter resources were operationally and geographically stretched to the limit. Luftflotte 2 had been severely depleted and its units were unable to interfere with the Allied advance and provided little opposition to the Allied landings at Anzio in January 1944. As far as the High Command was concerned, the defeat in North Africa and now the Allied progress through Italy meant that the Mediterranean had become a forgotten theatre.

Chapter 7

The Tide Turns in the East

By the opening days of 1942 the situation on the Eastern Front had changed. Russian forces had launched a successful second counter-offensive to drive a wedge between the German's central and northern sectors, and a breach more than fifty miles wide seriously threatened the German forces at Leningrad to the north. With the benefit of a much shorter supply line, the Soviet Air Force was better equipped and more experienced to fight a winter war.

As the air fighting intensified once more, Hannes Trautloft's JG 54 became torn between applying pressure on the beleaguered city of Leningrad and allocating resources to the fighting in the area of Lake Ilmen to the south. Friedrich Beckh's JG 51 faced similar decisions in the central sector as to whether to try and counter the Russian advance westwards from Moscow or allocate resources against the new counter-offensive on its left flank.

Richthofen's VIII. Fliegerkorps now faced at least eight Soviet fighter regiments in the Moscow area alone, all operating from airfields with good facilities for winter operations. The best his units could do was to slow down the Soviet advance but it would take until March to bring it to a halt. The following month Richthofen handed over responsibility for air support in the central region to Robert Ritter von Greim's V. Fliegerkorps, now to be designated Luftwaffenkommando Ost (Luftwaffe Command East), while Richthofen took VIII. Fliegerkorps south to the Crimea.

The increased air activity over the Eastern Front provided the Jagd-waffe with the opportunity to gain further success. Many units, such as JG 51, were now relieved of their ground-attack missions to counter the increased Soviet aerial threat and were able to operate more freely. Many pilots started to add to their personal scores and amongst those decorated for their achievements during the early months of 1942 were Hauptmann Heinz Bär, Kapitän of 12./JG 51, who became the seventh recipient of the Swords having been credited with ninety victories; Leutnant Hans Strelow of 5./JG 51 who became the Wehrmacht's youngest holder of the Knight's Cross with Oak Leaves at the age of just nineteen for his sixty-six victories; and Oberfeldwebel Franz-Josef Beerenbrock of 10./JG 51, who became the first member of the Geschwader to surpass Mölder's century of victories, for which Beerenbrock received the Oak Leaves to his Knight's Cross.

While Richthofen led the assault by VIII. Fliegerkorps on Sevastopol, which commenced in June, thousands of miles away at the other end of the Eastern Front a very different air battle was taking place around the ports of Archangel and Murmansk, through which the Allies had been supplying Stalin with arms and equipment. A new unit, JG 5, had been formed from elements of JG 77 and JG 1 with the responsibility of providing fighter cover over the Arctic Front. The new Jagdgeschwader found itself in a rather unusual situation as it fought aircraft of both the Western Allies and the Soviets at the same time. One Gruppe was based on the west coast of Norway to counter Allied anti-shipping attacks across the North Sea while two Gruppen were based in Finland to support operations in the east.

The war in the Arctic became a rather insular affair. Conditions were extremely cold and ranged from near twenty-four hours of daylight when the sun never fully set to long periods of almost total darkness. The Jagdflieger were always outnumbered. Nonetheless, they still achieved much success and amongst JG 5's leading scorers on the Arctic Front were Leutnant Heinrich Ehrler, Kapitän of 6./JG 5, who scored more than sixty victories operating in the extreme north, Leutnant Theodor Weissenberger, a former Zerstörer ace, now serving with 6./JG 5, Oberleutnant Walter Schuck of 7./JG 5 and Feldwebel Rudolf Müller of 6./JG 5 who claimed five Russian Hurricanes in one day over the Kola Inlet.

By mid-1942 about two-thirds of the Luftwaffe's total combat strength, more than 4,000 aircraft, was based on the Eastern Front and operating with the four major commands. From north to south these were: Luftflotte 5 under the command of Hans-Jürgen Stumpff; Luftflotte 1 commanded by Alfred Keller; Ritter von Greim's Luftwaffen-kommando Ost; and Luftflotte 4 led by Alexander Löhr. The size of these commands varied considerably and the number of combat aircraft available to each ranged from more than 1,500 available to Löhr to less than 200 available to Stumpff.[27]

Of greatest concern was the fact that the Red Air Force outnumbered the Luftwaffe along parts of the front by as much as 3 : 1. The number of Bf 109s across the entire Eastern Front now totalled around 550, only 70 per cent of the number available the previous year for Barbarossa. Apart from the fifty Bf 109Es allocated to Stumpff in Finland the rest of the single-engine fighter force along the front were Bf 109Fs. While Trautloft's JG 54 continued to watch over the northern sector and JG 51, now under the command of Oberstleutnant Karl-Gottfried Nordmann, provided fighter cover for the central sector, almost half of the Bf 109s were allocated to Löhr's Luftflotte 4 in the southern sector ready for the next German offensive. Three Gruppen of JG 3 were under the command of Oberstleutnant Günther Lützow and based at Morosovs-kaya and Millerovo, two Gruppen JG 52 and a single Gruppe of JG 53, all under the command of Major Herbert Ihlefeld, occupied airfields at Taganrog and Kharkov, and two of JG 77, led by Major Gordon Gollob, were based at Kastornoye and Kerch.

Hitler now renewed his offensive in the east, known as Fall Blau (Case Blue), a continuation of Barbarossa and soon to be expanded to become Operation Braunschweig (Brunswick), with the intention of knocking the Soviet Union out of the war. Oil had always been Germany's achilles heel and before the war the country had to import 85 per cent of its needs but Hitler could now only rely on two main sources of supply: Germany's own synthetic plants and the oilfields of Romania. With almost all of his oil reserves gone, and supplies in Romania in decline and continuously vulnerable to attack, Hitler had no option other than to seek out new supplies.

The immense Caucasus region, bounded by the Black Sea to its west and the Caspian Sea to the east, had two main oilfields. The area north of the mountains produced 10 per cent of all Soviet oil while the region to the south, around Baku on the Caspian, contained some of the largest oilfields in the world and produced 80 per cent of the Soviet Union's oil supply, while also offering large supplies of coal and peat along with other rare materials.

In response to Hitler's order for all available forces to be made available for his new offensive in the east, Jeschonnek included training units amongst the forces he sent to the Eastern Front. As General der Jagdflieger, Galland protested and argued that a reduction in training in Germany would have longer-term consequences on the Luftwaffe. While Jeschonnek was seemingly sympathetic to Galland's view, he was adamant that the short-term priority was the defeat of the Soviet Union as this would have a far bigger consequence on the outcome of the Second World War and so all available units were sent east.

The new offensive carried out by Army Group South commenced on 28 June along a front stretching 500 miles from Kursk in the north to the Sea of Azov in the south. It was essentially a two-pronged advance, aiming ultimately to reach the rich oilfields of Baku and the key industrial city of Stalingrad on the Volga River, a move that would cover the flanks of the drive towards the oilfields. Initially the advance resulted in rapid gains, including vast amounts of territory and a number of oilfields, but the Red Army often chose to retreat rather than fight.

Despite having entered this new offensive with less than half the number of combat aircraft it would have liked, the Luftwaffe gained initial control of the sky. Amongst those who achieved successes in the air during the opening period of this new campaign was Gordon Gollob, leading JG 77 over the Kerch Straits opposite the Crimea peninsula. Gollob was the highest scorer at the time having become the first to reach 150 victories and had been fortunate to have a number of experienced pilots under his command. They included the very capable Heinz Bär, Kommandeur of I./JG 77, who had been awarded the Swords earlier in the year while Staffelkapitän of 1./JG 51 for his ninety victories. Also serving with JG 77 were three centurions, all Staffelkapitäne and all of whom had been awarded the Oak Leaves to their Knight's Cross: Hauptmann Heinrich Setz commanding 4. Staffel; Hauptmann Anton Hackl of 5. Staffel; and Oberleutnant Erwin Clausen of 6. Staffel.

With air-combat leaders of such high quality, it is hardly surprising that JG 77 dominated the sky over the Kerch–Taman area. Gollob often adopted the tactic of operating at low level with his wingman and waiting for a Soviet formation to appear. They would then climb in a spiral, keeping the enemy formation above them while carefully manoeuvring into a firing position, and then strike; more often than not, two unsuspecting Soviet aircraft would disappear from the form-ation. For his leadership on the Eastern Front, Gordon Gollob became the third recipient of the Diamonds. He was then given a well-earned rest with promotion to Oberstleutnant and a posting to a staff appoint-ment on the Channel Front as JG 77 moved south to the Mediterranean.

Another to achieve a notable milestone was Oberleutnant Hermann Graf, Kapitän of 9./JG 52, who became the first fighter pilot to shoot down 200 enemy aircraft. At the start of September 1942 he had been credited with 140 victories but his achievement during the month that followed was most impressive: five victories on 2 September; four more the following day; then thirteen more during the next week; fifteen during the week after that; and then ten more in the next five days. Then, on 23 September, he claimed ten aircraft during the day and his score reached a staggering 202 on 26 September, earning him the coveted Diamonds. Hermann Graf had become the fifth recipient of the Diamonds as the announcement of his award came just days after Hans-Joachim Marseille's in North Africa.

It can be no coincidence that the five recipients of the Diamonds so far were all Jagdflieger; such was their contribution in all theatres as their achievements were recognized at the highest level. Graf had earned the four highest decorations – Knight's Cross, Oak Leaves, Swords and Diamonds – in the space of just eight months, a remarkable achievement considering he had scored his first success just over a year before. Graf's former wingman, Oberfeldwebel Leopold Steinbatz, would also be highly decorated and became the Wehrmacht's first non-officer to be awarded the Swords, albeit posthumously, for his ninety-nine victories on the Eastern Front.

There were so many examples of aerial success on the Eastern Front during this period. Another young man to score consistently was the Austrian-born Leutnant Walter Nowotny. Still only twenty-one years old,

Nowotny was serving with JG 54 and had claimed his first victories during Barbarossa the previous year. Known to be superstitious, he wore the same pair of trousers on combat missions that he had been wearing a year before when he had spent three days in a dinghy having been shot down over the Gulf of Riga. During July and August 1942 Nowotny took his total to more than fifty victories for which he was awarded the Knight's Cross. Having then been given some well-earned leave, he was able to return to Vienna to spend some valuable time with his brother, Hubert, also an officer in the Wehrmacht. It would be the last time the brothers were to meet as both would soon return to the Eastern Front and while Walter was celebrating his appointment as Staffelkapitän of 1./JG 54 in October, Hubert was killed at Stalingrad.

It was also during October 1942 that the FW 190 made its first appearance on the Eastern Front with I./JG 51 being the first Gruppe to convert to the type. The Gruppe had been temporarily withdrawn from the front line and retired to Jesau near Königsberg for conversion to the FW 190A-3. Having returned to the front, I./JG 51 was initially deployed to the northern sector where the 190s were given the freedom to roam as a Rotte or Schwarm during *freier Jagd* sorties to the south-east of Leningrad, before they were moved to the central sector where the FW 190 would soon be at the heart of the air war over the Eastern Front.[28]

The new FW 190A proved more manoeuvrable than the Bf 109F, which to some was starting to seem a little tired, and its introduction was a timely counter to the improving Russian fighters, particularly the Lavochkin La-5 and the Yakovlev Yak-7B. The other Gruppen of JG 51 soon converted to the FW 190A and made an immediate impact, although the tried and tested Bf 109 still remained a favourite for many pilots.

Scores in the air were still rising as German forces advanced on Stalingrad, including those of I./JG 53, who accounted for more than 900 victories during the summer of 1942. Hauptmann Friedrich-Karl Müller, Kapitän of 1./JG 53, claimed twenty-five during August, including five in one day on 12 August, and during the first three weeks of September he added another thirty-five, including seven on 19 September; this took Müller's total past 100 and earned him the Knight's

Cross and Oak Leaves within the space of just four days. Two others to stand out were Oberleutnant Wolfgang Tonne, Kapitän of 3./JG 53, who was credited with eighty-eight Russian aircraft in just four months between May and September, for which he received the Knight's Cross and Oak Leaves within two weeks during September, and Oberfeldwebel Wilhelm Crinius of the same Staffel. Crinius had initially flown as wingman to Tonne but went one better than his Staffelkapitän by scoring 100 victories during the same period and was awarded the Knight's Cross and Oak Leaves on the same day.

There were losses as well for I./JG 53 and amongst the thirty Bf 109s lost were four in two days of heavy combat during 9–10 September, including three *Experten*. The first was Oberfeldwebel Alfred Franke with sixty victories. Having been bounced, surprisingly, by an Il-2 Sturmovik, Franke was shot down and killed on 9 September, after which he was posthumously promoted to the rank of Leutnant and awarded the Knight's Cross. The following day, the Bf 109G of Leutnant Walter Zellot was hit by flak over Stalingrad. Zellot managed to bail out but was too low for his parachute to deploy fully and was killed; Zellot, also a holder of the Knight's Cross, had recorded eighty-three victories over the Eastern Front. The Gruppe's second *Experte* to be killed that day was Feldwebel Franz Hagedorn who was shot down by a Sturmovik having been credited with thirty-seven victories.

Along with other vital air assets, I./JG 53 soon departed for the Mediterranean, which weakened the Jagdwaffe's presence in southern Russia to the point that only two Jagdgeschwader were now left to cover the vast area; JG 3 to support the advance on Stalingrad and JG 52 to cover the Caucasus and Black Sea.

Now led by Major Wolfe-Dietrich Wilcke, JG 3 was tasked to support General Friedrich Paulus's Sixth Army as it made its final assault on Stalingrad. Wilcke was fortunate to have some of the finest pilots on the Eastern Front under his command, including two centurions and holders of the Oak Leaves; Hauptmann Kurt Brändle, Kommandeur of II./JG 3, and Oberleutnant Viktor Bauer, the Kapitän of 9./JG 3. Amongst Wilcke's other notable pilots were Leutnant Joachim Kirschner of 5./JG 3 and Leutnant Wilhelm Lemke of 9./JG 3. Lemke was already a holder of the Knight's Cross and would soon pass a century of victories for which he was awarded the Oak Leaves, and Kirschner would soon be awarded the Knight's Cross for passing fifty victories during the battle of Stalingrad and would go on to become JG 3's highest scorer for which he, too, would be awarded the Oak Leaves.

JG 3 faced enormous resistance in the air but Wilcke was able to move his units forward to a small airstrip at Pitomnik, just over ten miles from the suburbs of Stalingrad, from where it would operate for the next couple of months. While JG 3 was maintaining air superiority over the city, JG 52, led by Herbert Ihlefeld, was left to shuttle between the southern and central sectors to cover the vast area from the Black Sea to Moscow, highlighting just how stretched the Jagdwaffe had now become, although JG 52 would later become the highest scoring Bf 109 Jagdgeschwader on the Eastern Front.

Unlike previous campaigns earlier in the war, the lack of air assets meant that German troops on the ground had become increasingly exposed by the lack of superiority in the air. Despite a long and extremely bloody struggle, Paulus and the Sixth Army were unable to dislodge the determined defenders of Stalingrad, who refused to give an inch and chose to defend every ruined building and every stronghold on the west bank of the Volga to the last. Then, just as the fighting at Stalingrad was reaching a climax, the Russians suddenly counter-attacked. A massive two-pronged counter-offensive beginning on 19 November saw Soviet forces cross the Volga to the north and south of Stalingrad, crashing through the enemy forces and joining up to the west of the city just three days later.

The German Sixth Army was now surrounded and cut off with more than 250,000 Germans trapped within Stalingrad. Also cut off were the ground crew of JG 3 who had been unable to escape, although most of the aircraft had earlier withdrawn to airfields at Tazinskaya and Morozovskaya, nearly 200 miles to the south-west of Stalingrad, from where the Luftwaffe would mount its supply mission to the beleaguered forces trapped within the city. But not all of JG 3's aircraft and pilots had left Pitomnik. A volunteer detachment, consisting of twenty-two pilots led by Hauptmann Rudolf Germeroth, Kapitän of 3./JG 3, had remained behind to form the Platzschutzstaffel Pitomnik as an airfield-defence squadron to offer some protection to the defenceless Ju-52 transport aircraft while in the perimeter and on the ground as they continued to fly supplies into the city.

With his Sixth Army cut off at Stalingrad, Hitler realized that the capture of the Caucasus oilfields before the onset of another winter was extremely unlikely. He decided that if he could not capture the oilfields then he was at least determined to deny them to the enemy and so Luftflotte 4, now under the command of Wolfram von Richthofen, was ordered to carry out bombing attacks against the oilfields. However, the events at Stalingrad soon resulted in Richthofen withdrawing his units north and bringing his offensive against the oilfields to an end. The distance to the oilfields was on the range limit for his twin-engine bombers, making their transit route predictable. It was also beyond the range of his fighters, and an unescorted bombing campaign would have proved too costly.

JG 52 was moved up to the Stalingrad area during December to support the futile attempt to relieve the beleaguered forces from the south-west. It was soon engrossed in the air battle and one young pilot to distinguish himself was 22-year-old Oberleutnant Heinz Schmidt of 6./JG 52. Like many of the Luftwaffe's top pilots of the war, Schmidt had been a relatively slow starter but he came into his own during 1942 and was awarded the Knight's Cross in August for more than fifty victories. While it had taken him a year to reach his first fifty, his next fifty came at a staggering rate after he was transferred to 5./JG 52. Operating over the Caucasus, he passed his century of victories just one month later, for which he was awarded the Oak Leaves to his Knight's Cross. Having now moved to the Stalingrad area, Schmidt would continue his run of success and soon took his total to 130 victories while operating over the beleaguered city.

The fact that the Red Army had not only refused to give up Stalingrad but also had the strength to launch the mass counter-offensive in mid-November took Hitler by surprise. Although his forces refused to give in and fought on, Stalingrad proved to be the decisive moment in the east. The Luftwaffe did what it could to establish an air bridge into the city and started to resupply the garrison during the winter months but it was always going to prove an impossible task.

The Platzschutzstaffel Pitomnik operated in desperate and appalling conditions while keeping the airstrip open for more than a month to enable the transport aircraft to bring in supplies. However, a lack of spares meant that more often than not there were just two or three 109s serviceable at any one time. The Luftwaffe simply did not have the number of transport aircraft nor the serviceability to deliver the 500 tons of supplies needed by the beleaguered force each day, particularly at a time when the transport fleet was in great demand elsewhere, such as to re-supply Rommel's retreating forces in North Africa. The best that was ever achieved was 300 tons on one day but the average daily total was around a hundred tons; nor was the whole relief effort helped by adverse weather.[29] Attempts by German forces on the ground to relieve the Axis forces trapped at Stalingrad also proved fruitless but Hitler ordered his forces to stay. There was to be no break-out.

Despite the best efforts of Germany's highest-ranking officers on the Eastern Front to persuade him otherwise, Hitler would not back down nor would he visit the Eastern Front to assess the situation for himself. His men were left to their fate and only one third would ever return to Germany. By mid-January 1943, as the Stalingrad pocket continued to shrink, the airstrip at Pitomnik was close to being overrun and so the surviving remnants of the Platzschutzstaffel flew out. It had surpassed all expectations, claiming more than a hundred victories during the month, and amongst those recognized was Feldwebel Kurt Ebener, the highest scorer inside the perimeter, who claimed thirty-five victories over Stalingrad to earn him the Knight's Cross. But inevitably there were losses and amongst those to fall was Leutnant Georg Schentke, already a holder of the Knight's Cross with ninety victories to his name, who died on Christmas Day.

The Red Army then commenced its last crushing assault and the German forces at Stalingrad finally surrendered on 31 January. The German Army had suffered its most decisive defeat. For once, Hitler took full responsibility but he still continued to criticize Göring for the Luftwaffe's part and from that moment on the relationship between Hitler and Göring steadily deteriorated.

The German position in southern Russia had also become critical and it took until March to halt the Soviet winter offensive, resulting in a temporary stalemate on the ground, although the Luftwaffe continued to dominate the air and hassle the Soviet supply lines. However, by the spring of 1943 the industrial might of the Soviet Union was starting to tell and the Red Air Force now enjoyed numerical superiority in the region of 5 : 1.

Despite being so heavily outnumbered, the Jagdflieger continued to achieve success, particularly if they were able to gain a tactical advantage. One example occurred on 29 January when a pair of FW 190s of 9./JG 51 based at Orel, led by Oberleutnant Günther Schack, encountered eight Petlyakov Pe-2s. The Pe-2 was a twin-engined bomber and the formation was crossing the German lines in line astern. Schack's proven technique was to fire while in a steep turn against his opponent, a manoeuvre requiring considerable skill but against such benign opposition it proved lethal and within five minutes all eight Russian aircraft had been shot down; five of them were credited to Schack.

Two new names were now appearing regularly on the score sheet of success and both were long-serving members of JG 51. One was Leutnant Joachim Brendel, who had taken his personal score to twenty during February and would go on to be credited with 189 victories by the end of the war, all achieved while serving with JG 51 and making him the Geschwader's highest scorer, for which he was awarded the Knight's Cross with Oak Leaves. The second was Oberfeldwebel Josef Jennewein, an alpine skier and world champion, whose tally had risen to forty-five during March. Jennewein would later take his total to eighty-six victories but then in July 1943 he had to force-land his FW 190 behind Soviet lines and was never seen again.

JG 54 was also enjoying considerable success. Superbly led by Hannes Trautloft, who had developed a successful tactic of intercepting nuisance raiders on bright moonlit nights, his Jagdgeschwader had destroyed more than fifty Russian aircraft during a six-month period without suffering any losses. Many blossomed under his command and one was Hans Philipp, Kommandeur of I./JG 54 and the first member of JG 54 to be awarded the Swords, who had now taken his tally past 170 victories. Another was the tall and slender Oberleutnant Hans Beisswenger, Kapitän of 6./JG 54 and holder of the Knight's Cross with Oak Leaves, who had now passed 140 victories, and others included

Oberleutnant Max Stotz of 5./JG 54, who passed 150 victories during this period, and Major Hans 'Assi' Hahn, Kommandeur of II./JG 54, who also became a centurion at the end of January 1943.

These were successful times for JG 54 but two of these four pilots went missing in the space of just a few weeks. The first was Hahn who met a number of Soviet La-5 fighters near Staraya on 21 February 1943 and had to force-land his Bf 109G behind Soviet lines and was taken prisoner; Hahn would have to wait until 1950 before he was released. The second was Beisswenger who had taken his tally to 152 victories before he was posted as missing in action on 6 March after engaging LaGG-3s near Staraya. It is possible that his aircraft was rammed by a Soviet fighter but his fate remains unknown. Neither of the other two would survive the year. Max Stotz became Kommandeur of II./JG 54 and was credited with 189 victories but was shot down during combat with Yak fighters on 19 August 1943. Stotz bailed out of his aircraft and was last observed drifting towards Soviet lines but was never seen again. Hans Philipp would soon be transferred back to the west for defence of the Reich duties as Kommodore of JG 1 and would become only the second pilot to pass 200 victories but would be killed in action on 8 October.

JG 54 started receiving its first FW 190s during February 1943 and with JG 51 provided the main FW 190 presence on the Eastern Front. The Luftwaffe High Command then decided to rotate fighter units between the Western and Eastern Fronts and during early 1943 III./JG 54 was replaced by I./JG 26, led by its accomplished Kommandeur, Johannes Seifert, an experienced campaigner of many air battles and holder of the Knight's Cross with forty-two victories already to his name.

The FW 190s of JG 26 were in action almost immediately and by the end of March I./JG 26 had claimed seventy-five victories, with Hauptmann Walter Hoeckner, Kapitän of 1./JG 26, claiming six in one day. While I./JG 26 would be the only Gruppe of JG 26 to serve on the Eastern Front, a single Staffel, 7./JG 26, under the command of Hauptmann Klaus Mietusch, was sent to Krasnogvardeisk-Gatschina, to the west of Leningrad, to replace 4./JG 54.

Another FW 190 unit to serve on the Eastern Front, again only in Staffel strength, was 14./JG 5 under the command of Hauptmann

Friedrich-Wilhelm Strakeljahn, which operated along the Arctic coast-line as an autonomous fighter-bomber unit to combat Soviet coastal vessels. The only other FW 190s to see action in the east were those serving with the ground-attack Gruppen.

The number of FW 190s on the Eastern Front peaked at nearly 200 but the idea of rotating Jagdgruppen between west and east proved misguided. Pilots new to the Eastern Front soon found that operating in the east was quite different from operating in the west. In the east they usually flew around in smaller formations at low level where they were vulnerable to Russian ground defences. There were further problems when operating in the east. The vast and often featureless snow-covered landscape made navigation that much harder, and maintaining an awareness of the position of the front line, which frequently changed, was much more difficult. Furthermore, some airfields, such as Krasnogvardeisk-Gatschina, had good facilities whereas others, such as Ryelbitzi to the west of Lake Ilmen, first occupied by the Luftwaffe during Barbarossa, were little more than a basic airstrip, known as a Feldflugplatz, with no domestic facilities and personnel had to be accommodated in the local villages.

Conditions on the Eastern Front were quite different from those in the west and the tactics employed against the Russian fighters differed from those used against the Western Allies, and so the idea of exchanging fighter units between the two fronts was soon abandoned. The FW 190s of I./JG 26 and 7./JG 26 soon returned to France. They had both spent more than four months on the Eastern Front during which I./JG 26 had claimed 126 victories and 7./JG 26 sixty-three. Klaus Mietusch, leading 7./JG 26, was credited with fifteen during a period of four weeks between the end of May and the end of June, including five victories in one day on 18 June. The first two that day, both LaGG-3s, were shot down soon after 06.00 near Kinderovo and Podborovye, while the last, a Yak-7 over Lake Ladoga, was claimed during the evening, more than fourteen hours after his first success.

By now German forces had been driven well back and any hope of launching a new offensive against Moscow had disappeared. After a period of such intense fighting there was a brief lull on the Eastern Front as both sides reinforced. Hannes Trautloft was appointed as Jagdflieger

Inspizient Ost, an appointment within Adolf Galland's office giving Trautloft responsibility for all fighter units operating on the Eastern Front, and was replaced as Kommodore of JG 54 by Major Hubertus von Bonin, who had spent the previous two years on the Eastern Front as Kommandeur of III./JG 52. However, the brief lull which had descended over the Eastern Front was not to last long and would soon come to a sudden and dramatic end.

Chapter 8

Air War at Night

The campaign fought by the Luftwaffe over Germany at night to prevent the destruction of its industrial power involved thousands of aircraft and proved to be one of the fiercest fought during the Second World War.

The Luftwaffe's reliance on a strategy of offensive operations to achieve air superiority over the enemy, rather than recognizing the need for an effective defensive system as well, meant there had been little investment in the defence of the Reich. During the early months of the war the Luftwaffe lacked an effective and co-ordinated air-defence system but this did not cause any great concern because the amount of aerial activity over Germany had been limited.

As the war progressed, the RAF was forced to conduct its operations at night following heavy casualties suffered by unescorted bombers during the day. The Luftwaffe started to allocate more resources to the defence of Germany but crucial weaknesses in leadership, and the failure to recognize that it was going to be a long war, meant that strategic decisions were often delayed and resulted in resources being committed too late. Furthermore, the combination of poor communications and co-ordination between ground and air units, the lack of training for ground-based personnel serving with defensive units and an overall ineffective ground-to-air control system meant that Germany's industrial effort was not getting the protection it required.

The failure to protect Berlin from a number of small-scale raids carried out by the RAF during the summer of 1940 played a part in the development of an air-defence system that included the formation of Luftgaukommando III, under the command of Hubert Weise, to protect the area of Berlin. Weise formed Luftwaffenbefehlshaber Mitte, the Central Air Force Command, with the responsibility of protecting the area covering the Netherlands and northern Germany, and also created the Nachtjagddivision (Night-Fighter Division) under the command of Josef Kammhuber to combat the increasing number of night operations being carried out by RAF Bomber Command.[30]

An early influencer of Germany's night war was Major Wolfgang Falck, Kommodore of the Luftwaffe's first dedicated night-fighter unit, Nachtjagdgeschwader 1 (NJG 1), which was formed at Düsseldorf in June 1940 from elements of I./ZG 1 and IV./ZG 26. Until that point, a handful of Bf 109 and Bf 110 Staffeln had been designated as dual day- and night-fighter units because the Luftwaffe did not possess a night-fighter force at the time. There were no specialist aircraft or trained crews and there was no technical ability to aid the detection of aircraft at night, and so any night aerial activity was conducted using existing aircraft and methods, and by making the best of whatever weather conditions prevailed at the time.

Unsurprisingly, these traditional methods of trying to adopt daylight fighter tactics at night brought no success but it soon became clear that the twin-engine Bf 110 offered potential as a night fighter. Based in Holland, NJG 1 was part of Kammhuber's Night-Fighter Division. The appointment of Falck as its Kommodore in the relatively junior rank of Hauptmann had caused murmurs amongst many senior officers within the Luftwaffe. But Göring had confidence in his junior officers and Falck's appointment signalled the start of a number of rapid advancements for junior officers within the Jagdwaffe.

Setting up a new night-fighter unit was never going to be easy. There was no template to follow and a completely new training programme was required. The aircraft were initially standard daytime Bf 110s and in addition to painting the aircraft in an all-black scheme there were further modifications required, such as the fitting of flame dampers to the engine exhausts and modifying the aircraft's cockpit lighting. Gradually, the Bf 110s were adapted for night operations as Falck worked on identifying an area from which to operate. He decided to move his unit to Gütersloh from where NJG 1 could provide defence of the industrial heartland of the Ruhr as well as offering some protection against any raids on Berlin.

Using searchlights and listening posts for detection, the concept was for the 110s to get airborne once a raid had been detected and to patrol

Hauptmann Hans Philipp, Gruppenkommandeur of I./JG 54, pictured on 31 March 1942 after achieving his 100th victory. Philipp was the fourth Luftwaffe centurion and became only the eighth recipient of the Swords to the Knight's Cross and Oak Leaves. (*John Weal*)

Hauptmann Heinrich Krafft (*right*) pictured at the end of May 1942 on his appointment as Gruppenkommandeur of I./JG 51. Krafft would be killed later in the year after achieving his seventy-eighth victory having been forced down behind Russian lines only to be beaten by his captors. On the left is Hauptmann Wilhelm Hachfeld. (*John Weal*)

Left: As Geschwaderkommodore of JG 77 on the Eastern Front during 1942, with the difficult task of supporting the hard fighting over the Kerch straits on the east of the Crimea peninsula, Major Gordon Gollob became only the third recipient of the coveted Diamonds to the Knight's Cross, having passed 150 victories, making him the highest-scoring Luftwaffe *Experte* at the time. (*Chris Goss collection*)

Below: Lake Ivan to the west of Moscow during the winter of 1942–3, home to a detachment of FW 190A-3s of I./JG 51. (*John Weal*)

Operating in harsh conditions was never easy. This FW 190 is 'White 10' of Unteroffizier Otto Gaiser of IV./JG 51 and is shown after an accident while taxiing at Bryansk in March 1943. (*John Weal*)

An FW 190A-4 of II./JG 54 pictured alongside a Bf 109G at Siverskaya early in 1943. (*John Weal*)

Above: During the early stages of the night war it became clear that the twin-engine Messerschmitt Bf 110 offered potential as a night fighter. The aircraft were initially standard daytime Bf 110s and so in addition to painting them in an all-black scheme there were further modifications required, such as fitting flame dampers to the engine exhausts and modifying the aircraft's cockpit lighting for night operations. (*Chris Goss collection*)

Left: Major Heinz-Wolfgang Schnaufer was awarded the Knight's Cross with Oak Leaves, Swords and Diamonds, all in less than a year while serving with NJG 1 during 1943–4. When he took command of NJG 4 in November 1944, Schnaufer was the youngest Kommodore in the Luftwaffe at the age of just twenty-two. All of his 121 victories were achieved at night, making Schnaufer the highest-scoring night-fighter ace in history. (*Chris Goss collection*)

Adolf Glunz (*far right*) prepares to receive the Oak Leaves to his Knight's Cross from Hitler in July 1944. Other recipients (*L to R*) are: Friedrich Lang, Erich Hartmann and Heinz-Wolfgang Schnaufer (all receiving the Swords) while Horst Kaubisch and Eduard Skrzipek are receiving the Oak Leaves. *(Glunz via Caldwell)*

The Jagdwaffe's ground crews had to work extremely hard to keep the aircraft flying all along the Eastern Front, particularly at its northern most extremity. This Bf 109 of JG 5 is pictured at Petsamo in Finland where conditions were particularly harsh. *(John Weal)*

Serving extensively on the Eastern Front with the *Grünherz* ('Green Hearts') of JG 54, Hauptmann Walter Nowotny became a double centurion in September 1943. At that time he was Gruppenkommandeur of I./JG 54 and when his score passed 215 later that month, he was the highest-scoring Luftwaffe *Experte* at the time. His Oak Leaves and Swords were both presented personally by Hitler on 22 September 1943. (*Chris Goss collection*)

A heating trolley connected to the front of an FW 190F in late 1943 during another harsh winter on the Eastern Front. (*John Weal*)

Above: A FW 190 of Schlacht-geschwader 10 at Koscoff airfield during January 1944. SG 10 was a close air-support wing formed in October 1943 and had been transferred to southern Russia for ground-attack operations with Luftflotte 4. (*Chris Goss collection*)

Right: Hauptmann Gerhard Barkhorn, Gruppenkommandeur of II./JG 52, after another successful sortie on the Eastern Front. Barkhorn became only the second triple-centurion and ended the war with 301 victories, having flown well in excess of a thousand combat missions, making him the second-highest-scoring fighter pilot of all time. (*John Weal*)

An investiture of the Swords to the Knights' Cross in the Wolf's Lair during July 1944.
From left: Hitler, Josef Priller, Anton Hackl, Friedrich Lang, Erich Hartmann, Heinz-Wolfgang Schnaufer.
(*Cranston via Caldwell*)

to the rear of the detection area so that the night-fighters did not interfere with the detection methods being used. Once an enemy bomber was caught in the searchlights then the night-fighter could strike but it had to be quick because of the depth of the searchlight belt, and also because the amount of time the searchlights could be expected to maintain contact with an enemy bomber was no more than a few minutes. The first success for NJG 1 using this tactic occurred on the night of 20 July 1940 when Oberleutnant Werner Streib shot down a Whitley of RAF Bomber Command to claim the Luftwaffe's first official night victory.

The greatest challenge in Germany's night war remained how to find the enemy bombers. Using searchlights to locate an attacking bomber was fine but searchlights were generally positioned in and around the target area, which meant the bombers could only be attacked once overhead the target, which was all too late. It was also quite difficult to spot a bomber caught in searchlights from above and so night-fighter pilots often chose a lower altitude from where the pilot could look up to see a bomber caught in the beam of a searchlight. This often resulted in the Nachtjagdflieger being dazzled by the searchlights and they almost invariably came under attack from overly eager flak batteries below. The searchlights were then moved away from the target areas to form a protective belt, which helped, but weather conditions often meant that cloud cover would make the searchlights completely ineffective.

Rather than rely totally on a defensive system over German-occupied north-west Europe, another early tactic favoured by Kammhuber was to fly intruder missions across the Channel and to engage RAF bombers over English soil. The fighters based in occupied Europe lacked the range for an intruder mission to be successful and so Junkers Ju 88Cs were used with a new intruder unit, I./NJG 2, being formed in September 1940 as a Nachtjagdgruppe for long-range intruder missions over England with the aim of harrying the RAF's returning bombers and disrupting its training at night.

Based at Gilze-Rijen in Holland, I./NJG 2 was initially equipped with just seven Ju 88C-1 and C-2 night-fighters, although a few Dornier Do 215B-5s would later be converted and used for night operations.

Early intruder operations used basic visual techniques to find airfields, such as spotting flare paths, and looking out for bombers returning from operations that had switched on their navigation lights once back over England. Use was then made of intercepted radio signals to pin-point active Bomber Command airfields in eastern England so that the intruders from I./NJG 2 could be scrambled to intercept the bombers as they returned home.

Within a year more than a hundred claims were made against Bomber Command aircraft and techniques were further improved by making use of German radio operators to listen to RAF transmissions. Those successful as intruder pilots included Feldwebel Wilhelm Beier who was credited with fourteen victories in this role; Leutnant Hans Hahn of 3./NJG 2 (not to be confused with the day fighter pilots, Hans 'Assi' Hahn and Hans von Hahn), who was the first Nachtjagdflieger to be awarded the Knight's Cross with twelve intruder victories at night; Oberfeldwebel Alfons Köster with eleven; and Feldwebel Heinz Strüning of 1./NJG 2, who flew sixty-six intruder missions over England and was credited with nine victories.

The tactics used by the intruder pilots varied. Some would follow the bombers back across the North Sea and carry out an attack near the English coast whereas others had the audacity to locate the bomber airfield and then join the circuit to prosecute an attack at low level and from very close range. However, the intruder missions never really impacted on Bomber Command's war against Germany and occasionally proved costly for the Luftwaffe. Hans Hahn, for example, was killed in 1941 when he collided with his thirteenth victim and, as technology improved, radar-equipped RAF night-fighters started to achieve success against the intruders. Furthermore, Hitler did not favour intruder missions as he felt the German people should see RAF bombers being shot down over Germany so that claims of success could not be doubted.

While intruder operations had their place, it was the development of a night-fighter force and an associated network of defence that was required to counter the increasing number of night raids by Bomber Command. Operational trials began using a Freya radar installation in Holland that was designed to be co-ordinated with ground stations to direct individual fighters against detected bombers. This form of close control achieved its first success on the night of 16/17 October 1940 when a Wellington bomber was shot down by Leutnant Ludwig Becker flying a Bf 110.

Becker was directed to the Wellington by ground control. He was fortunate as the conditions that night were completely in his favour and he could see the bomber silhouetted in the bright moonlight as he slowly closed in from astern. Once within 50 yards of his target Becker opened fire, scoring hits on the fuselage and starboard engine. The Wellington flew on for a short distance while losing height before it caught fire and spun into the ground.

Ludwig Becker thus paved the way during the early night war against Bomber Command, and he would later carry out the Luftwaffe's first night interception using airborne radar, but what was needed was a system that was not dependent on favourable weather conditions, and this required the development of a new method of radar detection, combined with a successful tracking and reporting system.

Radar installations were set up along the Dutch and German coastlines in front of the searchlight belt and Kombinierte Nachtjagd-gebiete (combined night-fighter zones) were established around areas considered a priority. The stations used Würzburg gun-laying radar and searchlights; a tactic known as *Helle Nachtjagd* (bright night fighting). This idea would have limited success and so a second system, known as *Dunkel Nachtjagd* (dark night fighting), was developed using a Freya early-warning radar slaved to a searchlight.

Over the next two years Kammhuber set up a defensive chain of radar stations with overlapping coverage and divided into zones, which ranged from Denmark to central France. This was known to the British as the Kammhuber Line. Each zone was controlled by a control centre, called a Himmelbett, and used Freya radar that was capable of detecting aircraft out to a range of 60–70 miles. The concept was based on the fact that RAF bombers had to cross the line at some point and the radar would direct a searchlight to illuminate the bomber with a night fighter then being directed to intercept the illuminated bomber.

This system failed to yield any real success and so the next move was to use a Bf 110 in a pre-arranged holding area and in contact with the radar station. This also failed to achieve any results of note and so the idea was later refined using the more accurate Würzburg tracking radar. The system had its weaknesses in the early days because of the lack of air-mounted IFF (Identification Friend or Foe) equipment, meaning that only one fighter in the zone could be controlled from the ground at any one time. There were also inaccuracies caused by having to use one of the radars to track the bomber while another controlled the night fighter, which could lead to the night fighter ending up to half a mile away from its intended target.

Although the development of a night fighter-defence system was still in its infancy, there were successes and by the end of 1940 the Nacht-jagd had achieved more than forty victories with Falck receiving a well-earned Knight's Cross. Although this figure is modest when compared to achievements later in the war, it was a start and with an operational air-defence system now online tactics were further refined.

However, these tactics relied on ground-based systems rather than on the development of airborne radar, as the Luftwaffe lacked a suitable aircraft for the night-fighter role. Germany was well behind Britain in this highly technical branch of aerial warfare and it would be another year or more before operational radar sets were widely installed into German night fighters.

One of the earliest developments was the FuG 202 Lichtenstein B/C radar as fitted to the Ju 88R night fighter. The complex *Matratze* ('Mattress') arrangement of antennae meant the idea was not altogether popular amongst the night-fighter crews as the installation increased drag on the aircraft and reduced its performance. Many night-fighter pilots preferred instead to maintain the performance of their aircraft and seemed quite happy to be guided to the bomber stream from the ground, and then acquire their target visually once amongst the bombers.

The first successful use of Lichtenstein took place on the night of 9 August 1941 and was claimed by Ludwig Becker,[31] now an Oberleutnant, flying a Do 215. Becker's technique involved waiting above the esti-mated height of the main bomber stream and then positioning himself behind his target. He would then descend to just below the bomber, usually to within 1,000 feet but keeping out of the visual scan of the aircraft's gunners, so that he could look up and silhouette the bomber against the night sky. Using any ambient light to his advantage, Becker would take up a position below the bomber and then edge his aircraft closer to his intended victim to a final position within a matter of yards. He would then open fire, aiming at a point where the bomber would fly through his burst of cannon shells and machine-gun rounds.

Ludwig Becker was a true pioneer of night air combat but he would not survive the war. As Staffelkapitän of 12./NJG 1 he was promoted to Hauptmann and awarded the Knight's Cross in July 1942 but he and his radar operator, Oberfeldwebel Josef Straub, were posted as missing on 26 February 1943 during a daylight attack against American bombers over the North Sea. Their Bf 110G crashed off the Dutch island of Schiermonnikoog and Becker, with forty-six victories, all at night, was posthumously awarded the Oak Leaves to his Knight's Cross.

The normal tactic when using Lichtenstein was to scramble the experienced night-fighter crews first because of the limited capacity of the control system, in order to give them the maximum time to get into the main bomber stream and shoot down as many bombers as possible. The number of successes at night continued to rise and by the end of 1941 the Nachtjagd units had claimed more than 400 aircraft, accounting for nearly 60 per cent of Bomber Command's losses at night. The night defensive network had widened during the year with NJG 3 forming near Hamburg, under the command of Major Johann Schalk, to protect the port and Kriegsmarine (German Navy) installations.

Winter weather often made operating conditions most difficult. Climbing through seemingly endless layers of cloud, causing the night fighter to buffet and bounce around in the turbulent air, it would take several minutes to climb up to the altitude of the main bomber force. The close control from the Jägerleitoffizier (fighter control officer) on the ground rarely seemed to take into account the harsh conditions faced by the night-fighter crew. There was also the bitterly cold air from operating at such heights, which even managed to penetrate the thick, electrically heated flying suits worn by the crew.

Conditions were hard and opportunities for scoring success at night remained elusive but it was the RAF's first thousand-bomber raid, against Cologne on the night of 30/31 May 1942, that marked the start of a new Allied intent to use large numbers of bombers concentrated against specific targets. Until then, Bomber Command crews had essentially been responsible for finding their own way to the target, which meant they passed through the night-fighter engagement zones in relatively low numbers. Now, however, Bomber Command had changed its tactic for night bombing and had chosen to saturate Germany's defences in order to get large numbers of aircraft onto a target within a short space of time.

This change of tactic by the RAF came at a time when the defence of German airspace was still considered to be a low priority as the Reich continued to expand on all fronts. Nonetheless, the saturation of German defences during the raid against Cologne had presented a target rich environment and the 600th night victory was achieved. Amongst the successes that night were two bombers claimed by Hauptmann Werner Streib, now Staffelkapitän of 2./NJG 1 and holder of the Knight's Cross; they were his twenty-fifth and twenty-sixth victories at night.

Another successful pilot that night was 23-year-old Oberleutnant Reinhold Knacke of 3./NJG 1, who scored his twentieth night victory, for which he would also be awarded the Knight's Cross. The Cologne raid, while successful as far as RAF Bomber Command was concerned, was still seen by the German High Command as a bit of a 'one-off' as the RAF had failed to make much mark in other raids against Germany, and the United States had yet to enter the fray in any considerable numbers.

The night-fighter force continued to expand with the formation of NJG 4 and NJG 5 from elements of the earlier Nachtjagdgeschwader, and tactics continued to evolve as training improved. While the training carried out at the Nachtjagdschule (Night-Fighter Training School) taught the rudiments of night fighting, such as how to operate on and off the ground at night, and basic cross-country night navigation, there was still much to learn. The more advanced phases of training taught navigation using radio beacons, essential for operations in the Kammhuber Line when the night fighter had to hold in the right area, and integration with the network of defences, such as searchlight and anti-aircraft batteries. However, the advanced training syllabus was not helped by the lack of technical equipment. While there was some teaching of air interception, it was left to the operational units to teach the final and most decisive aspects of night fighting using the scarce specialist equipment that could not be released for the training schools.

The night of 5/6 March 1943 saw the beginning of what RAF Bomber Command later called the Battle of the Ruhr. Many night-fighter crews found themselves posted to Holland and Belgium as, for the next few weeks the Allies concentrated on industrial targets in the Ruhr, although Bomber Command did not limit its effort to Germany's major industrial district and many other targets were hit, such as Munich, Frankfurt, Stuttgart and Düsseldorf. The Battle of the Ruhr lasted four months, during which the RAF flew nearly 20,000 sorties and lost nearly 900 aircraft. Having suffered such high losses, Bomber Command temporarily brought a halt to large-scale night raids.

Bomber Command's next major offensive, the Battle of Hamburg, began on 24 July. This new offensive saw the RAF introduce a new radar countermeasure known as Window. This deception tactic made use of strips of aluminium foil, cut at a specific length and packed into bundles, dropped from bombers to create a cloud of false radar returns by re-radiating the radar signal and making it almost impossible for the German defences to distinguish real aircraft from the false returns generated by Window. Unable to track individual bombers, all the ground controllers could do was to make a general assessment of the position of the main bomber stream.

No longer able to rely on ground radar, the German night-fighter crews found their task had become much harder and were forced to change tactics. The ground controller was now required to provide a running commentary to the night-fighter crews to try and get them into the right area from where they could make an attack. This form of loose control of the night fighter took some time to settle down but it did start to meet with success and the number of bomber losses soon started to mount.

Nonetheless, approaching an enemy bomber from the rear was still a risky manoeuvre and would not always guarantee success. The bomber's rear gunner maintained a watch for night fighters and if one was spotted then he was able to warn his pilot to take defensive action. Furthermore, approaching the rear of the bomber from below would mean having to pull up sharply to open fire and this caused the night fighter to lose valuable speed while also making it vulnerable to the bomber's defensive fire.

In response to the growing threat of Bomber Command's night raids on the Reich during mid-1943, which had started to see the RAF gain the ascendancy over the Nachtjäger, through the tactical use of Window and other decoy methods, Kammhuber looked for solutions and the result was a concept known as *Wilde Sau* ('Wild boar').

The *Wilde Sau* tactic was developed by Major Hans-Joachim Herrmann, a former bomber pilot who had gained a reputation while serving with the operational staff as one of the leading tacticians. His idea was to form a new unit equipped with single-engine day fighters manned by experienced night-fighter pilots with the freedom to hunt the bombers visually in the target area. They would use a combination of the light created by searchlights and fires below, and special flare-equipped Ju 88s that would position themselves at the rear of the bomber stream.

Standard FW 190As and Bf 109Gs were initially borrowed from day-fighter units, mainly from JG 1 and JG 11, and used to test the theory. The tactics were used operationally for the first time on the night of 3/4 July 1943 during a raid on Cologne with twelve bombers being shot down in the target area, although some of these were jointly claimed with anti-aircraft batteries on the ground. The tactic had proved successful and led to the formation of JG 300 the following month. JG 300 enjoyed much early success and so two more units, JG 301 and JG 302, were formed along the same lines, which then led to the formation of 30. Jagd Division under Herrmann's command.

When the tactic was first used, the single-engine fighters were not specially equipped but once the tactic was proven as a concept variants of the Bf 109G were adapted for the night-fighter role eventually using the Naxos Z passive homing detector and an interception radio system. In addition, a number of Bf 109Gs and FW 190A-6s would be fitted with the FuG 217/218 Neptun active search radar and serve with NJGr 10 and NJG 11 as radar-equipped night fighters.

One of the most successful of JG 300's *Wilde Sau* pilots was Oberleutnant Klaus Bretschneider of 5./JG 300. Bretschneider had joined the unit when it first formed and had claimed his first victory, a Lancaster to the south of Mannheim, on the night of 5/6 September 1943. By early 1944 he had been credited with fourteen victories and appointed Staffel-kapitän of 5./JG 300, and would eventually be credited with thirty-four victories, including fourteen RAF heavy bombers at night, for which he was awarded the Knight's Cross.

Hans-Joachim Herrmann went on to fly more than fifty night-fighter missions and claimed the destruction of nine enemy bombers but the introduction of radar for the main night-fighter force and the high wastage of pilots and aircraft due to accidents during the winter months brought a close to *Wilde Sau* tactics at the end of 1943, after which Herrmann became the Luftwaffe's Inspector-General of Night Fighters and was awarded the Swords to his Knight's Cross with Oak Leaves.

The first radar sets were fitted to German night fighters in September 1943 and by early 1944 the majority of aircraft, such as the Ju 88R-1 and Bf 110G-4, had been suitably equipped. The eight-dipole-element *Hirschgeweih* ('Stag's antlers') antenna was an improvement on earlier designs but the installation added considerable weight to the aircraft and reduced its performance, which in turn made the night fighters a target for the RAF's own night fighters that had now gone over to the offensive.

Nonetheless, the Bf 110 proved an ideal aircraft for development as a night fighter. It was fast enough to chase down the RAF's bombers and its benign handling, endurance and relatively heavy armament made it adequate for such a role. Most importantly, though, it was big enough to accommodate the new technology and an additional crew member to operate the radar and to assist the pilot with getting the Bf 110 into the right part of the sky to make his attack. In addition to the Bf 110, the Ju 88 and Do 17 were also performing well; although designed as high-speed bombers, both had been suitably adapted for the night-fighter role.

Following on from the success of *Wilde Sau*, the development of *Zahme Sau* ('Tame boar') as a night-fighter tactic gave freedom to the radar-equipped night fighters to operate alone rather than under the direction of the Himmelbett. The concept behind *Zahme Sau* was for the ground-based radars to detect a raid and night fighters to be scrambled to designated holding points where the crews would wait to be directed into the main bomber stream in large numbers. Once amongst the stream the night-fighter crews would use their own radar to detect an individual bomber and to press home their attack.

Bomber Command losses started to rise once more but the fact remained that the Luftwaffe was still some way behind the RAF when it came to the technological war. The limited capability of the technology during the early days of *Zahme Sau* meant it was not an easy tactic to execute well but it did become more successful over time as radar detection ranges increased, particularly with new equipment such as the FuG 220 Lichtenstein SN-2, operating in the low VHF band and therefore impervious to Window.

As technology and night tactics continued to evolve, the improved Bf 110G-4 was fitted with the upward-firing twin-cannon installation known as *Schräge Musik* (from the German colloquialism for 'Jazz Music' with *schräg* meaning 'slanted'), mounted just above the rear cockpit, which allowed the night fighters to attack RAF bombers from below and outside the scan of the bomber's air gunners. The idea was not entirely new as it had been first trialled during the First World War[32] but the concept of using upward-firing cannons for night fighting during the Second World War was developed by Rudolf Schönert who had first experimented with upward-firing guns as early as 1942 while Kapitän of 4./NJG 2. The first installation was in a Lichtenstein-equipped Do 17Z but the idea was initially rejected by his Gruppenkommandeur, Helmut Lent, although Schönert persisted with his idea and managed to convince Kammhuber of its potential. Further trials were carried out during the following months, and when Schönert was given command of II./NJG 5 his armourers mounted two MG FF 20 mm cannon in the rear compartment of the upper fuselage of one of the unit's Bf 110s and designed to fire through the canopy. Schönert's first success using his modified aircraft came in May 1943 and from the following month modifications were also authorized for the Ju 88 and Do 217.

The introduction of *Schräge Musik* now meant that the night fighter could approach the bomber from the rear and below without the need to pull up sharply. Instead, the pilot slowed down his approach speed and then rose up gently underneath the bomber. Holding formation, the optimum firing position was with the bomber positioned at 65–70 degrees above the fighter where the pilot could clearly see the silhouette of the bomber. The fighter's gunsight was modified by placing a reflecting mirror above the pilot's head, in line with a similar mirror behind the actual gunsight. It was complicated in theory but the final positioning of the night fighter was achieved by the radar operator giving commands to the pilot until the pilot could see the large silhouette of the bomber above him and take up his final position to open fire. For a well-practised and experienced crew the whole manoeuvre could be done in seconds rather than minutes.

When first used, the tactic came as a complete surprise to the unsuspecting crews of Bomber Command but the RAF was slow to react because initial losses were believed to be due to flak. It was only when detailed analysis was done of returning bomber aircraft that the damage was acknowledged to have been caused by night fighters firing from below. The only real problem for the night-fighter crew was that they had to get out of the way quickly once they had carried out their attack. Their guns were so accurate and the ease of the firing solution from such a position meant that any damage to the bomber, such as debris or parts of the aircraft falling off, or even worse its bomb load exploding, presented a real risk to the night-fighter crew. Many chose to aim at the wing to cause structural damage and hit the wing fuel tanks rather than aim at the central fuselage where the risk of hitting the bomb bay was too great.

Within the year a third of all German night fighters were fitted with *Schräge Musik* and later installations included more powerful MK 108 30 mm cannon. While these more powerful guns meant that only a handful of hits were required to bring down a large bomber, the extra weight and drag reduced fighter performance and heavier cannon were also criticized by crews because the low muzzle velocity meant that the fighter had to get even closer to its target to achieve success. Nonetheless, *Schräge Musik* proved to be a great success. Schönert went on to serve with NJG 100 on the Eastern Front and was eventually credited with sixty-four victories, including eighteen using *Schräge Musik*, making him the seventh-highest-scoring Nachtjagdflieger, for which he was awarded the Knight's Cross and Oak Leaves.

The combination of Lichtenstein SN-2 and *Schräge Musik* had made the German night fighter an extremely effective weapon and Bomber

Command losses continued to mount. The Germans also used intercept stations to listen to and track the IFF devices fitted to the RAF bombers. Bomber Command belatedly directed crews to turn these off when over Germany but the night-fighter crews were then able to track the Monica and H2S transmissions of the RAF bombers; H2S could be tracked by Naxos radar detectors and Monica could be tracked on Flensburg radar detectors, both of which were mounted on the night fighters.

Bomber Command's latest offensive, the Battle of Berlin during the winter of 1943–4, failed to win the war outright as had been hoped, and cost the RAF more than 1,000 bombers with a similar number severely damaged. The Luftwaffe lost just 250 fighters during the campaign but amongst those killed was the high-scoring Heinrich Prinz zu Sayn-Wittgenstein, Kommodore of NJG 2, who was shot down while taking part in a *Zahme Sau* mission on the night of 21 January 1944. Having already claimed four Lancasters during the mission, Sayn-Wittgenstein was engaging a fifth when his aircraft was hit. Although his two crew members managed to escape the stricken aircraft, the Ju 88R crashed near the town of Stendal to the west of Berlin; the body of Sayn-Wittgenstein was found near the wreckage. Credited with eighty-three night victories, Sayn-Wittgenstein was the third-highest scorer at night and was posthumously awarded the Swords to his Knight's Cross with Oak Leaves two days later.

The death of Sayn-Wittgenstein had been a loss to the Nachtjagd and the same night there was another when Hauptmann Manfred Meurer, Kommandeur of I./NJG 1 and holder of the Oak Leaves with sixty-five night victories, was killed after colliding with a Lancaster attacking Berlin. These losses were hard to take amongst what had become a very close and compact night-fighter force.

Although the RAF had inflicted severe damage on the Big City, Berlin proved to be a difficult nut to crack. For the Luftwaffe, its losses were not entirely unexpected from such a long and intense bombing campaign but the psychological effect on its night-fighter crews, having regularly seen their capital city ablaze as Berlin's citizens took a seemingly endless pounding, must have been considerable.

Night-fighter operations were now being directed from Berlin under Wolfgang Falck, by this point an Oberst and Kammhuber's representative within Luftwaffenbefehlshaber Mitte. In his appointment as Einsatzleiter Nachtjagd (Head of Night Operations), Falck was responsible for the night fighter defence of the Reich and was updated at his headquarters on the developing night air war by using a large map divided into a system of grid squares so that he could direct the air battle each night as it evolved.[33] Falck was able to evaluate the number of bombers taking part in the raid and where the likely target was so that he could direct the German night defences accordingly.

The demands of the night war were quite different from those of fighting by day. A successful night interception was often the result of teamwork rather than operating in isolation. It not only depended on the skill of the ground controller to position the night fighter in the right place and at the right time; the introduction of airborne radar now meant in addition that better crew co-operation was required between the radar operator and the pilot. It took skill and patience to get the night fighter into a position from where it could strike, and closing in on a large aircraft at night, often in bad weather, meant that any misjudgement could be fatal.

One of the best was Major Helmut Lent, Kommodore of NJG 3. Lent had been the first to reach fifty night victories in January 1943 while Kommandeur of IV./NJG 1, and in July 1944 he became the first to pass a century of victories at night to earn the coveted Diamonds; the first Nachtjagdflieger to be so recognized. Lent's life would soon be cut short by a fatal accident on 5 October during a routine transit flight to visit Hans-Joachim Jabs, Kommodore of NJG 1, at Paderborn. As Lent was making the approach to land, his Ju 88 suffered an engine failure and then struck a power cable before it crashed. Also on board were Lent's long-term radio operator, Oberfeldwebel Walter Kubisch, a second radio operator, Oberleutnant Hermann Klöss, and a wartime correspondent, Leutnant Werner Kark. Although all four were pulled out of the wreckage alive, Kubisch and Kloss died soon after while Kark died the following day. Lent finally succumbed to his injuries two days after the crash.

Lent was given a state funeral in Berlin with the guard of honour consisting of Hans-Joachim Jabs; Oberstleutnant Günther Radusch, Kommodore of NJG 5; Major Rudolf Schönert, Kommandeur of NJGr 10;

Hauptmann Heinz Strüning, Staffelkapitän of 3./NJG 1; Hauptmann Paul Zorner, Kommandeur of III./NJG 5; and Hauptmann Heinz-Martin Hadeball, Kommandeur of I./NJG 6. Ahead of the coffin and carrying his impressive array of decorations was Oberstleutnant Werner Streib, now Inspector of Night Fighters, while Göring took the salute.

At the time of his death, Lent was twenty-six years old and had been credited with 110 victories, of which all but seven were achieved at night. Lent had been the first of only two Nachtjagdflieger to receive the highest recognition of the Knight' Cross with Oak Leaves, Swords and Diamonds. The other was Major Heinz-Wolfgang Schnaufer who surpassed a century of victories just two days after Lent's death. Schnaufer had begun his night-fighter career with II./NJG 1 at the end of 1941, claiming his first night victory in June 1942 before being appointed Staffelkapitän of 12./NJG 1 in August 1943. As an Ober-leutnant he was awarded the Knight's Cross at the end of the year, having been credited with forty-two victories, after which he was promoted to Hauptmann and appointed as Kommandeur of IV./NJG 1 in March 1944. The award of the Oak Leaves soon followed and then the Swords a month later when his personal score had reached eighty-nine victories. Then, in October 1944, came the coveted Diamonds and Schnaufer would go on to become the Luftwaffe's youngest Kommodore at the age of just twenty-two, ending the war as the highest-scoring Nachtjagdflieger with 121 victories.

In addition to the achievements of Schnaufer, Lent, Sayn-Wittgenstein, Streib, Meurer and Schönert, others to achieve success during the night war over Germany included Oberstleutnant Günther Radusch, Kommodore of NJG 5, with sixty-four victories at night for which he was awarded the Oak Leaves, and Hauptmann Heinz Rökker, Kapitän of 2./NJG 2, with sixty-three night victories, another holder of the Oak Leaves. A further thirteen pilots achieved fifty victories or more at night, including Paul Zorner with fifty-nine, Martin Becker and Gerhard Raht (each with fifty-eight) and Wilhelm Herget (fifty-seven).

There were others who also achieved fifty victories but not all at night, although they proved to be great leaders of their night-fighter units and formed a small elite group who demonstrated skill and ability by day and by night. One was Hans-Joachim Jabs, Kommodore of NJG 1 and a former Zerstörer pilot with ZG 76, who added twenty-eight night victories to his twenty-two by day for which he was awarded the Oak Leaves to his Knight's Cross. Extremely intelligent and a master when it came to assessing a tactical situation quickly, Jabs was an excellent leader and was always held in very high regard by his crews.

The night war was a hard, and at times horrific, campaign for both sides and proved to be a titanic struggle for survival in the air.

Chapter 9

Struggle in the East: Zitadelle

The brief lull on the Eastern Front came to a sudden and dramatic end on 5 July 1943 when the Germans launched Operation Zitadelle, the Battle of Kursk, which would develop into the largest battle of armoured units in history. The Germans hoped to eliminate Soviet troop concentrations in the Kursk salient by a pincer attack, supported by Luftflotte 6 (previously Luftwaffe Command East) from the north and Luftflotte 4 from the south, but the huge German build-up prior to launching the offensive had simply indicated to the Russians that an attack was imminent and so vast Soviet reinforcements had been brought in.

The Jagdwaffe in the east had around 550 single-engine fighters stretched along the entire Eastern Front. While this figure is almost identical to the number of fighters available the year before when Hitler had launched Braunschweig, the composition of the Jagdwaffe was now quite different. The introduction of the FW 190 had seen the balance change from an all-109 fighter force just a year before to a mixed force of approximately 60 per cent FW 190As and 40 per cent Bf 109Gs.

The FW 190s were mainly allocated to Luftflotte 6, although a number had gone north to the Leningrad area to operate with the Bf 109s of JG 54 under Luftflotte 1. The four Gruppen of 190s operating with Luftflotte 6 (three of JG 51 and one of JG 54), some 160 fighters in all, were under the command of Oberstleutnant Karl-Gottfried Nordmann and were to provide fighter cover along the northern flank of Kursk. A hundred more FW 190s were to operate with Luftflotte 4 on the southern flank of Kursk in the ground-attack role. The Bf 109s were mainly allocated to Luftflotte 4 (although Luftflotte 5 had retained its Bf 109E/Fs of JG 5 in Finland) to operate in the southern sector and these consisted of three Gruppen of JG 52, under the command of Oberstleutnant Dietrich Hrabak, and two of JG 3 commanded by Major Kurt Brändle and Major Walther Dahl.

For the Luftwaffe, Zitadelle was over almost before it had even begun. During the early hours of 5 July, just as the bombers and dive bombers were being prepared for the opening offensive, large numbers of Russian aircraft attacked their airfields. It was only the alertness of JG 3 and JG 52 that saved a disaster and their quick reaction in scrambling to intercept the raids led to a fierce air battle between the force of nearly 150 Bf 109Gs and the Russian hordes, resulting in more than 400 Soviet aircraft claimed for the loss of fewer than thirty German fighters. The most successful during this opening encounter was 23-year-old Oberleutnant Joachim Kirschner, Kapitän of 5./JG 3. His nine victories that day took his personal total past the 150 mark for which he was awarded the Oak Leaves to his Knight's Cross.

Throughout the opening morning of Zitadelle, the Jagdwaffe provided escort for the bombers and Ju 87 Stukas and it was not until the afternoon that more encounters with the Red Air Force took place. Two Staffelkapitäne serving with JG 52 scored double figures on the opening day of Zitadelle. One was Johannes Wiese of 2./JG 52, who claimed twelve Russian aircraft, and the other was Walter Krupinski of 7./JG 52 who was credited with eleven.

But arguably the best performance of the opening day came from a relatively unheard-of FW 190 pilot, Oberfeldwebel Hubert Strassl, a young Austrian serving with 8./JG 51. Strassl claimed fifteen victories in four sorties during the afternoon and early evening to the south of Orel and would add a further ten victories the following day, followed by two more the day after. But then, with his score on sixty-seven, Strassl was killed on 8 July, when he was shot down by LaGG-3s to the south of Ponyri. Strassl had been forced desperately low during the encounter and although he was seen to bail out of his aircraft there was no time for his parachute to deploy fully.

The Jagdwaffe soon gained local air superiority and maintained a level of dominance during the opening days of the new offensive. JG 52 passed the 6,000 mark for its total number of victories during early July, followed soon after by JG 51. These were quite staggering achievements and would become even more so during the following year when JG 51 surpassed 8,000 victories, as did JG 54, with JG 52 boasting an even higher tally when it passed 10,000 victories.

There were, nonetheless, losses and one to be shot down on the second day of Zitadelle was Major Reinhard Seiler, Kommandeur of I./JG 54. With his personal score on ninety-nine, Seiler was seeking his 100th victory but having chased and claimed an Airacobra he was then shot down by another. Seiler had achieved his century of victories, for which he would later be awarded the Oak Leaves to his Knight's Cross, and was fortunate to escape with his life, although he was badly wounded and would take no further part in air operations for the rest of the war. But not all were fortunate enough to escape with their life, including Major Rudolf Resch, Kommandeur of IV./JG 51, who was killed on 11 July. Resch, a holder of the Knight's Cross credited with ninety-four victories, was shot down by Soviet fighters to the south of Ponyri.

Despite the efforts of the Luftwaffe over the Kursk salient during July 1943, Zitadelle was struggling and by the end of the first week it was evident that it had failed. The Allied invasion of Sicily on 10 July resulted in Hitler abandoning Zitadelle on 16 July as he ordered the transfer of key assets to Italy. This decision to call off a major operation at the height of a tactical battle would, understandably, later lead to severe criticism of Hitler but the Allied landings and the immediate threat to southern Italy had now become a greater priority.

The last day of Zitadelle witnessed the death of one young pilot, 21-year-old Leutnant Günther Scheel of 3./JG 54, who had the impressive record of shooting down more enemy aircraft than he had flown operational missions. Scheel had only joined his unit earlier in the year on completion of his pilot training and had quickly adapted to air combat on the Eastern Front. His unit was transferred from the northern section of the front to Orel in early July to support the Kursk offensive and he quickly made a name for himself, shooting down more than forty Russian aircraft in a little over two weeks. But with such intense air activity his luck ran out on 16 July when, at low level, the wing of his FW 190A clipped the Yak-9 that he had just shot down. Scheel stood no chance. In an operational career lasting just six months he had claimed seventy-one aircraft in seventy sorties for which he was posthumously awarded the Knight's Cross.

The intensity of the air activity over the Eastern Front had reached new heights and the end of Zitadelle did not bring an end to the losses. In its immediate aftermath a number of the Jagdwaffe's influential combat leaders were killed in action and these included Heinrich Jung, Kommandeur of II./JG 54, who was shot down to the south-east of Leningrad on 30 July with his score on sixty-eight victories. A few days later, on 2 August, Gerhard Homuth, who had replaced Reinhard Seiler as Kommandeur of I./JG 54, failed to return from a sortie near Orel. Homuth, with sixty-three victories, had been one of the leading scorers of the North African campaign and had only just arrived on the Eastern Front. Replacing Homuth as Kommandeur of I./JG 54 was Hans Götz, with eighty-two victories and a holder of the Knight's Cross, but just two days later, on 4 August, Götz was also killed. Three days later, Heinrich Höfemeier, Kapitän of 3./JG 51 and holder of the Knight's Cross with ninety-six victories over the Eastern Front, was killed over Karachev. And so it went on.

The Soviet Air Force had come a long way in two years of fighting and it had become increasingly hard for the Jagdwaffe to score success. The Soviet aviation industry was producing better fighters by keeping the design simple and based on earlier production aircraft so that vast numbers could be produced in quick time. One example was the Lavochkin La-5, a development of the LaGG-3 that had been designed to accommodate a more powerful radial engine, giving the La-5 a top speed in excess of 400 mph. The latest variant, the La-5FN, entered service in 1943 and would be further developed as the much improved La-7, arguably the Soviet's best fighter of the war, which would enter service during the following year and designed to counter the FW 190A-8. Another example was the Yak-9, a further development of the Yak-7, which itself had been developed from the Yak-1, that had entered the combat arena at Stalingrad during the last weeks of 1942 and would become the most- produced Soviet fighter of all time. The Yak-9 performed exceedingly well at lower altitudes but was similar in appearance to the Yak-3 that performed well at higher altitudes, and this gave the Jagdflieger the problem of having first to identify what variant of Yak he was up against and then decide how best to counter it.

The Russian pilots were now operating as pairs or in formations of four, constantly weaving and maintaining their speed, thus improving their own chances of surprising an opponent, while being less vulnerable to unobserved attacks. The two air forces were now more evenly matched in quality but, despite being heavily outnumbered, the Jagdgeschwader had inflicted heavy losses on their opposition and at least maintained parity in the air over the crucial sectors.

Stalin then unleashed the might of his armies in a series of decisive blows along the Kursk sector. To the north there were offensives against cities such as Smolensk and Orel, while to the south there were similar thrusts towards the city of Kharkov, the second-largest city in the Ukraine. This time the offensives would prove decisive and from now on there would be no stopping the Red Army. The Wehrmacht was forced to withdraw and this retreat set the pattern for the rest of 1943 as the air war on the Eastern Front raged on.

German strength in the east was now in decline as aircraft and spares had to be abandoned and more units were recalled to Germany to defend the Reich, and this all came at a time when the Soviet Air Force was increasing in strength. As Focke-Wulf's production line struggled to meet the increasing demand for new fighters, some units reverted back to the Bf 109 as those left to resist the might of Stalin's forces in the east did so in the knowledge they had effectively been forgotten by their High Command back home.

Despite facing increasing challenges, the Jagdwaffe continued to resist the relentless might of the Red Air Force and one young pilot rapidly making his name known on the Eastern Front was Leutnant Erich Hartmann of JG 52. Known as 'Bubi' (young boy) because of his youthful looks and age, twenty-year-old Hartmann had been posted to the Eastern Front in October 1942. Based at Maykop and flying the Bf 109G, he quickly learned from some of the Luftwaffe's finest but it still took time for him to establish himself in combat. By March 1943 he had claimed his first two victories but it was while he was flying as wingman to the experienced Walter Krupinski, Kapitän of 7./JG 52, that Hartmann learned the art of close-quarter attacks and how to get closer and closer to his victim. The teaching worked well. Hartmann would soon add to his total and during the next five months took his personal tally to ninety victories, more than forty of which were achieved during one month.

Hartmann had a lucky escape on 19 August 1943 when he was in combat with Sturmoviks and his aircraft was damaged. Forced to land behind enemy lines he was taken prisoner but quick to try and find a way out, Hartmann faked internal injury. He was placed on a stretcher and put in a truck where he waited for an opportunity to make his escape. Then, under the cover of a Stuka attack, Hartmann jumped from the truck and made a break into a field. Evading his pursuers, Hartmann hid and waited for night fall before continuing his escape back towards German lines under the cover of darkness by following a Soviet patrol heading for the front. Even then, just as he was making his way back to German lines, Hartmann had to survive a shot from an overly eager German sentry, which passed through his trousers.

Allowing Hartmann to escape would prove extremely costly for the Soviets as he would continue to be a thorn in their side. At the end of the month Hartmann was appointed Staffelkapitän of 9./JG 52 at the age of just twenty-one when he replaced the centurion Leutnant Berthold Korts who went missing on 29 August having been last seen engaging P-39 Airacobras.

Even at such a young age, Hartmann proved to be an inspirational leader. He would always make sure, as best he could, that his pilots remained as safe as possible and took enormous pride in the fact that he never lost a wingman in combat. His technique was often based on first seeking out his enemy and then ambushing them, using the power and performance of the Bf 109G to his advantage. Although he was extremely capable when it came to close air combat, he was not one to be drawn into lengthy manoeuvres but chose instead to use his speed and height to set up an attack and, where possible, to use the sun to his advantage so that he could sweep through a formation and then capitalise on the confusion he had just caused, either to disengage or to attack another victim. If conditions and the altitude of an enemy formation dictated otherwise, then he would often attack from below so that he could silhouette the enemy aircraft against the white cloudy sky.

Tactically, Hartmann learned how to be patient and he became a master at deciding whether to attack at once or to hold off and wait for a better opportunity to develop. Against the Sturmoviks, the Soviet's main ground-attack aircraft, which usually flew in formations that were more akin to those of heavier bombers, Hartmann often found his enemies did not even take evasive action. This would enable him to close to a ridiculously short range, sometimes to within forty or fifty yards, before opening fire. This was a technique he had learned from Krupinski and made a kill almost a certainty. Closing to point-blank range made it all but impossible for his victim to escape and enabled Hartmann to be as accurate as possible and to expend the minimum amount of ammunition in one engagement. There was always the risk that Hartmann's aircraft would suffer damage from the debris from his opponent, and that often proved to be the case, but the technique worked well; many Soviet airmen became victims without ever seeing him.

Defensively, Hartmann had perfected the use of speed and rudder to point his aircraft into an unexpected direction so that he could deceive an opponent into misjudging the amount of deflection required when opening fire. Should his opponent open fire then Hartmann would use full control stick deflection to put his Messerschmitt into an outside loop to make his escape.

Hartmann reached a century of victories in September 1943 and, by the end of the following month, when he was awarded a long overdue Knight's Cross his total stood at 148; it was the highest number of victories required by anyone on the Eastern Front before the Knight's Cross was awarded. By now his call-sign of Karaya One (Karaya meaning sweetheart) was feared by the Soviet pilots who came into contact with him. There was even a price put on his head by the Soviet command.

The award of Hartmann's Knight's Cross coincided with another milestone being passed by a fellow member of JG 52 when Günther Rall, Kommandeur of III./JG 52, passed his double century of victories, which earned him the Swords. Also proving to be a thorn in the Soviet's side was Walter Nowotny, now Kommandeur of I./JG 54. Nowotny had converted to the FW 190 earlier in the year and had adapted to the new type better than most. His personal score had risen at a rapid rate to pass a century of victories, and he was now leader of a feared Schwarm that included his loyal wingman, Karl Schnörrer, Anton Döbele and Rudolf Rademacher, and known as the Nowotny Schwarm or sometimes as the 'Chain of Devils'. During August 1943 alone Nowotny claimed a staggering forty-nine victories, and during the following month he took his total past the 200 mark. At that time Nowotny was the highest-scoring *Experte* in the Luftwaffe; he was awarded the Oak Leaves and Swords to his Knight's Cross. He was then promoted to Hauptmann and, on 14 October 1943, became the first pilot to reach 250 victories to earn him the coveted Diamonds at the age of just twenty-two. The decoration was presented to him personally by Hitler at the Wolfsschanze at Rastenburg.

It was not long before Günther Rall became the second to pass 250 victories. Many consider Rall to have been the best marksman of all those serving on the Eastern Front when it came to air-to-air gunnery due to many of his victories being achieved from extreme ranges or high crossing angles, although, like others, he was just as comfortable when attacking from very close in. Rall was undoubtedly a master of deflection shooting, a technique that many found difficult, which required aiming ahead of the target so that the target arrived at exactly the same point in the sky as the rounds fired by Rall.

Another young pilot to enjoy success in the east was Gerhard Barkhorn. Barkhorn was still only twenty-four but he was already a veteran of the campaigns against France and Britain, although it took him more than a hundred combat missions to achieve his first aerial success. Two years on, he was now an Oberleutnant and Staffelkapitän of 4./JG 52, and holder of the Knight's Cross with Oak Leaves having taken his personal score past a hundred victories.

Using the art of surprise, Barkhorn found that he was often able to get into a Russian formation unobserved, particularly when attacking from high and line astern, or from low and beneath the formation from the rear, tactics that he had clearly mastered. He often found the lookout of the Russian pilots to be poor and their tactics lacking in flexibility but air combat was far from easy, and against a good opponent Barkhorn was known to temper aggression with caution.

Barkhorn was given command of II./JG 52 in September 1943 but his appointment coincided with the loss of Heinz Schmidt who was posted as missing in action on 5 September after being shot down near Markor. Schmidt's death had come just two weeks after the loss of Max Stotz and these losses were a blow to the Jagdwaffe in the east.

There were, however, further successes for Hartmann, who now passed 150 victories, and for Barkhorn who took his tally to 200 during November. These two *Experten* would become the best of friends and both would go on to score at a very high rate; Barkhorn's 250th victory came on 13 February 1944 and just a few weeks later, on 2 March, Hartmann would pass 200. Along with Walter Krupinski and Johannes Wiese, also of JG 52, Barkhorn and Hartmann were summoned to the Berghof in Berchtesgaden where Hitler personally presented Barkhorn with the Swords and Hartmann with the Oak Leaves to his Knight's Cross; Krupinski and Wiese also received the Oak Leaves.

While JG 52 boasted the highest-scoring Jagdflieger, JG 51 had its achievers too. Major Erich Leie, Kommandeur of I./JG 51 since January 1943, claimed his century of victories in November 1943, an achievement matched by the Kapitän of 1./JG 51, Oberleutnant Joachim Brendel. Two other Staffelkapitäne amassed a century of victories in the aftermath of Kursk: Oberleutnant Karl-Heinz Weber of 7./JG 51 and Oberleutnant Günther Schack of 9./JG 51.

Although many stories of great success continued, the fact was the number of *Experten* was slowly reducing. Just two years earlier during the opening phase of Barbarossa, many had performed well and had achieved numerous victories. They had been well trained and were prepared for air combat. Their prospects of survival, albeit against moderate opposition at the time, were generally good but much had now changed. The Red Air Force could no longer be considered to be moderate opposition and new pilots arriving on the Jagdgruppen along the Eastern Front had not received the same level of training or the preparation enjoyed by their predecessors. After Zitadelle, 25 per cent of new pilots did not survive more than their first four operational sorties. The Jagdwaffe had to rely on the skill and courage of its *Experten* but in a war of attrition they were gradually disappearing one by one.

The Luftwaffe continued to defy the advancing Soviet forces and one to stand out above others was Oberfeldwebel Otto Kittel serving with 2./JG 54 who was awarded the Knight's Cross at the end of October 1943 for achieving 120 victories. Kittel's award demonstrates just how many victories were now required for an NCO pilot to get recognition. Kittel had scored his first victory during Barbarossa and initially found aerial success hard to come by but during Zitadelle his score started to mount. He quickly took his total past fifty and then averaged a kill a day, passing a century of victories in mid-September.

Another of JG 54's excellent tacticians was Leutnant Emil Lang who enjoyed great success on 3 November when he claimed a record eighteen aircraft in one day, making him the most successful fighter pilot in one day of aerial combat in the history of air warfare. Lang was previously a civil pilot with the German airline Lufthansa and so had served as a transport pilot during the early period of the war. Eventually transferred for training as a fighter pilot in 1942, Lang was nearly thirty-four years old by the time he arrived on the Eastern Front in January 1943. He initially served with 1./JG 54, scoring his first success in March, before he was appointed Staffelkapitän of 5./JG 54 in August, after which his personal score mounted quickly. During October and November Lang claimed seventy-two victories in just three weeks of aerial fighting around the Kiev area, and was awarded the Knight's Cross having taken his total to 119.

Lang's achievement on 3 November was almost repeated just three days later when Hauptmann Erich Rudorffer, Kommandeur of II./JG 54, claimed thirteen aircraft in one day; all were reportedly shot down in one sortie during a period of just seventeen minutes. But Rudorffer did not always have things his own way. He was shot down sixteen times and on nine occasions owed his life to his parachute.

While the third winter on the Eastern Front did not prove as harsh as the previous two, endless amounts of mud made operating from some of the more basic airfields extremely hazardous and individual achievements in the air were seemingly having little impact on the ground. While Stalin's major offensives following Kursk had been focused on the central and southern sectors of the Eastern Front, the situation in the northern sector had been one of relative stability as the siege of

Leningrad continued. Then, in January 1944, the northern sector burst into life when Stalin launched a new offensive that resulted in the ending of the siege, 872 days after it had begun, making the siege of Leningrad amongst the longest and most destructive in history.

It was impossible to prevent the Red advance in the north, just as it was further south, and the overall situation was not helped because many fighter units had already been transferred back to Germany for the defence of the Reich. While things may have already seemed bad in the east, things were about to get worse as more fighters were sent west to counter the Allied invasion of mainland Europe, leaving the Luftwaffe with fewer than 400 single-engine fighters along its entire Eastern Front while the Soviets boasted more than 13,000 aircraft, of which nearly half were fighters. The Red Air Force now outnumbered the Jagdwaffe in the east by more than 15:1. The tide had well and truly turned.

Chapter 10
America Enters the Fray

The entry of the United States into the war in December 1941 could not have been welcomed by many in Germany but it would be some time before the Americans would influence the air war over Europe. Along the Channel Front the pattern during the first half of 1942 was similar to the previous year as JG 2 and JG 26 continued to counter the RAF's incursions across northern France. The two Jagdgeschwader had also taken part in the highly successful Operation Donnerkeil during February when the Jagdwaffe provided an umbrella of more than 250 FW 190s and Bf 109s above three of the German Navy's principal warships – the *Scharnhorst*, *Gneisenau* and *Prinz Eugen* – as they made their daring daylight dash up the Channel.

The FW 190A was now fully embedded in the west and it would be some time before the RAF's latest mark of Spitfire, the Spitfire IX, would appear in sufficient numbers to counter its dominance along the front. The newer Bf 109G had also started to replace earlier variants of the Bf 109, with the Gustav combining the airframe of the Friedrich with the more powerful DB 605 engine, and a reinforced wing structure and improved armament to enable it to fulfil a greater variety of roles.

While the air war over the Channel Front had become somewhat predictable during the summer of 1942, the air activity suddenly intensified on 19 August when the two Geschwader were called upon to help counter the large-scale Allied amphibious raid on the harbour town of Dieppe as the RAF provided air cover above the beachhead.

Due to the close proximity of their airfields to the town, JG 26 was the first to react just after daybreak with nearly thirty 190s of the I. Gruppe, led by Johannes Seifert, scrambled from their base at St-Omer. Once the scale of the attack had become clear, more FW 190s of Gerhard Schöpfel's JG 26 were called upon with the II. Gruppe, led by Wilhelm-Ferdinand 'Wutz' Galland, Kapitän of 5./JG 26 and younger brother of

Adolf Galland, scrambled from Abbeville, while the III. Gruppe, led by Klaus Mietusch, was scrambled from Wevelghem near Courtrai.

By mid-morning it had become apparent that the amount of Allied air activity was greater than anything ever seen before and so the FW 190s of Walter Oesau's JG 2, based further west in the Normandy and Cherbourg area, were also called into action. Like Schöpfel, Oesau had excellent Gruppenkommandeure. Leading the I. Gruppe from Tricqueville was Oberleutnant Erich Leie, with Hauptmann Helmut Bolz leading the II. Gruppe from Beaumont-le-Roger while the III. Gruppe, based at Maupertus, was led by Hauptmann Hans 'Assi' Hahn.

The air activity peaked in the late morning, with the German fighters countering Allied fighters and escorting bombers attacking the invading forces. During the course of the day the two Jagdgeschwader flew 800 missions between them and accounted for nearly a hundred Allied aircraft for the loss of nineteen fighters.

JG 2 was in the thick of the action over Dieppe with fifty-nine confirmed victories for the loss of fourteen of its own fighters. The 9. Staffel, in particular, had been at the centre of the fight, with its Kapitän, Oberleutnant Siegfried Schnell, shooting down five Spitfires during the day to bring his overall total to seventy, and Oberfeldwebel Josef Wurmheller claiming six Spitfires and a Blenheim. Wurmheller had achieved his success despite suffering from a broken leg, the unfortunate result of an earlier crash-landing, but he still managed to claim three victories during the morning and three more during the afternoon before his seventh victim of the day, a Spitfire over the harbour, came in the early evening. Wurmheller was immediately promoted to Leutnant and the following evening claimed two more Spitfires north of the Normandy coast to take his total past sixty, for which he was awarded the Oak Leaves to his Knight's Cross.

Other successes over Dieppe included Oberleutnant Egon Mayer, Kapitän of 7./JG 2. The Spitfire he shot down during a late-morning encounter was his fiftieth success of the war. Others to score during the same action included Erich Leie, who claimed his forty-second victim of the war, a Spitfire just a mile to the north of Dieppe, and Leutnant Günther Seeger of the Stab who claimed two Spitfires just further to the north to add to a Spitfire he had claimed earlier that morning; Seeger's total now stood at twenty-two. Other JG 2 successes that day included two Spitfires during the late afternoon for Leutnant Erich Rudorffer, to bring his total to forty-five, a Spitfire for Oberleutnant Kurt Bühligen, who would become a centurion, and two Spitfires for Leutnant Julius Meimberg, who would go on to achieve fifty-three victories.

JG 26 accounted for thirty-eight Allied aircraft over Dieppe for the loss of just five of its own fighters. The most successful was Ober-leutnant Kurt Ebersberger of the II. Gruppe who claimed four Spitfires during the day to bring his total to twenty-eight. Amongst the many other claims from JG 26 were two Spitfires for the Kommodore, Gerhard Schöpfel, bringing his total to forty, and for the three Gruppen-kommandeure there was a Spitfire each for Johannes Seifert and Wutz Galland, while Klaus Mietusch claimed two Spitfires during the late morning encounter. Oberleutnant Fulbert Zink of the I. Gruppe claimed three victories during the day to bring his total to twenty-six.

Other multiple scorers from the Geschwader included Oberleutnant Rolf Hermichen, Kapitän of 3./JG 26, who claimed two victories during the day to bring his total to seventeen, Oberfeldwebel Emil Babenz, who claimed three Spitfires taking his total to twenty-one, and Oberfeldwebel Wilhelm Philipp of the fourth Staffel who claimed two Spitfires; Philipp would eventually achieve eighty-one victories. Another who would later become a high scorer was Feldwebel Adolf Glunz, also of the 4. Staffel, who claimed a Spitfire during the late morning over Dieppe, his twenty-first victim of an eventual total of seventy-two.

While the FW190A and Bf 109G were both excellent fighters, other new aircraft types under development had disappointingly failed to materialize and, as 1942 drew to a close, there was a danger that Germany was starting to lose the technical edge. But as long as the Luft-waffe continued to enjoy a certain level of dominance over the Channel Front and Germany during the day, there was seemingly little for the High Command to worry about, for the time being at least, given that there was no Allied fighter over Europe considered to be superior to those of the Jagdwaffe.

Although the pattern of Bomber Command raids would continue at night, the air war over Germany was about to see a sudden and dramatic change by day. Many senior American commanders considered that night bombing lacked accuracy and had proved to be wasteful, and so decided that American bombers would take the air war to Germany by day. They felt that precision bombing, which at that stage of the war could only effectively be carried out in daylight, would make better use of American resources and so plans were drawn up to defeat the Luftwaffe in the air and on the ground, and to destroy Germany's aviation industry to the point that it could no longer pose a threat to an Allied invasion of Europe.

When the American Eighth Air Force prepared to wage war against the Reich in January 1943, there was no American fighter (or British one for that matter) with sufficient range to escort the bombers all the way to their targets. There was also an air of arrogance amongst some American commanders that the defensive armament of the American bombers, such as the B-17 Flying Fortress and the B-24 Liberator, was sufficient to prevent any great losses. Some even believed that no escort was required at all.

Seemingly the Luftwaffe's High Command, including Göring and Jeschonnek, had little respect for the American air force and believed that heavy four-engine bombers could be shot down in large numbers. Jeschonnek would soon become better informed on the performance and potential of the American bombers, and would subsequently change his mind, but his views were not shared by Göring or Hitler. Jeschonnek faced a difficult problem, which was not helped by concerns within the Luftwaffe about the capabilities of its existing fighters compared to improvements being made to Allied fighters at the time.

The first large American raid was carried out on 27 January by a mixed force of B-17s and B-24s against the North Sea naval base at Wilhelmshaven. The combination of poor weather conditions, which hampered navigation, and an intercepting force of FW 190s off the Dutch coast meant that only half of the bomber force, all B-17s, made it to the target area where they encountered the Bf 109Gs of I./JG 1. The 109s carried out a conventional stern attack against the bomber formation but were met by heavy return fire from the B-17s.

This first encounter against such numbers of heavily armed American bombers resulted in only a handful of bombers being claimed for the loss of five Bf 109s. One of the bombers was claimed by Oberleutnant Hugo Frey of 2./JG 1 who would go on to become one of the highest scoring B-17 destroyers.

Over the following weeks there were further attempts by the American bombers but poor weather in the target areas hampered the raids, as did the FW 190s and Bf 109s of JG 1. One young pilot to gain early success against the Americans during these opening exchanges was 21-year-old Leutnant Heinz Knoke of 2./JG 1 who claimed his first American 'heavy', a B-24, on 26 February 1943.

Knoke achieved his success using a frontal attack and from slightly below the bomber. The initial head-on pass had damaged the bomber sufficiently to force it away from the relative safety of its formation and from then on he was able to mount further attacks from above and behind as the return fire from the bomber diminished. A fire broke out and then the wing broke away as the bomber entered its final lunge to earth, spiralling and spinning as it fell, before exploding and dis-integrating shortly before it hit the ground. It was the young Knoke's third kill of the war and his victim that day was the first B-24 shot down over German soil. Although it had been a victory it had proved hard work, as it would always be when coming up against large formations of heavy well-defended American bombers.

While poor weather conditions during the opening weeks of 1943 meant that the American bombing campaign against the Reich got off to a slow start, penetrations into Germany soon deepened and increased in numbers. Those bombers that survived the initial encounters over the North Sea then had to run the gauntlet of several Jagdgruppen as the large bomber formations made their way across Germany to their targets. Then, because their transit over Europe could take several hours, the American bomber crews had to face the German fighters again during their return as the Jagdgruppen had been able to land and refuel before rejoining the air battle once more.

Units equipped with the Bf 109Gs and FW 190As started to inflict heavy losses on the American bomber groups and on average one in seven American bombers carrying out daylight raids over Europe did not return; this figure would become nearly one in five during the coming months. While the Bf 109G offered less punch when it came to bringing a heavy bomber down, the very capable FW 190A-5 was already becoming the scourge of Allied bomber crews over Europe. Its engine was mounted slightly further forward than earlier variants, in an attempt to rectify problems of over-heating that had been experienced since the early days of production, and in addition to its 20 mm cannon, the MG 17 machine guns, which lacked the firepower needed when attacking large aircraft such as heavy bombers, had been replaced by two MG 131 13 mm machine guns.

The optimum range for the FW 190 pilot to open fire was within 400 yards of his target as the trajectory of the rounds would fall away if firing from beyond. Furthermore, the pilot had a limited number of rounds for his larger-calibre weapons and so it was vital that ammunition was not wasted. This meant sitting in a line-astern position and closing gradually on the target but when attacking a bomber the fighter was vulnerable and predictable, and so it was not uncommon for him to open fire too early. This was particularly the case when attacking a four-engine bomber with a large wing span, which made it difficult to assess the range to the target visually and because he would usually be under fire, not only from the bomber he was attacking but also from others within the tight bomber formation.

The Luftwaffe's tactics were evolving all the time, some of them proving to be quite radical. For example, Heinz Knoke of 2./JG 1 and his colleague, Leutnant Dieter Gerhardt, developed the idea of aerial bombing a tight bomber formation using a time-fused 250 kg bomb dropped from 3,000 feet above the bombers to break up the formation. Knoke used this novel tactic for the first time on 22 March 1943 against a formation of B-17s. With the additional weight of the bomb under his fuselage, it took Knoke more than twenty minutes to climb to the height of the bombers at 30,000 feet and by the time he had reached sufficient altitude for his attack, the B-17s had already bombed their target of Wilhelmshaven and were now heading for home. The technique used by Knoke required him to sit above the formation, even though he was under continuous fire from the bombers, while he lined up his attack. He edged forward until he was above the lead bomber, having to dip his wing periodically to align himself accurately above the B-17. Then, having fused the bomb, Knoke released it and climbed away looking over his shoulder to see the impact.

The bomb detonated in exactly the right spot amongst three B-17s, tearing off the wing of one and causing damage to two more. The B-17 he brought down crashed into the sea west of Heligoland killing its crew and Knoke became the first fighter pilot known to have brought down an enemy aircraft with a bomb. He rightly received plaudits from the hierarchy and his new tactic reverberated around the American crews. However, this tactic was short-lived as the carriage of a 250 kg bomb reduced the high-altitude performance of the 109 and the technique required to deliver the weapon meant that the fighter was always vulnerable to attack. But Knoke was a great tactician and knew how to get the best out of the 109. He would finally be credited with thirty-three victories, earning him the Knight's Cross days before the end of the war.

At the beginning of April 1943, JG 1's four Gruppen were split into two pairs and a new third Gruppe was added to each pair to form two separate Geschwader. From this came the new JG 11 under the command of Major Anton Mader with responsibility for the protection of Germany's North Sea coastline while JG 1, now commanded by Oberstleutnant Hans Philipp, was responsible for protecting the more westerly approaches to the Reich over Holland.

The Luftwaffe had managed to maintain its fighter strength in France at around 200 FW 190s and fifty Bf109s but the increase in Allied air power in north-west Europe led to Hitler ordering the numbers of fighter units allocated for the defence of the Reich (called Reichsverteidigung) to be increased. Jagdgruppen were recalled from other theatres as five Gruppen were deployed along the continental coastlines of the English Channel and the North Sea, the main approach routes for the American heavy bombers. Two of the Gruppen were allocated to Luftflotte 3 and became responsible for defending the outer airspace of north-west Europe, while the other three were allocated to Luftwaffenbefehlshaber Mitte (later to become Luftflotte Reich) for the defence of Germany. This increased the total number of Bf 109s available for defending Germany to nearly 200: I./JG 3 at Mönchengladbach led by Major Klaus Quaet-Faslem; I./JG 11 at Jever under Hauptmann Günther Specht; and III./JG 54 at Oldenburg under Hauptmann Siegfried Schnell.

Two specialist units were also formed to counter the increasing number of high-level reconnaissance sorties over Germany, usually flown by RAF Mosquitoes. These were Jagdgruppe 25 (JGr 25) at Berlin under the command of Herbert Ihlefeld and Jagdgruppe 50 (JGr 50) at Wiesbaden led by Hermann Graf. These were elite units, equipped with pressurized Bf 109G-5s and with some of the finest pilots. Their aircraft were amongst the first to be fitted with WGr 21 air-to-air rocket launchers mounted in a tube under the wing and designed to bring down heavy bombers. The idea was for the weapon to be fired at a large formation in the hope that it would achieve a direct hit or at least cause enough devastation to break up the bomber formation. While it was a good theory the reality was the tubes caused drag and reduced the fighter's performance and so very few units used the weapon when flying against escorted bomber formations.

Other variations of the Bf 109G included the G-6 Kanonenboote, designed as a bomber-killer, which had the option of being armed with two 20 mm cannon in under-wing gondolas. Units operating this sub-variant included III./JG 3 led by Walther Dahl, which was tasked as one of the anti-bomber Jagdgruppen. The unit commenced its work-up during June 1943 and although the build-up would, at times, be frustratingly slow, the concept proved worthwhile and it was not long before the Gruppe was achieving some success.

JG 3 was fortunate to have some notable pilots. These included many veterans of the Eastern Front such as Wilhelm Lemke of 9./JG 3 with more than a hundred victories, Hans-Joachim Kirschner, the long-serving Staffelkapitän of 5./JG 3 and holder of the Oak Leaves with more than 150 victories, and Hans Schleef of 7./JG 3 with more than ninety.

Not all of the greatest tactical leaders were high scorers. An example was Major Günther Specht, Kommandeur of II./JG 11, who was considered to be amongst the finest fighter commanders, although he was only credited with a modest thirty-four victories during the war. Specht led his Gruppe on every mission and after each one would write a detailed and analytical report. His unit quickly gained a reputation as one of the finest Jagdgruppen and Specht was soon leading combined formations against the American heavies, although he had become increasingly critical of the relatively weak armament of the Bf 109.

The intensity of the bombing campaign increased at the end of July 1943 when the Allies launched Operation Gomorrah, known to the

Americans as 'Blitz Week', a six-day continual bombing campaign by day and night against key targets in the Reich, particularly Hamburg which was devastated after a series of night raids by the RAF's Bomber Command. The Jagdwaffe enjoyed much success during the days of the Allied offensive but there were also losses, such as Major Karl-Heinz Leesmann, Kommandeur of III./JG 1 and holder of the Knight's Cross with thirty-three victories, who was lost on 25 July over the North Sea having been shot down by the B-17 he was attacking.

The US Ninth Air Force joined the European air war at the beginning of August 1943, operating from bases in North Africa, but often suffered losses inflicted by I./JG 4 and IV./JG 27 operating out of Romania and Greece. There then followed a series of shuttle raids carried out by American bombers operating from bases in England and then landing at Allied bases in North Africa.

The tactics employed by the American formations at times bordered on futile and this period marked the Jagdwaffe's finest hour in north-west Europe. Three raids in particular led to heavy losses for the American bomber crews. The Schweinfurt-Regensburg mission on 17 August, the deepest penetration yet by the Americans, resulted in sixty B-17s lost plus more than 170 aircraft damaged, of which four were later scrapped (approximately 20 per cent of the attacking force). This was followed by a disastrous attempt against Stuttgart on 6 September that resulted in forty-five B-17s failing to return, ten of which fell to the fighters of the Kanonenboote-equipped III./JG 3. A further attempt against the ball bearing factory at Schweinfurt on 14 October, known as 'Mission 115', resulted in the loss of another sixty B-17s and nearly 140 aircraft damaged, with seven of those scrapped (a total loss of approximately 29 per cent of the attacking force).

The Luftwaffe was now enjoying some of its finest moments, so much so that the Americans temporarily suspended daylight deep-penetration missions until the bombers could be provided with some suitable fighter cover. Amongst the most successful Jagdgeschwader was JG 27 led by Oberstleutnant Gustav Rödel, but the wide dispersal of his four Gruppen gives an indication of the problems faced by a Geschwaderkommodore during early 1943; I./JG 27 had returned from North Africa and was assigned to Luftflotte 3 in northern France,

II./JG 27 was based in Sicily and Italy to protect the supply convoys, III./JG 27 had remained in Crete and the Greek islands and IV./JG 27 had been formed in Greece to protect the Romanian oilfields at Ploesti.

While command and communications proved an occasional problem for a Kommodore such as Rödel, most things had been going the way of the Jagdwaffe so it came as something of a shock during September when the Bf 109Gs of Anton Mader's JG 11 encountered more than a hundred P-47 Thunderbolts fitted with drop tanks over Germany's North Sea coastline. The JG 11 pilots initially believed the fighters were friendly FW 190s; it was only when their 109s came under attack that it became clear what was going on.

More than twice the weight of many of its contemporaries, the P-47 Thunderbolt was the largest and heaviest single-engine, single-seat propeller-driven fighter aircraft ever built.[34] The addition of belly tanks and wing tanks meant that the P-47 was able to fly deeper into occupied Europe, with fighter escort missions lasting more than five hours. While the appearance of American fighters over Germany was not entirely unexpected, German intelligence reports stating that P-47s had been brought down as far to the east as Aachen had been largely ignored. Göring believed such cases to be insignificant and that American fighters could only have reached so far by being shot down or damaged at height, and the aircraft then having glided eastwards where they eventually crashed.

The Jagdflieger quickly learned how best to deal with the escorting fighters. Once they had located an American formation coasting in over Europe they would often shadow the bombers from a safe distance until the escorting fighters had reached the limit of their range and turned for home. The waiting pack of Jagdgruppen would then strike at what was now an unescorted bomber formation. Using this tactic of patience paid dividends and dozens of bombers could be downed in as many minutes.

Personal scores continued to increase as the Jagdflieger became more familiar with the American tactics. Amongst the leading B-17 destroyers was Anton Hackl, now Kommandeur of III./JG 11, already a holder of the Oak Leaves with more than 120 victories. Hackl would go on to claim thirty-two heavy bombers amongst his final tally of 196 victories, for which he would be awarded the Swords. He would be one of only a small number of flyers to serve with the Jagdwaffe through the entire war.

Although the P-47C started to appear in increasing numbers, the American pilots often lacked combat experience and their tactics were initially poor as they struggled to provide suitable protection for the heavy bombers. The Thunderbolt simply could not match the manoeuvrability of the Bf 109G, or the later Bf 109K, nor could it match the rate of climb, although very few Thunderbolts were actually lost in air combat. Similarly, while the P -38 Lightning offered good range as an escort fighter, it also struggled in combat against the FW 190A and the Bf 109G.

While American fighter pilots initially lacked combat experience, they did not lack ability as pilots. Their flying training in the United States had been long and they arrived in the European theatre with typically between 300 and 400 flying hours. They were generally very capable pilots, well taught as far as aircraft-handling was concerned, and they were instilled with an aggression and confidence about their abilities and in the aircraft they flew.

Gradually, the early advantage of the Jagdflieger, born mainly of his previous combat experience and the superior tactics he used, was slowly being eroded. The Jagdwaffe had to adapt its tactics to meet the changing air battle and decided to use one Gruppe of fighters to counter the American escorting fighters while two Gruppen attacked the bombers. Those tasked with the anti-bomber role were equipped with the high altitude Bf 109G-5/6s. Produced from early 1943, the G-6, powered by the improved DB 605A engine, became the standard sub-variant. It was unpressurized and differed from earlier Gustavs by the inclusion of two cowling-mounted MG 131 13 mm machine guns rather than the nose-mounted MG 17s, in addition to the hub-firing MG 151 20 mm cannon.

As more American fighters appeared over Germany, the Jagdwaffe suffered increasing losses as Göring again blamed his pilots rather than recognizing there might be a problem elsewhere. Criticism worsened following a heavy raid against Frankfurt when the local Gauleiter (political leader) complained personally to Hitler about the Luftwaffe's failure to protect the city and Hitler, in turn, passed on his annoyance to Göring.

In a meeting with his High Command, Göring insisted something needed to be done and decided that his fighters should be fitted with barographs to provide evidence that the aircraft had climbed to a sufficient height to engage the American bombers and for those aircraft not already fitted with a gun camera, one would now be fitted to provide further evidence that the fighter had engaged in combat. There was even talk of employing aerial observers or commissars.

Not for the first time, Göring had doubted the courage and ability of his units and the direction he now gave was very clear. As far as he was concerned there were no reasons whatsoever why his Jagdgruppen could not engage the bombers. Poor weather would be no excuse, nor would the lack of ammunition or a weapon malfunction; as far as Göring was concerned his fighters could still ram the bombers. He even went as far to state that any pilot returning to his airfield without a victory, or at least without having visible signs of air combat, such as damage to his own aircraft, would face a court martial!

Once again, there was no question of his pilots lacking courage. Göring's allegations were completely unfounded and had he taken the trouble to ask the American bomber crews who had been on the receiving end of such aggression, they would never have agreed with him. The direction given to the men under his command had clearly demonstrated Göring's lack of belief and confidence in them and simply drove a wedge between him and the Luftwaffe that he led.

Somewhat fortunately for the Jagdgruppen, the heavy American raids during early October provided an opportunity for the Jagdwaffe to claim considerable success. For the time being at least they managed to keep their leader off their backs but the fierce air battles inevitably resulted in casualties and one to fall was Oberstleutnant Hans Philipp, Kommodore of JG 1. On 8 October, Philipp, holder of the Knight's Cross with Oak Leaves and Swords, and with a quite staggering total of 206 victories, was shot down and killed near Neuenhaus while engaging P-47s escorting a raid against Bremen and Vegesack.

It was a painful loss but the Reich defenders had done so well in such a short period of time that the second half of October saw just one

American raid. While the Allies were not prepared to continue suffering such losses, the American raids had sent shivers through the German High Command.

The balance of experience levels on the front line was now changing. Just a year before, fewer than half those flying with the Jagdgruppen were new to the front line and the majority had at least some level of combat experience but the pendulum had now swung to the point that fewer than half had any combat experience at all. Defence of the Reich was not Hitler's highest priority. He had seemingly lost faith in Göring and had lost confidence in the Luftwaffe. Jeschonnek, having decided that he could no longer work with Göring, and who had come under an increasing amount of criticism from Hitler, committed suicide.

Jeschonnek was replaced by Günther Korten, who recognized the importance of maintaining a strong fighter defence of Germany, even if this meant depleting units on other fronts. One of Korten's first tasks was to transfer a number of fighter units back to Germany from the Eastern Front and these withdrawals would soon lead to Germany conceding air superiority in the east. Further changes to the hierarchy during the autumn of 1943 included Josef Kammhuber being sent to command Luftflotte 5 in Norway to replace Hans-Jürgen Stumpff, who now returned to Germany to command the newly created Luftflotte Reich tasked with the defence of the Reich.

There was also the creation of I. Jagdkorps (Fighter Corps) under the command of Joseph Schmid to control the fighter units based in Germany for the defence of the Reich, with three air divisions allocated to the defence of German airspace. The first line of defence was 3. Jagddivision with the task of providing defence from the French border to Luxembourg and into western Belgium. The Netherlands and north-west Germany was to be protected by 1. Jagddivision and responsibility for the defence of Denmark and north–central Germany fell to 2. Jagddivision. The defence of the area surrounding Berlin was given to 4. Jagddivision, and 5. Jagddivision was tasked with the protection of central and southern Germany.

At the tactical level, the Bf 109 Gruppen were tasked with engaging the American fighter escorts, with two Gruppen specifically taking off ahead of the others to intercept and disperse the escorting fighters, while the more heavily armed FW 190 Gruppen were to attack the heavy bombers once they had been stripped of their fighter escort. Other units, such as those equipped with Bf 110s and Ju 88s, were only to attack the American formations if the bombers had been deprived of their escort or if the bombers had penetrated beyond the range of their escorting fighters.

A new aircraft to enter service as a bomber destroyer was the twin-engine Messerschmitt Me 410 'Hornisse' (Hornet), a straightforward modification of the earlier Me 210 that had never gone into full production. With a crew of two (pilot and gunner) and the size of a Bf 110, the Me 410 was capable of a top speed approaching 400 mph and had a good rate of climb up to its operating height of around 32,000 feet. It was well armed with two MG 151 20 mm cannon and two MG 17 7.9 mm machine guns, with a further two MG 131 13 mm machine guns, these each firing rearward from a remotely-operated barbette on either side of the fuselage. Deliveries of the Me 410A commenced during 1943 with its main task being to break up the large formations of heavy American bombers. Sub-variants were modified with a 50 mm BK 5 Bordkanone instead of the two MG 151s in the under-nose weapons bay or four under-wing tubes with 21 cm mortar rockets. In this role the Me 410 proved moderately successful, particularly if the bombers were unescorted.

One unit to enjoy success with the 410 was II./ZG 26 based at Hildesheim under the command of the former Zerstörer pilot, Eduard Tratt. Tratt was given command in October 1943 and personally claimed a number of victories while flying the 410. His thirty-eighth and final victory, a B-17, came on 20 February 1944. Two days later Tratt was shot down and killed while single-handedly attacking a formation of B-17s near Nordhausen; he was later posthumously awarded the Oak Leaves to his Knight's Cross.

Although the Me 410 enjoyed some success against the American bombers, it was no match for the Allied fighters and losses increased, resulting in it later being withdrawn from defence of the Reich duties and assigned to reconnaissance duties instead.

The end of 1943 saw the entry into the air-combat arena of the most significant American fighter to be introduced into the European theatre. Capable of speeds well in excess of 400 mph, the North American P-51B Mustang was the fastest fighter at the time and also benefitted from lower fuel consumption than other American fighters. When fitted with under-wing drop tanks, the additional fuel gave the Mustang a range of around 2,000 miles, far enough to accompany the long-range bombers to any target deep into Germany. The Mustang would go on to become America's best fighter of the Second World War and its introduction would soon tip the balance of air power in favour of the Allies.

The Mustang's arrival coincided with the Luftwaffe's introduction of the FW 190A-6 variant with a redesigned wing and four MG 151 cannon, although the aircraft retained the two MG 17 machine guns mounted above the engine. It would not be long before the final variant of the FW 190 to enter large scale production, the A-8 with an additional internal fuel tank, would appear and by the end of the war more than 20,000 FW 190s had been built; 13,000 were built as fighters and nearly 7,000 as fighter-bombers. The latest variants of 190 out-performed the Bf 109Gs and Ks, although the Bf 109s were employed in large numbers and it was still an extremely potent fighter in the hands of a capable pilot. However, the FW 190 was nearly 50 mph slower than the Mustang, although there was little to choose between the two in combat when the Mustang pilot would always have to keep his speed up, and maintain a height advantage when possible, because not even the later variants of the Mustang could match the roll rate of a FW 190.

By the beginning of 1944 the air war over Germany had taken a dramatic turn in favour of the Allies as the number of American aircraft taking part in each raid regularly exceeded a thousand. The number of Jagdgruppen defending the Reich had now increased to more than twenty, which meant the air fighting was always intense. While the Jagdgruppen continued to inflict losses on the American formations, as far as the fighter versus fighter air war was concerned, the best the Jagdwaffe could usually achieve was parity and its losses were now equivalent to a Jagdgruppe for every heavy raid. While poor weather often offered some respite, and losses could be rectified with new fighters delivered off the production lines, pilot numbers and experience levels had rapidly been diluted.

The last week of February, known to the Americans as 'Big Week', saw the heaviest daylight raids so far. The combined effort of the US Eighth and Fifteenth Air Forces, flying from bases in England and Italy respectively, escorted by a thousand fighters, saw the deepest-penetrating raids to date.

One of the main objectives of Big Week was to disrupt Germany's aircraft manufacturing industry but this failed. In fact, German aircraft production would continue to rise and would not peak for another six months. As for other objectives, the Americans achieved some success with a number of Luftwaffe airfields being put out of action and many aircraft being destroyed or damaged on the ground.

Days later, the Americans turned on Berlin to continue the strategic bombing campaign by day that Bomber Command had started by night. On 4 March, bombs dropped by American bombers fell on the capital of the Reich for the first time and the raid was followed up two days later by an even greater effort when a force of more than 700 bombers attacked the city. The Luftwaffe responded with twenty-five Jagd-gruppen entering the cauldron. As the bomber formations were tracked approaching Germany, large numbers of fighters were scrambled from various bases in the northern part of the country. Typically, more than a hundred fighters – a mix of FW 190As and Bf 109Gs – were assembled at holding points to wait for the bombers before the Jagdgruppen then struck, shooting down nearly seventy bombers and severely damaging 350 more. It was the Americans' heaviest losses in a single day.

One to enjoy success on 6 March was Hermann Graf, now promoted to the rank of Oberstleutnant and Kommodore of JG 11. His victory that day, a B-24, took his total to 209 victories but it would be one of his last: just three weeks later he was severely injured after colliding with a Mustang having just claimed his 212th victory. Graf managed to bail out of his aircraft but he would take no further part in the air war over the Reich. Although the Jagdwaffe had inflicted heavy losses on the Americans during the day, more than sixty of its pilots had been killed or wounded; 6 March 1944 would be remembered amongst many *Experten* as their hardest day of fighting of the war.

The American heavy bombers were now being escorted by large numbers of Mustangs seeking to engage the Luftwaffe at every oppor-tunity. The Mustangs also introduced area patrols along the planned route of the bombers, with each fighter unit given the responsibility of protecting the American bombers as they passed through its area. While this tactic enabled the Jagdflieger to determine where the main bomber force was routed, there was still the problem of dealing with the patrolling fighters, either before the bomber force had reached each area or by having to tackle the fighters at the same time as trying to shoot down the bombers.

While Göring chose to take another holiday, his Jagdflieger were directed to focus on shooting down the American bombers and to ignore the fighter escort. This was easier said than done and proved all but impossible, particularly as the new P-51D was now appearing and proved a most formidable fighter. Not only was it capable of providing long-range escort for the American heavy bombers but the Mustang's performance had improved so much that in the hands of a capable pilot it could out-perform both the Bf 109 and FW 190.

With the introduction of the Mustang in large numbers, the Jagdwaffe was forced to engage the large bomber formations even earlier if there was to be time to counter the fighter escort while trying to shoot down the enemy bombers, and this brought its fighters into contact with Allied short-range fighters such as RAF Spitfires and the American Lightnings and Thunderbolts.

The aerial fighting was relentless and at times resulted in carnage. During the first four months of 1944 the Luftwaffe lost more than a thousand pilots,[35] including some of its most experienced combat leaders and commanders. Losses in March alone included Wolf-Dietrich Wilcke (162 victories), Emil Bitsch (108), Egon Mayer (102), Gerhard Loos (92) and Hugo Frey (32, of which all but six had been four-engine heavy bombers). Losses were particularly high amongst the Bf 109G Gruppen and were in fact unsustainable, but the Jagdgruppen continued to inflict whatever damage they could.

The direction for the Bf 109s to leave the engagement of the American bombers to the more heavily armed FW 190s, and only to counter the escorting fighters, may have seemed reasonable guidance at the time but the reality was the Bf 109G also proved very capable against the heavy bombers. Nonetheless, the Jagdwaffe faced an unenviable task. The Bf 109 that had once ruled the skies over Europe had now met its match and the performance of the FW 190 deteriorated at altitude.

Furthermore, its tactics had essentially remained unchanged from those used earlier in the war and continued to be based on the four-aircraft Schwarm. While these tactics had previously served the Jagdflieger well, he now faced an enemy that was increasing in numbers, had better-performing fighters and was adopting similar fluid tactics to his own. Not only did he have to cope with the evolving tactics of the American fighters, the defensive armament of the American bombers, combined with the mutual defensive fire provided by a number of bombers flying in a tight box formation, led to the Jagdwaffe having to change its own tactics.

The American box formation was typically based on three sections, with six aircraft in each section. The lead section was given protection from its flanks and rear by two more sections on either side, with one section being higher than the lead section and the other lower. This gave an overall large box formation that was staggered in height. The Jagd-flieger had learned they could gain success against the American box formations by making a frontal attack in pairs or in formations of three aircraft, and to be effective the attack had to be made as near head-on as possible where the heavy bombers lacked defensive armament and could provide little or no mutual defence.

To determine the exact height and heading of the bomber formation, the Jagdflieger would position himself abeam the bombers and outside the range of the gunners. This usually meant he could remain outside the visual range of the bomber's crew as it was far easier for him to see a large formation of heavy bombers than it was for the bomber's gunners to pick out a small fighter against the blue sky. Once he had established as accurately as possible the heading and height of the formation, he accelerated ahead of the bombers and then turned back to take up his position for the frontal attack, selecting his own target within the bomber formation.

The frontal attack also increased the chance of killing the bomber pilots, bringing it down that way, and so the attack was modified to be carried out from slightly above the bomber as it was more difficult for the bomber pilots to spot the attacker. So successful were the frontal attacks that they were soon widely adopted when attacking formations of large heavy bombers but they did require nerve and accuracy. When the pilot selected his target, the bomber at first appeared small in his gunsight but with a closing speed of the order of 600 mph it did not take long for the bomber to grow in apparent size.[36] It then took great nerve and flying skill to close at such a speed and there was always the fear of collision. There was little time for the attacker to position himself, assess the firing solution and to carry out his attack, with there being only a very brief window of opportunity – less than a second – when the attacker was within his optimum range to open fire.

The temptation to open fire early is obvious but this would usually result in wasted ammunition and the vibration caused by having already opened fire would not help; smoothness on the controls was required to give the best chance of success. It took a cool head and a nerve of steel to hit the target. Rarely would a heavy bomber be brought down in one head-on pass, although an accurate attack often succeeded in damaging the bomber enough to force it from its defensive formation, after which stragglers could then be picked off more easily.

While the FW 190 was a robust aircraft and capable of withstanding damage, its performance at high altitudes, particularly up around 30,000 feet, where much of the aerial combat was taking place, was lacking. If he ever found himself in high-altitude combat with a fighter such as the Mustang then a 190 pilot's best defensive manoeuvre was to roll over and pull towards the ground or escape as fast as he could towards any cloud cover in the area. To mitigate the FW 190's high-altitude failings the Jagdwaffe used dedicated high-altitude Bf 109G units such as II./JG 11, under the command of Major Günther Rall, with engines fitted with special superchargers, to counter the high altitude American escort fighters while the FW 190s engaged the heavy bombers.

While still very effective as a fighter, the Bf 109G lacked speed when trying to escape the fighter escort. It was also a great source of frustration to have climbed to altitude and to have achieved a position of advantage against the large bomber formations only then to get bounced from above by the escorting fighters. A technique used by many 109 pilots was to trim the aircraft so that it flew slightly tail heavy, requiring constant forward pressure on the control column to keep the aircraft level, so that when he needed to inject a sharp upwards movement to evade attack, the aircraft pitched far more quickly without the momentary hesitation that would otherwise have occurred and could well have proved fatal.

Although the number of Bf 109s allocated for defence of the Reich duties increased significantly in the previous year, by May 1944 Luftflotte Reich was down to fewer than 350 serviceable 109s across its sixteen Gruppen: four Gruppen of JG 27 under the command of Gustav Rödel; three of JG 3 under the command of Friedrich-Karl Müller; two of JG 5 led by Horst Carganico and Theodor Weissenberger; one of JG 11 led by Günther Specht; one Gruppe from each of JG 1 and JG 53 led by Hartmann Grasser and Julius Meimberg respectively; two from JG 300 (Gerhard Stamp and Iro Ilk) and a Gruppe from each of JG 301 (Richard Kamp) and JG 302 (Richard Lewens).

These were all very capable units but the demise of the Luftwaffe's fighter capability was unavoidable. While the Jagdflieger fought with great courage, the Allies now outnumbered the Jagdwaffe by as much as 10 : 1. Furthermore, the air war was being fought at high altitude and often against better opposition, which was a completely new experience for a pilot recently recalled to Germany from other theatres where much of the aerial combat had taken place at lower levels.

As the Jagdwaffe prepared for the Allies to invade north-west Europe, its losses continued to mount and included the influential and legendary Walter Oesau. A veteran of the Legion Condor, the Battles of France and Britain, and the Eastern Front, and one of a small elite group to have been awarded the Spanish Cross in Gold with Swords and Diamonds and the Swords to the Knight's Cross, Oesau was killed on 11 May defending his homeland when he was shot down by a group of P-38s after a dogfight lasting more than twenty minutes. Like many of the *Experten* now to have fallen, Oesau had been heavily outnumbered and completely out of luck.

It was not only in the west that the Luftwaffe encountered American fighters. Erich Hartmann, for example, engaged American fighters for the first time in the east at the end of May 1944 when III./JG 52 was briefly sent to protect the strategically important Romanian oilfields and installations against attacks by the American Fifteenth Air Force. During one extensive engagement over the Ploesti oilfields in June, Hartmann claimed a P-51 Mustang before he suddenly found himself on the receiving end from several more Mustangs. Eventually finding himself out of fuel and ammunition, Hartmann had to abandon his aircraft and was relieved when the Mustangs made a couple of close passes to him in his parachute before breaking away and heading for home.

Hartmann's Gruppenkommandeur, Willi Batz, also achieved success over the oilfields of Romania. Batz had been in the Luftwaffe since 1935 but his experience as an instructor had kept him away from operational flying until early 1943 when he was finally granted his request to transfer to a front-line unit. He initially joined II./JG 52 on the Eastern Front and was soon appointed Kapitän of the 5. Staffel. While his first six months of operational flying resulted in modest success, the following six months saw Batz take his personal score to seventy-five, for which he was awarded the Knight's Cross. He recorded his hundredth victory in March 1944 before he was appointed Kommandeur of III./JG 52 and by the end of May he had taken his score past 150 victories, including a staggering fifteen victories in one day on 31 May, to which he added two Mustangs and a B-24 over the oilfields in June.

Batz was fortunate to have other high scorers in his Gruppe. In addition to Hartmann he had Oberleutnant Friedrich Obleser of 8./JG 52, who had been awarded the Knight's Cross in March 1944 and would eventually be credited with 120 victories, and Leutnant Walter Wolfrum of the 5. Staffel, who would soon receive the Knight's Cross and would go on to achieve 137 victories before the end of the war.

Despite such individual achievements, the Luftwaffe was struggling. As the war approached the end of its fifth year, the Jagdwaffe was going around an ever-decreasing circle. The increasing losses at the front meant that more pilots were required, which meant that training time had to be cut and so led to a lower quality pilot, which in turn reduced his chances of survival in combat and so led to more losses at the front, which further increased the requirement for more pilots. And so it went on. The Luftwaffe could no longer sustain a lengthy defence of the Reich and was finally destined for defeat.

Chapter 11

Final Defence of the Reich

When the Allied invasion of north-west Europe came on 6 June 1944, the Jagdwaffe was heavily outnumbered over the beaches of Normandy and could only offer little resistance. Hugo Sperrle, commander of Luftflotte 3, only had two operational Jagdgeschwader, JG 2 and JG 26, in the region, neither of which had been reinforced prior to the invasion, and even allowing for support from other Jagdgruppen in north-west Europe, the Luftwaffe could initially muster fewer than 300 serviceable fighters to counter the 4,000 Allied fighters that were available to support the landings.

With the Allies quickly gaining a foothold in Normandy, Göring deployed more than twenty Jagdgruppen forward from their bases in Germany to northern France. These additional units would never be enough to influence the air battle over the invasion area and moving them forward from their home bases in Germany simply weakened the Luftwaffe's ability to defend the Reich. Furthermore, as their new airfields in northern France came increasingly under Allied attack, the Jagdwaffe was forced to operate from dispersed sites and remote landing strips with all the associated communications, logistical and maintenance problems that such moves always bring.

The air war over north-west Europe was now entering its final phase. In the weeks following the invasion, the Allies were able to mount six times more air sorties than the Luftwaffe and losses amongst the Jagdflieger were high: nearly 200 pilots in the first month after the invasion. However, the Allies did not have everything their own way and Allied losses exceeded 300 aircraft during the month of July alone. While the Jagdgruppen were struggling to achieve parity, the fact was that the Allies could afford such losses whereas the Luftwaffe could not. It was only a matter of time before the Jagdgruppen were forced to abandon their airfields in France and withdraw to Germany.

The Luftwaffe was now in retreat and could not sustain such losses and so changes were introduced to offer the more experienced pilots some protection. For example, a Staffelkapitän was only allowed to fly an operational mission if there were at least five other aircraft in the formation. For a Gruppenkommandeur the number of fighters required was at least fifteen and for a Geschwaderkommodore the number increased to forty-five but, while a good idea, the reality was the Jagd-waffe rarely had the numbers required to provide such protection for its combat leaders.

The nature of the air war over north-west Europe had also changed and the defence of the Reich was no longer straightforward. Before the invasion the general pattern was to counter the American heavy bomber raids by day and those of RAF Bomber Command at night but as the Allies took a foothold in Europe, the Jagdflieger were now facing many different types of aircraft on a daily basis. Not only were there the strategic-bomber raids deep into the heart of Germany but there were also numerous tactical raids over much shorter distances in and around the forward battle area, and carried out by a variety of aircraft ranging from single-engine fighters and fighter-bombers to twin-engine light or medium bombers.

As the Allies occupied more airfields then the task became even greater. The Luftwaffe responded by adapting its chain of command so that Jagdgruppen allocated to defending the Reich were part of Luftflotte Reich while those allocated to the local and more tactical battle in northern France were allocated to Luftflotte 3. In the end, these organizational changes made little or no difference to the Jagdflieger and he soon learned to engage whatever Allied aircraft came his way, whether it was a single-engine fighter at low level or a high-level four-engine heavy bomber.

Tactics against the heavy bomber raids now focused on the employ-ment of air battle groups, which started appearing over north-west Europe during the summer of 1944. Galland believed that better results could be achieved by using a mix of front and stern attacks and this led to the introduction of the *Gefechtsverband*, a large mixed fighter formation where the combination of frontal attacks and more con-ventional stern attacks was used to best effect. New specialist units, known as *Sturmgruppen*, were formed and equipped with heavily armed FW 190A-8 *Sturmbocks* ('Battering Rams'), armed with two MK 108 30 mm cannon and two MG 151 20 mm cannon.[37] Their pilots were volunteers and tasked with breaking up the large bomber formations but because the FW 190 continued to struggle at high altitude, the Sturmbocks were supported by two Gruppen of Bf 109Gs tasked with holding off any fighter escort.

The Sturmbocks were at the heart of the Gefechtsverband. One of the most successful units was JG 300 led by the very capable Walther Dahl, a pioneer of the Gefechtsverband, who had just been awarded the Knight's Cross for sixty-seven victories. An example of success came on 7 July when a large American raid, consisting of more than a thousand B-17s and B-24s, was dispatched to bomb aircraft factories in the Leipzig area and the synthetic oil plants at Böhlen, Leuna-Merseburg and Lütz-kendorf. The formation was intercepted by a Gefechtsverband consisting of a Sturmgruppe, IV./JG 3, led by Hauptmann Wilhelm Moritz, escorted by two Gruppen of JG 300 led by Dahl. It took just minutes to annihilate the B-24s: at least twenty-eight Liberators fell to the Sturmgruppe, earning Moritz the Knight's Cross; Dahl would later be awarded the Oak Leaves for 128 victories and his leadership of JG 300.

Although there were successes, there were inevitable problems when leading such a large formation of about a hundred fighters and one of the biggest challenges its leader faced was getting the Gefechtsverband into a position from where it could make its attack. It took time to take off and climb to height, and such a large formation proved unwieldy as far as manoeuvring was concerned, particularly in weather conditions other than clear sky. While the use of large numbers may have seemed a good idea, the tactic did not prove as successful as had been hoped as the problem of manoeuvring the Gefechtsverband meant that the Jagdflieger rarely found he was in a position to make an attack.

While the Jagdwaffe continued to struggle in the west, the Soviet summer offensive in the east was crashing through the German central sector and was already paving the way towards Berlin. Furthermore, a change of government in Romania, following the invasion by Soviet forces, had now seen this one-time member of the Axis powers change sides and declare war on Germany. The Jagdwaffe in the east now had fewer than 500 single-engine fighters with around 300 FW 190As and about 170 Bf 109Gs. The FW 190s were spread across the three main sectors. About seventy were operating as fighters with JG 54 and allocated to Luftflotte 1 in the north (based in Finland and Estonia) and a dozen more were operating in the central sector as a mixed force with Bf 109Gs of the Stab of JG 51, now led by Major Fritz Losigkeit. The other FW 190s, about 200 in all, were operating in the ground-attack role with Luftflotte 6 and Luftflotte 4 in the central and southern sectors respectively.

The Bf 109Gs were also spread across the Eastern Front, with a single Gruppe of JG 5 retaining twenty aircraft in Finland for the Arctic Front and about sixty aircraft operating with two Gruppen of JG 51 in the central sector under the command of Erich Leie. The remainder were operating in the southern sector, with three Gruppen from JG 52 and a single Gruppe of JG 53, all under the command of Oberstleutnant Dietrich Hrabak. This force totalled less than ninety aircraft as JG 52, like other Jagdgruppen on the eastern and southern fronts, had already been weakened by the loss of Staffeln to counter the American daylight raids on Germany in the west.

The Jagdwaffe in the east continued to face overwhelming odds; in some places the Red Air Force had an advantage of more than 30:1. Furthermore, as the Soviets pushed west, Germany's two fronts were slowly being squeezed closer together and it would not be long before units operating in the east would come under threat from long-range fighters operating from the west.

Despite such overwhelming opposition, the Jagdwaffe in the east still produced a number of high scorers including a trio of Staffelkapitäne serving with JG 51 – Oberleutnant Joachim Brendel of 1./JG 51, Leutnant Günther Josten of 3./JG 51 and Leutnant Günther Schack of 9./JG 51 – who all passed 150 victories for which each received the Oak Leaves to the Knight's Cross.

These were impressive achievements but they could not match that of Erich Hartmann, still serving as Kapitän of 9./JG 52, who claimed his 274th victory on 17 August to become the Luftwaffe's highest-scoring *Experte* by surpassing the score of Gerhard Barkhorn, his best friend and colleague in JG 52. Just a week later, on 24 August, Hartmann took his total to an unprecedented 302 victories after shooting down eleven aircraft in a period of just three hours during the afternoon to add to the eight he had claimed the afternoon before. Hartmann had become the first fighter pilot ever to reach a triple century of victories and by the end of the month he had added two more victories to bring his total for August alone to thirty-five, all achieved during the last two weeks of the month. It was a quite remarkable achievement and earned Hartmann the coveted Diamonds, which were presented to him personally by Hitler at the Wolfsschanze.

Stalin's offensive in the north had ended the siege of Leningrad and resulted in the two long-serving FW 190 Gruppen of JG 54 being withdrawn deeper into Latvia and to new bases on the Courland peninsula. Increasing problems of logistical support, resulting in a lack of fuel and spares, had now become a major concern as the Red Army's offensive in the central sector pushed German forces back towards the Reich.

With all but one Staffel of JG 51 having converted back to the Bf 109, JG 54's two Gruppen were the only fighter variants of the FW 190 now on the Eastern Front; the only other FW 190s along the Eastern Front were ground-attack versions. JG 54 had also suffered losses, most notably its Kommodore, Horst Ademeit, who had served with the Geschwader since Barbarossa. Ademeit was a holder of the Knight's Cross with Oak Leaves and was credited with 166 victories but he failed to return from a sortie on 7 August over Russian lines near Dünaburg.

Ademeit was just one of many losses in the east and others included Anton Hafner, Kapitän of 8./JG 51 and holder of the Oak Leaves with 204 victories before his death, and Otto Fönnekold of 5./JG 52 who was killed at Budak in Hungary. Having just landed, Fönnekold, holder of the Knight's Cross and with 136 victories, was taxiing back to the dispersal when the airfield came under attack from an American Mustang; Fönnekold stood no chance.

Meanwhile in the west, some of the Luftwaffe's finest had also fallen. In the immediate aftermath of the Allied invasion in Normandy, 22-year-old Hauptmann Karl-Heinz Weber of III./JG 1 (136 victories and holder of the Oak Leaves) was killed on 7 June, and Major Josef Wurmheller, Kommandeur of III./JG 2 (102 victories and holder of the Swords), was killed on 22 June.

There was also the death of Emil Lang, Kommandeur of II./JG 26. Lang's Gruppe had been the first to claim a hundred victories over Normandy and he had personally claimed twenty-nine victories in the west since his arrival in April 1944 to add to the 144 he had been credited with on the Eastern Front. Then, on 3 September, having just taken off from Melsbroek in Belgium, Lang's FW 190A suffered a technical problem and he was unable to raise the undercarriage. As Lang was trying to resolve the problem at a height of just over 500 feet, his wingman, Unteroffizier Hans-Joachim Borreck, spotted a formation of American fighters to the rear making an attack. Lang, holder of the Knight's Cross with Oak Leaves and with 173 victories, was last seen crashing to earth in flames; his aircraft's undercarriage was still down.

Hitler felt the Luftwaffe had retreated too quickly, particularly in the west. It was not so much that he questioned the courage of his pilots but that he felt the ground and support units had fled too hastily and accused them of running away. Hugo Sperrle was relieved of his command, although he was arguably a scapegoat. Given the vast strength of the Allied forces there was little he could have done but the Luftwaffe had indeed failed to have any real impact on the advancing Allied troops on the ground. Sperrle was replaced by Otto Dessloch as Luftflotte 3 was designated Luftwaffe Command West.

There were further changes forced on the High Command as Günther Korten, the Chief of the General Staff, died from injuries sustained during the attempted assassination of Hitler in the Wolfsschanze in July. Göring appointed Werner Kreipe as Korten's replacement, although Hitler would clearly have preferred Ritter von Greim.[38]

At just forty years old, Kreipe was young to be in command and may well have proved to be a good leader had Hitler not continued to interfere in the Luftwaffe's affairs due to the incompetence of Göring. After a devastating Allied raid on Darmstadt in September 1944 Hitler laid the blame well and truly on the Luftwaffe and considered replacing Göring with Greim but instead asked for Kreipe's resignation. Kreipe was eventually replaced by the uninspiring Karl Koller, who was appointed as the seventh and last Chief of the General Staff, but as it turned out his appointment would make little difference; at that stage of the war there was little that any chief could have done.

While changes were happening in the High Command, the struggle went on for the Jagdwaffe. Despite its precarious position, the Luftwaffe would not become short of aircraft and although more raw materials were being allocated to the Army for the construction of Panzers and artillery, aircraft production in Germany remained high. The German aviation industry produced about 36,000 aircraft during 1944 and during September alone, when German fighter production peaked, nearly 3,000 fighters were delivered, of which two-thirds were Bf 109s and a third were FW 190s.

Even though aircraft production had remained high, delays in the German jet-fighter programme meant that Bf 109s would have to be built until the end of the war. As materials became increasingly scarce, parts of the 109 were built out of wood, including the tail assembly, and other materials such as steel sheeting were used. The Bf 109K-4, which appeared towards the end of 1944, incorporated in one airframe the best of various upgrades to the earlier Gustav, and was produced in large numbers, but in reality its introduction made little or no difference to the air battle over the Reich.

The FW 190 had also evolved with the introduction of the F and G variants for the ground-attack role; these were essentially fighter-bomber versions of the 190A. There was also the FW 190D-9, known as the Dora 9, which was powered by a 2,000 hp Junkers Jumo 213 in-line engine; these started to appear in the latter half of 1944.

Pilots were initially wary of the Dora, mainly because its roll rate was less than earlier variants and its extended nose to house the engine (earning it the name of 'Long Nose' to the Allies) made it sluggish in pitch, but the pilots soon discovered that the Dora accelerated extremely well, was faster overall and could both climb and dive better than earlier FW 190 variants. Taking all this into account, the Dora was the most formidable piston-engine fighter to enter service with the Luftwaffe during the war and proved a true match for the American P-51D Mustang. However, the Dora was only ever intended to be an interim solution as Focke-Wulf's ultimate design for a high altitude fighter was the Ta 152H, featuring a wider wing span, stretched fuselage and with a pressurized cockpit. The Ta 152H first appeared at the end of 1944, although only about 150 were ever built and very few actually saw operational service, the only recorded examples being a handful delivered to JG 301.

It was an extraordinary effort by the German aviation industry which coincided with the Allies struggling at times to provide the logistical support required to maintain their advance across north-west Europe. There was even a slight lull in the air war, not for any great length of time but it did allow a number of Jagdgruppen to receive new aircraft. However, the fact remained that the latest variants of fighters appearing over Europe were starting to reach the performance limits of any piston engine, which meant that improved performance could only come with a new form of propulsion.

Germany had been researching new and far more advanced engines for a number of years, and the first new type to make a stunning entry into the combat arena during 1944 was the Messerschmitt Me 163 Komet, the only rocket-powered fighter aircraft of the war. At less than 20 feet in length, and with a wing span of only 30 feet, the Me 163 was a small but extremely potent aircraft. Having first flown as early as 1941, its performance far exceeded that of any piston-engine fighter; it immediately recorded a speed in excess of 620 mph. Powered by a Walter HWK 109 liquid-fuel rocket, the Komet's rate of climb of around 30,000 feet per minute meant that it could be up into the bomber stream in just a couple of minutes, but its endurance was limited to a few minutes only.

The Komet made its first operational appearance during May 1944. Because of its extremely high speed, Allied fighter pilots were at a loss as to how to counter it but the only realistic tactic for the Me 163 was to take-off and zoom up through an enemy formation to a height in excess of 35,000 feet, and then dive back down through the formation. This gave the pilot two very brief opportunities to fire at the enemy – once on the way up and then on the way down – before he had to land.

While the Me 163 was in a class of its own, its excessive fuel consumption limited its operational radius to about 25 miles and its two MK 108 30 mm cannon meant that the Komet's capability as a fighter was extremely limited. Although the aircraft generally handled well at high level, the cockpit was unpressurized and so the effectiveness of the aircraft at altitude was also limited by the personal endurance of the pilot. Also, to reduce weight, the Komet had no conventional under-carriage, which meant it had to be launched from a wheeled dolly and had to land back on a retractable skid, and this often caused back injuries to pilots if landing on an unprepared landing strip.

Fewer than 400 Komets were built and the only combat unit equipped with the Me 163 was JG 400 at Brandis near Leipzig under the command of Major Wolfgang Späte. The first aerial actions occurred at the end of July 1944 but the Me 163 proved largely ineffective with only a dozen or so confirmed victories by the end of the war, with the most successful Komet pilot being Feldwebel Siegfried Schubert with three victories.

The Komet was just the start of a new and exciting fighter pro-gramme as the long awaited Messerschmitt Me 262 Schwalbe, the world's first operational jet-powered fighter aircraft, arrived during the summer of 1944 and started to make its mark in the second half of the year. Although Germany had identified the potential of the jet fighter long before the outbreak of the war, engine problems had prevented the aircraft from becoming operational earlier, and a combination of main-tenance problems and a lack of fuel during the last months of the war would ultimately reduce its effectiveness as a fighter.

The Me 262 entered the war at too late a stage to influence its out-come seriously. Nonetheless, it was a potent fighter. Just short of 35 feet in length and with a wing span of just over 41 feet, it had first flown in 1941. Initially it was powered by a conventional Junkers Jumo 210 piston engine mounted on the prototype's nose but in July 1942 it first flew with Jumo 004 jet engines. Test flights continued over the next year but engine availability, combined with technical problems, continued to plague the project. The operational life of each engine was only expected to be about fifty hours, although in reality many did not last half that long and an engine change proved to be a lengthy task lasting several hours.

Hitler had believed the Me 262 would be most effective as an attack aircraft rather than a fighter, and at a top level meeting held at the Berghof in May 1943 – which included Milch, Göring and Galland – he demanded to know how many of his new jet aircraft were to be manu-factured as bombers. Milch informed him that without considerable design changes the answer would be none. Hitler was livid and transferred the jet aircraft programme away from the fighter branch of the Luftwaffe and gave it to the bomber, with Milch being stripped of his position, but the Me 262 was already late and changes to its design at such a late stage would only add further delays.[39]

A special test unit, Erprobungskommando 262, was formed at Lechfeld under the command of Hauptmann Werner Thierfelder, a veteran of many campaigns with twenty-seven victories and a holder of the Knight's Cross. Thierfelder would be killed soon after when, on 18 July 1944, his Me 262 crashed in unknown circumstances, although it is possible that his aircraft entered an unrecoverable dive.

Although the handling characteristics and tactics were yet to be properly worked out and developed for the new jet fighter, the first victory credited to a Me 262 occurred on 26 July 1944 when Leutnant Alfred Schreiber intercepted and damaged a Mosquito reconnaissance aircraft of the RAF, which subsequently crashed.

Regardless of opinion as to whether the Me 262 would best serve as a bomber or as a fighter, its performance was most impressive. Armed with four MK 108 30 mm cannon, it had a top speed of around 560 mph, was capable of operating at altitudes up to 35,000 feet and had a rate of climb of 4,000 feet per minute. Its high speed and excellent rate of climb made the Me 262 difficult to intercept but it did lack manoeuvrability when at high speed and its slow throttle response meant the jet engines required careful managing during combat to prevent flameout. Too much closing speed could also cause problems as it would mean flying through the opponent's turning circle. Nonetheless, despite its high wing loading and lack of thrust at lower speeds, the Me 262 pilot soon learned that the aircraft was quite manoeuvrable. It was able to maintain its high speed in tight turns better than conventional piston engine fighters and its leading-edge slats reduced the stalling speed in slower speed manoeuvring to a respectable 160 mph.

In September 1944, the highly decorated Walter Nowotny was given command of his own specialist Me 262 unit, called Kommando Nowotny, that operated from airfields near Osnabrück. Nowotny had already gained some experience on the jet fighter during his brief time in command of Erprobungskommando 262, having replaced Werner

Thierfelder, and his new unit was responsible for the development of tactics for the jet fighter.

Because of the Me 262's high performance, it was particularly important to develop new methods of attacking large formations of heavy bombers. When attacking head-on the closing speed was nearly 400 yards a second and far too high for an accurate attack. Even when attacking from astern the combination of having to close to within a suitable range and a high closing speed often meant the Me 262's cannon were ineffective. Therefore, the pilots soon learned how to adapt their attacks by developing a roller-coaster manoeuvre in which they approached the bomber formation from high and behind. Then, from a position about 3 miles astern and about 5,000–6,000 feet above the target, they went into a shallow dive. This enabled the 262 to avoid any fighter escort by its speed until, at a range of about a mile, the pilot would pull up sharply to reduce his rate of closing. Having then levelled off at a range of around a thousand yards from his target, and still with 100 mph of overtaking margin, the pilot would close quickly to 500 yards when he would open fire and maintain his attack until the minimum range of 200 yards when he had to break off. This tactic proved very effective. The bomber's gunners found it difficult to track the jet fighter due to the high closing speed and the relatively slow tracking of their electric gun turrets.

Although the aircraft was undeniably impressive in terms of performance, flying the Me 262 also proved quite dangerous. Not only did the pilot have to contend with the enemy but he also had to deal with continuing technical problems and unreliability; many Me 262s were destroyed or severely damaged in flying accidents. There was also increasing concern amongst senior officers about its lack of combat success, which had done little to offset the problem of Allied air superiority.

Nowotny's unit received a visit by Galland, accompanied by Alfred Keller, the commander of Luftflotte 1, on 7 November during which several pilots expressed their concerns about the suitability of the Me 262 for combat. Keller questioned them and came to the conclusion that some had lost their fighting spirit. This was not true, certainly as far as Nowotny was concerned. The following day he engaged a large formation of American bombers escorted by Mustangs and during the encounter that followed he was heard to report engine trouble and a fire. Whether this was a technical problem or due to enemy action is unclear but Walter Nowotny was killed; he was just twenty-three years old but had achieved a staggering 258 victories, making him the fifth-highest-scoring *Experte* of the war.

The sustained Allied bombing campaign against the German oil industry in Germany, Romania, Hungary and Poland was now having a severe impact on the Luftwaffe's ability to defend the Reich. The flying training schools, in particular, were given little or no allocation and were receiving only 10 per cent of the fuel required. The Jagdwaffe had become increasingly reliant on pilots with previous flying experience, such as bomber pilots, to reduce the training burden, and the night-fighter force, which had been so successful only a year before, was no longer able to make an impact on the war at night.

Galland continued to push for quality rather than quantity, believing one Me 262 jet fighter to be worth a handful of Bf 109s but delays in jet production meant this could not be achieved. Galland had also seen his earlier request for more units to be transferred back to Germany denied, although he did manage to persuade a number of commanders to give up some of their aircraft as the Reich units were reinforced for one last time. This was the last roll of the dice but the Jagdflieger were now expected to protect such a large number of potential targets across a vast area and facing all fronts, and all at a time when the Allies were enjoying such overwhelming air superiority. Losses reached an all-time high on 26 November when more than a hundred pilots were hit during the day; sixty were killed in action and a further thirty were wounded with others taken as prisoners of war, for the destruction of just twenty-five American fighters and a handful of bombers.

In what would effectively be one last attempt to inflict serious losses on the American heavy bomber force, Galland decided to hold back aircraft and fuel for one all-out effort. He hoped his aerial force of 2,000 fighters could shoot down 500 American heavy bombers in one day and compel the Allies to cease their bombing offensive over the Reich.[40] It was a desperate plan at a most desperate time but by the end of November Galland had assembled enough aircraft – thirty-three Gruppen – to mount an all-out attack. However, this ambitious plan did not materialize as Hitler decided instead to use the Jagd-gruppen to support his own surprise offensive in the Ardennes in what later became known as the Battle of the Bulge. Although the Jagd-gruppen suffered relatively low losses during the early stages of the new offensive, the situation changed when the offensive seemingly stalled and the Luftwaffe launched Operation Bodenplatte on 1 January 1945.

Originally planned to coincide with the launch of the ground offensive on 16 December, Bodenplatte was delayed by bad weather, and was then delayed again, before eventually, on New Year's Day 1945, the attack took place. The plan was to hit seventeen Allied forward operating airfields in the Low Countries and France to gain local air superiority above German forces advancing on the ground but this rather ambitious idea would prove to be the operation that finally brought the Jagdwaffe to its knees.

It was barely daylight when the FW 190s and Bf 109s of more than thirty Gruppen, a total of a thousand German fighters, supported by a number of night-fighter and bomber units, got airborne. All three Gruppen of JG 11 took off from their home airfields of Darmstadt-Griesheim, Gross-Ostheim and Zellhausen, some sixty-five aircraft in all, led by Günther Specht. Their transit took them across Koblenz at low level and then over Aachen to their nominated targets, the American airfield at Asch and the RAF airfield at Ophoven. Unfortunately for JG 11, a number of American fighters were already airborne and during the aerial combat that followed the Jagdgeschwader lost twenty-eight aircraft with twenty-five pilots killed. Amongst those killed was Günther Specht, a veteran of many campaigns and holder of the Knight's Cross.

The story was similar elsewhere. JG 26, led by Oberstleutnant Josef Priller and tasked to attack the airfields at Grimbergen and Evere, lost twenty-four of the sixty FW 190s taking part. It was Priller's last operational sortie of the war as a posting to the staff followed. Since the campaign against France in 1940 he had flown more than 1,300 operational sorties and was just one of eight to be credited with a hundred victories against the Western Allies for which he was awarded the Knight's Cross with Oak Leaves and Swords.

JG 26's losses during Bodenplatte were indicative of the Luftwaffe's casualties that day. JG 27 lost fifteen of its Bf 109 pilots during its raid on Melsbroek in Belgium and the FW 190s of JG 1, led by Oberst Herbert Ihlefeld, suffered similar losses as they attacked other airfields in Belgium, notably Ghent/Sint-Denijs where a Polish fighter wing of Spitfires was based, and two other airfields being used by RAF Spitfires near Maldegem and near Ursel. Although JG 1 claimed more than thirty Spitfires destroyed on the ground and a further eight shot down during aerial combat, ten of its pilots were killed, including Hauptmann Hans-Georg Hackbarth, Kommandeur of I./JG 1, with thirty victories.

While the losses of JG 1 had been bad, those of JG 2 and JG 4 were far worse. Their mission was to attack the airfield at Saint Truiden, used by American P-47 Thunderbolts, and at Le Culot, home to American P-38 Lightnings, and resulted in JG 2 losing thirty-seven pilots killed and JG 4 losing twenty-six; at nearly 40 and 50 per cent losses respectively, these were the most costly outcomes of all the Jagdwaffe's fighter units taking part in Bodenplatte.

Most units suffered badly but one of the few successful units that day was JG 3. Its twenty-two FW 190s taking part in the raid destroyed more than forty RAF Typhoons and Spitfires at airfields at Eindhoven and Gilze-Rijen in Holland. However, while some surprise and tactical success was achieved, the overall outcome of Bodenplatte was a disaster. Although several hundred Allied aircraft had been destroyed or damaged on the ground, these could easily be replaced and the fact that the Allies had lost aircraft, rather than pilots, meant that the Luftwaffe was not able to go on to achieve the local air superiority that it had tried so hard to achieve. Furthermore, there had been an unacceptable loss of aircraft, which was partly due to the fact the operation had been kept so secret. Many ground defence and anti-aircraft units were unaware that it was taking place and therefore many losses were due to friendly fire, before the attacks against the Allied airfields had even taken place.

Bodenplatte would prove to be the last major air offensive launched by the Luftwaffe during the war and having cost the lives of more than 200 Jagdflieger it effectively brought an end to Germany's fighter operations in the west. Amongst the losses were two Geschwaderkommodore, six Gruppenkommandeure and nine Staffelkapitäne; men that would be impossible to replace.

Following the disaster of Bodenplatte there were the occasional successes during the early days of 1945. Gerhard Barkhorn scored his 301st and final victory of the war before being appointed Kommodore of JG 6. His new unit was equipped with the FW 190D, although Barkhorn chose to retain his Bf 109G as well, but it was an inexperienced Geschwader and was suffering heavy losses against superior American opposition. Barkhorn would soon receive a brief rest from operations but he would later go on to fly the Me 262 during the final weeks of the war.

Losses continued to mount elsewhere and they included Heinz-Gerhard Vogt, Kapitän of 5./JG 26, a holder of the Knight's Cross with forty-eight victories, who had led his Staffel during Bodenplatte just two weeks before. On the morning of 15 January, Vogt was leading four FW 190D 'long-noses' from their home base of Nordhorn to attack American fighter-bombers near St Vith in Belgium. As the FW 190s passed Aachen they were spotted by a group of Mustangs escorting a large formation of heavy bombers heading towards Cologne. Heavily outnumbered and bounced from above, the 190s fought hard but Vogt was shot down. It was the sixth time he had been shot down but this time it proved fatal.

In one last desperate attempt to hold back the Red advance in the east, the Luftwaffe transferred more than 600 fighters to the Eastern Front at the end of January, bringing the total number of fighters in the east to nearly 900 but the Red Air Force had now expanded to a staggering 16,000 aircraft along the front.[41] Not only was there the problem of inferior numbers, the Jagdwaffe in the east had suffered a severe lack of fuel with many units only capable of mounting a handful of sorties at any one time. Even though they had received dozens of new FW 190s, the arrival of these fighters had come too late. Russian armour was already encroaching on German soil and the Jagdflieger, hopelessly outnumbered, could barely protect their ground forces from total annihilation.

One loss during this final phase in the east was Otto Kittel, Kapitän of 2./JG 54, who was killed on 14 February while attacking eight

Sturmoviks at low level. Having damaged one, Kittel was seen to be closing in on another when his FW 190 was hit by return fire from the rear gunner and crashed in flames. Kittel, holder of the Swords and credited with 267 victories, was the fourth-highest-scoring *Experte* of the war.

The death of Otto Kittel seemed to trigger an end to the Luftwaffe's resistance in the Courland peninsula and it was not long before German units caught up in the pocket were flying west to surrender to the western Allies, while some opted to head for neutral Sweden; anything was better than to surrender to the Russians.

Despite Germany facing an inevitable defeat, the struggles continued along the Eastern Front as the Red Army closed in on Berlin and there was still time for some to achieve success. One was Hauptmann Helmut Lipfert who had assumed command of I./JG 53 in February and continued to add to his personal total until the final days. During his two months in command Lipfert added more than twenty victories to his personal score, making him a double centurion and earning him the Jagdwaffe's last Oak Leaves of the war. Lipfert's award was announced on 17 April and came just four days before Major Willi Batz, now Kommandeur of II./JG 52, became the Jagdwaffe's last recipient of the coveted Swords for his 237 victories, all but three of which had been achieved on the Eastern Front.

During the later stages of the war, many decorations were being awarded on a points basis with the Jagdflieger earning points depending on the difficulty and importance of his victim. The highest number of points awarded for a kill was three and this was for the shooting down of a four-engined bomber, such as a B-17 or a Lancaster. A pilot who managed to force a bomber from its defensive formation scored two points and a pilot who completed the shooting down of an already crippled bomber received one point. Also worth one point was the shooting down of an enemy fighter, which demonstrates how little importance was placed on this. One point was enough to be awarded the Iron Cross Second Class with three points earning a First Class. The number of points needed for the Knight's Cross varied but was generally around forty, emphasising how much the award had retained its importance.

The early months of 1945 saw the introduction of another new German fighter, the Heinkel He 162 Volksjäger ('People's Fighter'). Powered by a single BMW 003 turbojet engine mounted in a unique pod nacelle on top of the fuselage directly aft of the cockpit, the Volksjäger was the last of the three new revolutionary types to enter service with the Luftwaffe. It was smaller than the Me 262 and capable of speeds in excess of 500 mph but was armed with only two cannon: either the MG 151 20 mm or MK 108 30 mm.

The Volksjäger was a final and desperate attempt to bring a new aircraft into service in large numbers, the idea being that it would be quick and cheap to build as it could be mass-produced by a semi-skilled labour force using readily available materials such as wood due to metals being in such short supply. Its first flight took place in December 1944, just three months after the requirement had been issued, and the evaluation unit, Erprobungskommando 162, was formed the following month. The Volksjäger entered operational service with I./JG 1 at Parchim during February but did not take part in combat until the last weeks of the war by which time just over a hundred had been delivered. Only one Allied aircraft, a Typhoon, is believed to have been lost to the type but this is unconfirmed. Like the Komet and the Schwalbe before it, the Volksjäger had arrived far too late.

However, the Me 262 continued to cause the Allied bombers significant problems until the end of the war, by which time more than 1,400 had been built. One of the 262 units was JG 7, which had formed at the end of 1944 under the command of Oberstleutnant Johannes Steinhoff and included Kommando Nowotny, now re-designated as III./JG 7 under the command of Major Erich Hohagen.

Steinhoff changed the more traditional fighter tactics that had been familiar to his pilots so that they were better suited to the capabilities of the Me 262. He dropped the four-aircraft Schwarm in favour of a three-aircraft Kette, not because he did not like the Schwarm but the speed of the 262 meant its pilots did not need to provide as much mutual cover for each other as had been the case with other fighters, and three Me 262s could take off together in a line abreast formation. It simply became easier to operate as a formation of three.

When Steinhoff departed to join another new Me 262 unit, command

Above: The Kommandeur of II./JG 26, Hauptmann Joachim Müncheberg, takes Hauptmann Egon Meyer of JG 2 on a tour of Abbeville in 1942. From left: Oberleutnant Kurt Ebersberger, the long-term Kapitän of 4./JG 26; Meyer; Müncheberg and Gerhard Schöpfel. (*Meyer via Caldwell*)

Right: Oberleutnant 'Wutz' Galland of II./JG 26 refights an air battle with his hands at Abbeville during 1942. (*Bundesarchiv-Bildarchiv 357-1853-8*)

Hauptmann Josef Priller, Kommandeur of III./JG 26, is interviewed beside his Fw 190A-3 at Wevelghem during August 1942. (*Bundesarchiv-Bildarchiv 613-2317-14*)

Leutnant Josef Wurmheller (*left*) of 7./JG 2 pictured at the end of 1942 soon after receiving the Oak Leaves to his Knight's Cross for sixty victories. He is pictured with Oberleutnant Erich Leie, Gruppenkommandeur of I./JG 2, at Beaumont le Roger in northern France, just days before Leie's appointment as Gruppenkommandeur of I./JG 51 (*Chris Goss collection*)

Hauptmann Josef Priller, photographed while Kommandeur of III./JG 26 in 1942. (*Genth via Caldwell*)

Oberfeldwebel Adolf Glunz of 4./JG 26 with his new Knight's Cross in August 1943. Glunz was the only NCO pilot of JG 26 to receive this award. (*Glunz via Caldwell*)

Leutnant Josef Wurmheller was appointed Staffelkapitän of 9./JG 2 in April 1943 and recorded his seventieth victory soon after when he shot down a B-17 heavy bomber. 'Sepp' Wurmheller would later be posthumously awarded the Swords to his Knight's Cross with Oak Leaves after being killed on 22 June 1944 while Kommandeur of III./JG 2 'Richthofen', having achieved 102 victories. (*Chris Goss collection*)

Günther Rall in front of his aircraft 'Yellow One'. After more than 250 victories on the Eastern Front, Rall was appointed Kommandeur of II./JG 27 in April 1944. Having been shot down and wounded the following month, he had the opportunity to fly a number of American fighters that had fallen into the Luftwaffe's hands in order to devise tactics to counter them. Rall ended the war with 275 victories and was the third-highest-scoring *Experte* of the war. (*John Weal*)

Oberleutnant George-Peter Eder while serving with JG 2. Eder was one of the pioneers of the head-on frontal attack to combat the American heavy bombers. He joined II./JG 26 in August 1944 as a post-D-Day reinforcement and became its Kommandeur after Hauptmann Emil Lang's death on 3 September. The following month Eder joined Kommando Nowotny, the first jet-fighter unit. (*Körner via Caldwell*)

Above: Oberstleutnant Josef Priller and Major Klaus Mietusch speaking informally with members of III./JG 26, probably at Villacoublay-Nord in June or July 1944. (*Genth via Caldwell*)

Right: Hauptmann Robert Weiss, Kommandeur of III./JG 54, photographed on the invasion front in the summer of 1944. (*Bundesarchiv-Bildarchiv 674-7785-8*)

Major Walter Nowotny was given command of a special Me 262 unit, dubbed Kommando Nowotny, in September 1944, flying from airfields near Osnabrück. Nowotny claimed three victories while flying the Me 262 before his death on 8 November 1944. This may have been as a result of an engine failure in his Me 262 or he could have been shot down by American fighters. At just twenty-three years old, Nowotny was the fifth-highest-scoring Jagdflieger of the war with 258 victories for which he was awarded the coveted Diamonds to the Knight's Cross. (*John Weal*)

The Messerschmitt Me 262 *Schwalbe*, the world's first operational jet-powered fighter, entered service during the summer of 1944. Hitler's vision had been for the Me 262 to be used as a ground-attack aircraft but it started to make its mark as a fighter in the second half of the year, although it had entered the war too late to influence its outcome. (*Chris Goss collection*)

Hauptmann Erich Hartmann of 9./JG 52 pictured on 23 November 1944 after achieving his 327th victory. (*John Weal*)

Hauptmann Heinz Knoke, Kommandeur of III./JG 11, was one of the last recipients of the Knight's Cross. While Staffelkapitän of 5./JG 11 in March 1943, he had brought down a B-17 with a 250 kg bomb dropped from his Bf 109 to become the first fighter pilot to achieve such a feat. (*Chris Goss collection*)

Still only twenty-two years old, Erich Hartmann became the highest-scoring fighter pilot in history with a quite staggering 352 aerial victories and was the Luftwaffe's eighth recipient of the coveted Diamonds to the Knight's Cross with Oak Leaves and Swords. (*John Weal*)

Few photographs capture the legacy of the Jagdflieger better than this picture of Oberleutnant Joachim Müncheberg in early 1941 during his highly successful Mediterranean tour as Staffelkapitän of 7./JG 26. He is seen wearing the Knight's Cross and would later add the Oak Leaves and Swords during his 135 victories but, like so many other gallant young Jagdflieger, Müncheberg's life was cut short when he was killed on 23 March 1943 while leading JG 77 in North Africa at the age of twenty-four. (*Bundesarchiv-Bildarchiv 435-1016a-31*)

of JG 7 was given to the double centurion Theodor Weissenberger who was elevated from his previous appointment as Kommandeur of I./JG 7 to lead the Geschwader until the end of the war; amongst his eventual total of 208 victories were seven B-17s and a Mustang he claimed while flying the 262.

JG 7 operated in small numbers from airfields at Parchim, Brandenburg-Briest and Oranienburg. It continuously suffered from an irregular supply of aircraft and spares and during the early months of 1945 it could rarely put into the air more than six Me 262s at a time. However, by March it was able to mount larger raids against the bomber formations and its heaviest attack took place on 18 March when thirty-seven Me 262s of JG 7 attacked an American force of 1,300 bombers and 700 fighters destined for Berlin, claiming twelve bombers and one fighter for the loss of three 262s.

Throughout its existence, JG 7 boasted some of the Luftwaffe's greatest amongst its ranks. In addition to Steinhoff and Weissenberger, its pilots included Erich Rudorffer (who achieved a final total of 222 victories), Heinrich Ehrler (209), Walter Schuck (206) and Franz Schall (137). Others included Wolfgang Späte (99), who had commanded JG 400 (the only combat unit equipped with the Me 163 Komet), and Georg-Peter Eder (78) who had led a charmed war, having been shot down no less than seventeen times, twelve of these events having resulted in quite serious injuries.

The loss of records makes it all but impossible to determine exactly how many Allied aircraft were shot down by JG 7 during its six-month existence but the details of almost 300 victory claims are known. Given the number of *Experten* serving with the unit during the last months of the war, this figure is not surprising. Hauptmann Franz Schall is known to have shot down eleven Allied aircraft (six American Mustangs and two B-17 heavy bombers and three RAF Lancasters) while leading 10./JG 7 from Oranienburg during March and early April, to add to his six victories while flying the Me 262 with Kommando Nowotny in late 1944. He died on 10 April 1945 during an emergency landing at Parchim when his aircraft rolled into a bomb crater, killing him instantly. Schall was the third-highest-scoring jet pilot of the war.

Schall's death came just days after the loss of the double centurion Major Heinrich Ehrler, a holder of the Knight's Cross with Oak Leaves. Ehrler had joined the Stab of JG 7 at the end of February and had quickly come to terms with the 262, claiming six victories during the past two weeks. On 4 April he took off from Brandenburg-Briest to engage a formation of B-24s to the east of Hamburg. Having claimed two of the bombers, he then ran out of ammunition and during his last radio transmission to his commanding officer, Theodor Weissenberger, Ehrler reported that he was about to ram the bomber. Whether he did is not clear but the B-24 crashed near the town of Havelberg and Ehrler's Me 262 came down in woods near Schaarlippe near Berlin; his body was recovered the following day.

JG 7 was a remarkable Jagdgeschwader and it may well be that the Luftwaffe's final aerial victory of the war went to one of its pilots, Ober-leutnant Fritz Stehle of I./JG 7, who claimed a Yak-9 over Freiburg at around 16.00 on 8 May, the final day of the war in Europe.

The Me 262 was also flown by 10./NJG 11, the only jet night-fighter unit to have been formed, based at Burg near Magdeburg under the command of Kurt Welter. Initially called Sonderkommando Stamp after its founder Major Gerhard Stamp, and then Sonderkommando Welter after its new commander, the unit's main task was to intercept the faster RAF Mosquito bombers that were operating in the Berlin area.

Initially there were no radar-equipped Me 262s and so the Nacht-jagdflieger had to rely on a mix of close control and searchlights in the target area to illuminate the attackers, and use proven *Wilde Sau* tactics. A single-seat Me 262 fitted with the FuG 218 radar was later delivered to the unit before a handful of radar-equipped two-seat Me 262s were introduced in the last weeks of the war. Welter's unit was eventually credited with shooting down more than forty Mosquitos. Although his personal score while flying the Me 262 remains unclear, Welter is believed to be the highest-scoring 262 pilot of the war and was awarded the Knight's Cross with Oak Leaves, finishing the war with sixty-three victories, of which fifty-six were at night.

Another Me 262 unit was formed in March 1945 after Adolf Galland, no longer amongst Göring's preferred generals after criticizing the Luft-waffe's policy and tactics, had been removed from his appointment as

General der Jagdflieger and replaced by Gordon Gollob. Hitler had always recognized Galland's huge influence amongst the Jagdwaffe and so ordered Göring to give Galland a fighter unit and challenged Galland to turn the Me 262 into the war-winning machine that they hoped it would be.

The unit Galland formed, Jagdverband 44 (JV 44), was an elite unit and eventually totalled some fifty pilots and twenty-five aircraft, although only a handful were ever serviceable at any one time. Known as *Der Galland Zirkus* ('The Galland Circus') or *Die Jet Experten* ('The Jet Aces'), JV 44 included several experienced and decorated pilots that had been transferred from other fighter units; all were considered capable of converting to the jet fighter in a very short period of time. Its top five *Experten* totalled more than a thousand victories between them: Gerhard Barkhorn (301); Heinz Bär (221, including 16 while flying the Me 262); Walter Krupinski (197, including 2 while serving with JV 44); Johannes Steinhoff, who had been transferred from JG 7, (178, including 6 with JV 44); and Günther Lützow (110, including 2 with JV 44).

JV 44 would not fly its first operational sorties until the final weeks of the war, by which time all the Me 262 pilots had further developed their tactics as Allied bomber crews had become more familiar with the jet fighters. A small number of aircraft were equipped with twenty-four 55 mm R4M rockets that enabled the pilot to approach the bomber formation from the side, but still outside the range of the bomber's guns. When he had a big enough target he would unleash his salvo of rockets; it only required one or two hits to bring a large bomber down.

The Allies had learned that the 262 was at its most vulnerable when on the ground or during take-off and landing, and so carried out numerous bombing raids against airfields known to be carrying out jet operations. Allied fighters were also tasked to patrol over these airfields and to attack the jets when they were coming in to land. Galland's response was to form his own protection flight of five FW 190Ds, led by Leutnant Heinz Sachsenberg, to provide his jets with fighter cover during take-off and landing.

Galland led JV 44 until 26 April, gaining seven victories while flying the Me 262, before he was wounded while leading twelve rocket-equipped 262s from München-Reim against a formation of American B-26 medium bombers attacking the airfield at Lechfeld. While claiming his second bomber, and the last of his 104 victories, he was hit by return fire and wounded in the knee. After disengaging from the bombers Galland was attacked by a Thunderbolt and his aircraft sustained further damage but Galland was able to recover his aircraft successfully back to his base, although he landed during an airfield attack and suffered further injury when he had to vacate his aircraft quickly. Galland's injuries prevented him from returning to operational flying and command of JV 44 was passed to Heinz Bär until the end of the war, now just a matter of days away.

As the Allies advanced, airfields and bases in western Germany were quickly overrun. The Allies enjoyed total air superiority, being able to attack the Luftwaffe where and when they pleased. One major loss during the final weeks of the war was Karl-Wilhelm Hofmann, one of the stalwarts of JG 26. Hofmann had gained his first victory in 1942 and, despite a serious injury to his eye following an incident on the ground involving the bolt of a machine gun, he continued to fly with an eye patch and was awarded the Knight's Cross following his fortieth victory. After leading 8./JG 26 against the airfield at Brussels-Evere during Bodenplatte, Hofmann was given command of 5./JG 26 but on 26 March 1945 he was leading eight FW 190s in the Wesel–Bocholt area when he claimed his forty-fourth victim but did not return from the mission. Although Hofmann had been shot down, he managed to bail out of his aircraft but was too low for his parachute to deploy fully. Hofmann was killed two days after his twenty-third birthday.

In a last desperate attempt to defend the Reich, one new unit to form was Sonderkommando Elbe ('Special Force Elbe'), whose young pilots were trained just enough to fly a Bf 109 and deliberately ram an enemy bomber's tail, causing the bomber to fall out of control, after which the pilot was expected to make his escape by bailing out of his aircraft. This idea was intended to generate one large all-out effort against American bombers that would hopefully curtail the daylight bombing offensive for just a few months. It did not work. When the unit went into action in April 1945 there was only enough fuel, aircraft and pilots for a force of about 150 fighters to mount an attack; only fifty returned and the bombing offensive continued.

It is quite fitting that one of the Luftwaffe's last aerial victories of the war belonged to Erich Hartmann, now Kommandeur of I./JG 52. Hartmann's last victory, and his 352nd overall, occurred on 8 May, the final day of the war in Europe, during a reconnaissance sortie over Brno in Czechoslovakia. From his vantage point at 12,000 feet, Hartmann and his wingman spotted two Yak-9s performing aerobatics over Soviet troops below in a victory show. Hartmann pounced and quickly sent one of the Yaks to the ground before taking up position to attack the second.

Before he could make his next attack, Hartmann spotted several American Mustangs approaching from the west. He was caught between the Allied lines, east and west, and decided against making a last stand. The war was all but over and there was nothing to be gained, and so Hartmann led his wingman away at low level and returned to base. With the Red Army just a few miles away, the members of JG 52 destroyed their remaining Bf 109s and fled west. Like most others, Hartmann chose to surrender to the Americans but he would later be handed over to the Russians and was not released until 1955; he was one of the last prisoners of war to be returned to Germany. Erich Hartmann died in 1993 at the age of seventy-one.

Within hours of Hartmann's final victory over the advancing Russian lines, the war in Europe was over. In the early years of the Second World War the Jagdflieger had achieved remarkable successes using surprise and cunning, combined with aggression and improvisation. Some of those qualities seemed to have been lost by the final stages of the war; relatively few of the top aces survived through the last days of the Reich. Their courage and ability had been beyond question but as the Third Reich fell apart, the Luftwaffe died with it.

The Highest-Scoring Experten

The table below gives brief details of pilots credited with more than one hundred victories. Where sources vary the range of victories is shown.[42] Only the individual's highest award is included. Only the main operational theatre(s) is/are shown and the approximate date of his first operation flown may vary slightly from other sources. The known units are also shown but these may not be complete and may also vary from other sources. (Abbreviations are Knight's Cross = KC; Oak Leaves = OL; Swords = Sw; Diamonds = Dia; Western Front = WF; Mediterranean = M; North Africa = NA; Eastern Front = EF; killed in action = KIA; missing in action = MIA; died of wounds = DoW).

Name	No. of victories	Highest award	Theatre(s) of operations	Approx. date 1st operation	Known units	Remarks
Erich Hartmann	352	Dia	EF	Oct 42	JG 52, JG 53	
Gerhard Barkhorn	301	Sw	EF	Aug 40	JG 52, JG 6, JV 44	
Günther Rall	275	Sw	EF, WF	May 40	JG 52, JG 11, JG 300	
Otto Kittel	267	Sw	EF	Sep 41	JG 54	KIA 14 Feb 45 (also reported as 16 Feb 45)
Walter Nowotny	258	Dia	EF, WF	Feb 41	JG 54, Kdo Nowotny	KIA 8 Nov 44
Wilhelm Batz	237	Sw	EF, WF	Dec 42	JG 52	
Erich Rudorffer	222–4	Sw	WF, NA, EF	May 40	JG 2, JG 54, JG 7	
Heinz Bär	220–1	Sw	WF, NA, M, EF	Sep 39	JG 51, JG 77, JG 1, JG 3, EJG 2, JV 44	
Hermann Graf	212	Dia	EF, WF	Jul 41	JG 51, JG 52, JGr 50, JG 11	First to reach 200 victori●
Heinrich Ehrler	209	OL	EF, WF	May 40	JG 77, JG 5, JG 7	KIA 4 Apr 45
Theodor Weissenberger	208	OL	WF, EF	Oct 41	JG77, JG 5, JG 7	
Hans Philipp	206	Sw	EF, WF	Sep 39	JG 76, JG 54, JG 1	KIA 8 Oct 43
Walter Schuck	206	OL	EF, WF	Oct 40	JG 5, JG 7	
Anton Hafner	204	OL	EF, NA	Jun 41	JG 51, JG 3	KIA 17 Oct 44
Helmut Lipfert	203	OL	EF	Dec 42	JG 52, JG 53	
Walter Krupinski	197	OL	EF, WF	Jan 42	JG 52. JG 5, JG 11, JG 26, JV 44	

Appendix 1: The Highest-Scoring Experten

Name	No. of victories	Highest award	Theatre(s) of operations	Approx. date 1st operation	Known units	Remarks
Anton Hackl	192–6	Sw	WF, EF	1939	JG 77, JG 11, JG 26, JG 300	
Joachim Brendel	189	OL	EF	Jun 41	JG 51	
Maximilian Stotz	189	OL	WF, EF	May 40	JG 54	MIA 19 Aug 43
Joachim Kirschner	188	OL	EF, M	1941	JG 3, JG 27	KIA 17 Dec 43
Kurt Brändle	180	OL	WF, EF	1939	JG 53, JG 3	KIA 3 Nov 43
Günther Josten	178	OL	EF	Nov 41	JG 51, JG 71	
Johannes Steinhoff	176–8	Sw	WF, NA, M, EF	Dec 39	JG 26, JG 52, JG 77, JG 7, JV 44	
Ernst-Wilhelm Reinert	174	Sw	EF, NA, M, WF	Jun 41	JG 77, JG 27, JG 7	
Günther Schack	174	OL	EF	Jun 41	JG 3, JG 51	
Emil Lang	173	OL	EF, WF	1942	JG 54, JG 26	KIA 3 Sep 44
Heinz Schmidt	173	OL	WF, EF	Aug 40	JG 52	MIA 5 Sep 43
Horst Ademeit	166	OL	WF, EF	May 40	JG 54	MIA 7 Aug 44
Wolf-Dietrich Wilcke	162	Sw	WF, EF	May 40	JG 53, JG 3	KIA 23 Mar 44
Hans-Joachim Marseille	158	Dia	WF, NA	1940	LG 2, JG 52, JG 27	Killed 30 Sep 42
Heinrich Sturm	157–8	KC	EF	Jul 41	JG 52	Killed 22 Dec 44
Gerhard Thyben	157	OL	EF, WF	Dec 42	JG3, JG 54	
Hans Beisswenger	152	OL	EF	1940	JG 54	KIA 6 Mar 43
Peter Düttmann	150–2	KC	EF	May 43	JG 52	
Gordon Gollob	150	Dia	WF, EF	1939	ZG 76, JG 3, JG 77	
Fritz Tegtmeier	146	KC	EF	Oct 40	JG 54, JG 7	
Albin Wolf	144	OL	EF	May 42	JG1, JG 54	KIA 2 Apr 44
Kurt Tanzer	143	KC	EF, WF	Mar 42	JG 51	
Friedrich-Karl Müller	140	OL	WF, EF	May 40	JG 53, JG 7, JG 3	Killed 29 May 44
Karl Gratz	138	KC	EF, WF	1942	JG 52, JG 2	
Heinrich Setz	138	OL	WF, EF	Jul 40	JG 77, JG 27	KIA 13 Mar 43
Rudolf Trenkel	138	KC	EF	Feb 42	JG 77, JG 52	
Walter Wolfrum	137	KC	EF	Jan 43	JG 52	
Franz Schall	133–7	KC	EF, WF	Feb 43	JG 52, Kdo Nowotny, JG 7	KIA 10 Apr 45
Horst-Günther von Fassong	136	KC	EF, WF	Jul 41	JG 51, JG 11	KIA 1 Jan 45
Otto Fönnekold	136	KC	EF	Nov 42	JG 52	KIA 31 Aug 44
Karl-Heinz Weber	136	OL	EF	May 42	JG 51, JG 1	KIA 7 Jun 44
Adolf Dickfeld	132–6	OL	WF, M, NA, EF	May 40	JG 52, JG 2, JG 11	
Joachim Müncheberg	135	Sw	WF, EF, M, NA	1939	JG 26, JG 51, JG 77	KIA 23 Mar 43
Hans Waldmann	134	OL	EF, WF	Aug 42	JG 52, JG 3, JG 7	Killed 18 Mar 45
Johannes Wiese	133	OL	EF	Jul 41	JG 52, JG 77	
Alfred Grislawski	133	OL	WF, EF	Jul 40	JG 52, JG 50, JG 1, JG 53	
Adolf Borchers	132	KC	LK, WF, EF	1937	JG 77, JG 51, JG 52	
Erwin Clausen	132	OL	EF, WF	Sep 39	LG 2, JG 77, JG 11	KIA 4 Oct 43
Wilhelm Lemke	131	OL	EF, WF	Nov 41	JG 3	KIA 4 Dec 43
Herbert Ihlefeld	123–30	Sw	LK, WF, EF	1937	LG 2, JG 52, JG 103, JG 25, JG 11, JG 1	

Name	No. of victories	Highest award	Theatre(s) of operations	Approx. date 1st operation	Known units	Remarks
Gerhard Hoffmann	125–30	KC	WF, EF	May 40	JG 52	Killed 17 Apr 45
Walter Dahl	128–9	OL	WF, EF	Jul 40	JG 3, JG 300	
Franz Eisenach	129	KC	WF, EF	May 40	ZG 76, JG 1, JG 54	
Heinrich Sterr	129–30	KC	EF, WF	May 42	JG 54	KIA 26 Nov 44
Franz Dörr	128	KC	EF, WF	Jun 41	EJGr 3, JG 77, JG 5	
Rudolf Rademacher	97–126	KC	EF, WF	Dec 41	JG 54, JG 7	
Josef Zwernemann	126	OL	WF, M, EF	May 40	JG 52, JG 77, JG 11	KIA 8 Apr 44
Dietrich Hrabak	125	OL	WF, EF	Sep 39	JG 76, JG 54, JG 52	
Walter Oesau	118–25	Sw	LK, WF, EF	1937	JG 51, JG 3, JG 2, JG 1	KIA 11 May 44
Wolf-Udo Ettel	124	OL	EF, M	1942	JG 3, JG 27	KIA 17 Jul 43
Wolfgang Tonne	122	OL	WF, EF, NA	May 40	JG 53	Killed 20 Apr 43
Heinz Marquardt	121	KC	EF, WF	Aug 43	JG 51	
Erich Leie	118–21	KC	WF, EF	Sep 40	JG 2, JG 51, JG 77	KIA 7 Mar 45
Heinz-Wolfgang Schnaufer	121	Dia	WF	1942	NJG 1, NJG 4	Highest scorer at night
Robert Weiss	121	OL	EF, WF	Jul 41	JG 26, JG 54	KIA 29 Dec 44
Friedrich Obleser	120	KC	EF	Jan 43	JG 52	
Franz-Josef Beerenbrock	117	OL	EF	Jun 41	JG 51	
Hans-Joachim Birkner	117	KC	EF	1943	JG 52	Killed 14 Dec 44
Jakob Norz	117	KC	EF	Nov 41	NJG 2, JG 1, JG 5	Killed 16 Sep 44
Heinz Wernicke	117	KC	EF	May 42	JG 54	KIA 27 Dec 44
August Lambert	116	KC	EF	Apr 43	SG 1, SG 2, SG 77	KIA 17 Apr 45
Wilhelm Crinius	114	OL	M, EF, NA	Mar 42	JG 53, JG 52, JG 27	
Werner Schroer	114	Sw	WF, M, NA, EF	Aug 40	JG 27, JG 54, JG 3	
Hans Dammers	113	KC	EF	Jun 41	JG 52	DoW 17 Mar 44
Berthold Korts	113	KC	EF	Jul 42	JG 52	MIA 29 Aug 43
Helmut Lent	110–13	Dia	WF	Sep 39	ZG 76, NJG 1, NJG 2, NJG 3	KIA 5 Oct 44
Kurt Bühligen	112	Sw	WF, NA	Jul 40	JG 2	
Kurt Ubben	110	OL	WF, M, NA, EF	Sep 39	JGr 186, JG 77, JG 2	KIA 27 Apr 44
Franz Woidich	110	KC	M, NA, EF	Jul 41	JG 27, JG 52, JG 400	
Emil Bitsch	108	KC	EF, WF	Jul 41	JG 3	KIA 15 Mar 44
Hans 'Assi' Hahn	108	OL	WF, EF	May 40	JG 2, JG 54	
Bernhard Vechtel	108	KC	EF	May 42	JG 51	
Viktor Bauer	106	OL	WF, EF	May 40	JG 2, JG 3, EJG 1, JG 77	
Werner Lucas	106	KC	WF, EF	Jul 40	JG 3	KIA 24 Oct 43
Günther Lützow	105–10	Sw	WF, EF	1937	LK, JG 3, JG 51, JV 44	MIA 24 Apr 45
Eberhard von Boremski	104	KC	EF, WF	May 40	JG 3, EJG 1	
Heinz Sachsenberg	104	KC	EF, WF	Nov 42	JG 52, JG 7, JV 44	
Adolf Galland	103–4	Dia	WF	1937	LK, JG 27, JG 26, JV 44	
Hartmann Grasser	103	OL	WF, EF, NA	May 40	JGr 152, ZG 52, ZG 2, JG 51, JG 11, JG 110	
Siegfried Freytag	102	KC	EF, NA, M	Jul 41	JG 77, JG 7	
Friedrich Geisshardt	102	OL	WF, EF, M, NA	Sep 39	LG 2, JG 77, JG 26	DoW 6 Apr 43

Appendix 1: The Highest-Scoring Experten

Name	No. of victories	Highest award	Theatre(s) of operations	Approx. date 1st operation	Known units	Remarks
Egon Mayer	102	Sw	WF	May 40	JG 2	KIA 2 Mar 44
Max-Hellmuth Ostermann	102	Sw	WF, EF	May 40	ZG 1, JG 27, JG 54	KIA 9 Aug 42
Josef Wurmheller	102	Sw	WF	May 40	JG 53, JG 2	KIA 22 Jun 44
Werner Mölders	101–15	Dia	WF, EF	1937	LK, JG 53, JG 51	Killed 22 Nov 41. First to achieve 100 victories
Rudolf Miethig	101	KC	EF	Jul 41	JG 52	KIA 10 Jun 43
Josef Priller	101	KC	WF	Sep 39	JG 51, JG 26	
Ulrich Wernitz	101	KC	EF	May 43	JG 54	
Reinhard Seiler	100–9	OL	WF, EF	1938	LK, JG 54, JG 104	WIA 6 Jul 43
Paul-Heinrich Dähne	99–100	KC	EF, WF	1942	JG 52, JG 11, JG 1	Killed 24 Apr 45

The names of those credited with 30–99 victories are listed below with their number of victories, although sources are known to vary:

99   Heinrich Bartels, Hans Schleef, Wolfgang Späte, Leopold Steinbatz

98   Horst Hannig, Gustav-Siegfried Rödel, Helmut Ruffler

97   Helmut Mertens, Hermann Schleinhage

96   Heinrich Höfemeier, Siegfried Lemke, Dieter von Eichel-Streiber

95   Leopold Munster

94   Anton Döbele, Heinrich Klopper, Rudolf Müller, Rudolf Resch

93   Helmut Bennemann, Edmund Rossmann, Siegfried Schnell

92   Gerhard Loos, Oskar Romm

91   Anton Resch

90   Georg Schentke

89   Heinz Kemethmüller

86   Ulrich Wohnert, Josef Jennewein, Gerhard Köppen, Anton Mader, Friedrich Wachowiak

85   Alexander Preinfalk, Walter Zellot

84   Heinz Ewald, Peter Kalden, Werner Quast

83   Franz Beyer, Walter Ohlrogge, Emil Pusch, Heinrich Prinz zu Sayn-Wittgenstein, Otto Wessling

82   Hans Götz, Hans Grünberg, Emil Darjes, Horst Haase, Helmut Missner

81   Hugo Broch, Willi Nemitz, Wilhelm Philipp, Rudolf Wagner, Max-Hermann Lucke

80   Herbert Bachnick

79   Otto Wurfel

78   Wolfgang Ewald, Georg-Peter Eder, Heinrich Krafft, Karl-Gottfried Nordmann

77 Hubertus von Bonin, Josef Haibock, Johannes-Hermann Meier

76 Hans-Joachim Kroschinski, Maximilian Mayerl, Alfred Teumer, Edwin Thiel,
    Klaus Mietusch

75 Johannes Bunzek, Helmut Grollmus, Hans Roehrig, Joachim Wandel,
    Johannes Pichler

74 Gustav Frielinghaus, Otto Gaiser, Friedrich Haas, Karl-Heinz Meltzer

73 Wilhelm Herget, Anton Lindner, Gerhard Michalski, Otto Schultz

72 Wilhelm Mink, Karl-Heinz Schnell, Adolf Glunz

71 Hans Füss, Alfred Heckmann, Herbert Rollwage, Günther Scheel

70 Hans Döbrich, Heinz Gossow, Karl Hoffmann, Herbert Hüppertz, Hermann-
    Friedrich Joppien, Heinz Lange, Rudolf Linz, Emil Omert, Rudolf Richter,
    Ernst Süss

69 Armin Köhler, Ernst Weissmann, Eugen-Ludwig Zweigart

68 Konrad Bauer, Kurt Dombacher, Walter Hoeckner, Heinrich Jung, Herbert Kaiser,
    Richard Leppla, Fritz Losigkeit, Günther Freiherr von Maltzahn, Hans Strelow,
    Otto Tange

67 Gustav Denk, Fritz Dinger, Herbert Findeisen, Karl Fuchs, Erbo Graf von Kageneck,
    Franz Schiess, Franz Schwaiger, Hubert Srassl, Werner Streib

66 Erwin Fleig, Reinhold Hoffmann

65 Franz Czech, Heinrich Fullgräbe, Berthold Grassmuck, Karl-Heinz Kempf,
    Manfred Meurer, Günther Radusch, Waldemar Semelka

64 Bernd Gallowitsch, Jürgen Harder, Rolf Hermichen, Walter Lindner, Viktor
    Petermann, Heinz Rökker, Franz Ruhl, Rudolf Schönert

63 Walter Borchers, Franz Götz, Karl Hammerl, Heinrich Hoffmann, Gerhard Homuth,
    Hermann Staiger, Kurt Welter

62 Wilhelm Hübner, Helmut Neumann

61 Hannes Trautloft

60 Hans-Ekkehard Bob, Gerhard Beutin, Horst Carganico, Franz Hrdlicka,
    August Mors, Karl Munz, Alfred Rauch, Kurt Tangemann, Walter Wever

59 Herbert Brönnle, Franz Eckerle, Alfred Franke, Hans-Arnold Stahlschmidt,
    Karl Steffen, Paul Zorner

58 Martin Becker, Hermann Buchner, Lutz-Wilhelm Burckhardt, Siegfried Engfer,
    Herbert Friebel, Hans-Joachim Langer, Gerhard Raht

57 Heinz-Wilhelm Ahnert, Walter Brandt, Hugo Dahmer, Heinrich Dittlmann,
    Kurt Ebener, Adolf Kulkum, Johannes Seifert, Edmund Wagner, Hermann Wolf

56   Herbert Bareuter, Helmut-Felix Bolz, Alfred Burk, Manfred Eberwein,
     Gustav Francsi, Heinrich Hackler, Isken Hermann, Helmut Holtz, Eduard Isken,
     Josef Kraft, Helmut Schönfelder, Günther Seeger, Heinz Strüning, Helmut Wick

55   Hans-Dieter Frank, Wilhelm-Ferdinand Galland, Erich Hohagen, Gabriel Tautscher,
     Rudi Zwesken

54   Johann Badum, Karl-Heinz Bendert, Wilhelm Hauswirth, Kurt Knappe,
     Heinz Leber, Herbert Puschmann, Siegfried Simsch, Hans Reiff, Heinz Vinke

53   Heinz-Edgar Berres, Albert Brunner, August Geiger, Herbert Lütje,
     Hans-Joachim Heyer, Julius Meimberg, Friedrich Rupp, Karl Sattig, Franz Barten,
     Wilhelm Kientsch

52   Heine Cordes, Martin Drewes, Hans Ehlers, Alfred Gross, Ludwig Hafner,
     Werner Hoffmann, Rudolf Pflanz, Heinrich Wefers, Heinz Knoke

51   Egmont Prinz zu Lippe-Weissenfeld, Otto Schulz

50   Walter Duellberg, Hermann Greiner, Hans-Joachim Jabs, Emil Knittel,
     Franz Lisendahl, Fritz Luddecke, Wilhelm Schilling, Fritz Schroeter, Karl Willius,
     Herbert Koller, Helmut Merkel

49   Rudolf Ehrenberger, Klaus Quaert-Faslem

48   Friedrich Beckh, Peter Seigler, Heinz-Gerhard Vogt, Oskar Zimmermann

47   Wilhelm Balthasar, Heinz Golinski, Günther Hannack, Eckhard Hubner, Fritz Karch,
     Herbert Kutscha, Georg Seidel, Günther Rübell, Erich Schmidt, Werner Stumpf

46   Ludwig Becker, Wolfgang Bowing-Treuding, Günther Fink, Rudiger von Kirchmayr,
     Erwin Laskowski, Hans-Karl Meyer, Günther Rammelt, Karl Schnörrer,
     Franz Schulte, Alfred Surau

45   Ernst Borgen, Ernst Drünkler, Jürgen Brocke, Ernst-Erich Hirschfeld,
     Alois Lechner, Wilhelm Kuken, Lothar Mai, Karl-Wolfgang Redlich,
     Gerhard Schöpfel, Hans-Johannes Stollenberger

44   Hans Frese, Jürgen Hoerschelmann, Karl-Wilhelm Hofmann, Reinhold Knacke,
     Walter Matoni, Wilhelm Moritz, Richard Quante, Wilhelm Steinmann,
     Otto Vinzent

43   Karl Boris, Ludwig Franzisket, Kurt Goltzsch, Hubert Muetherich, Josef Pohs,
     Paul-August Stolte

42   Dietrich Schmidt, Rudolf Klemm, Emil Reinhard, Rudolf Schmidt,
     Herbert Schramm

41   Robert Olejnik, Gerhard Schneider

40   Heinz Arnold, Rudolf Busch, Karl Boehm-Fettelbach, Peter Bremer,
Wolf-Dietrich Huy, Wolfgang Neuhoff, Georg Seckel, Günther Steinhausen,
Hermann Segatz

39   Heinz Bretnütz, Alfons Klein, Kurt Lasse, Bernhard Lausch, Georg Seelmann,
Rudolf Sinner, Fritz Stendel, Eckart-Wilhelm von Bonin, Robert Fuchs

38   Hans Dortenmann, Pepi Gabl, Walter Loos, Stefan Litjens, Detler Rohwer,
Erwin Sawallisch, Wolfgang Schellmann, Kurt Sochatzky

37   Franz Hagedorn, Gerhard Koall, Karl-Heinz Leesmann, Klaus Neumann,
Waldemar Radener, Wolfgang Traft

36   Helmut Belser, Helmut Bergmann, Georg Keil, Friedrich Körner, Elias Kuehlein,
Herbert Wehnelt, Hans Weik, Fulbert Zink

35   Günther Bertram, Graf Heinrich von Einsiedel, August Luy, Bruno Stolle,
Martin Ulbrich, Joachim Harner

34   Paul Brandt, Klaus Bretschneider, Hans von Hahn, Heinz-Horst Hissbach,
Wilhelm Johnen, Karl Kennel, Johannes Naumann, Karl-Heinz Plucker,
Herbert Schob, Walter Stengel, Horst Tietzen, Helmut Wettstein

33   Heinz Beyer, Harro Harder, Erwin Leykauf, Wolfgang Lippert, Waldemer Soffing,
Hans Stechmann, Ferdinand Vogel

32   Hugo Frey, Rudolf Glockner, Joachim Hacker, Werner Husemenn,
Werner Machold, Gunther Specht, Gerhard Weigand, Ralph Furch

31   Peter Crump, Carl von Lieres, Hermann Seegatz, Gustav Sprick, Alfred Seidl

30   Erich Bartz, Max Bucholz, Gerhard Friedrich, Josef Fözoe, Werner Gerth,
Hans-Georg Hackbarth, Friedrich Heimann, Harry Koch, Karl-Heinz Langer,
Hans-Karl Mayer, Rolf Pingel, Werner Schumacher

Highest-Scoring Experten by Operational Theatre

The first figure is the number of victories achieved in that theatre with the total number of victories shown in brackets.

Eastern Front			Western Front*		
Erich Hartmann	350	(352)	Hans-Joachim Marseille	158	(158)
Gerhard Barkhorn	301	(301)	Heinz Bär	125	(221)
Günther Rall	271	(275)	Kurt Bühligen	112	(112)
Otto Kittel	267	(267)	Adolf Galland	104	(104)
Walter Nowotny	255	(258)	Joachim Müncheberg	102	(135)
Wilhelm Batz	234	(237)	Werner Schroer	102	(114)
Hermann Graf	202	(212)	Egon Mayer	102	(102)
Helmut Lipfert	200	(203)	Josef Priller	101	(101)
Heinrich Ehrler	198	(208)	Gustav Rödel	97	(98)
Walter Schuck	189	(206)	Josef Wurmheller	93	(102)

* Including Channel Front, North-West Europe, Germany, North Africa & Mediterranean

Appendix 3

Highest-Scoring Experten at Night

The first figure gives the number of victories achieved at night with the total number of victories shown in brackets.

Heinz-Wolfgang Schnaufer	121	(121)
Helmut Lent	103	(110)
Prince Heinrich zu Sayn-Wittgenstein	83	(83)
Werner Streib	67	(68)
Manfred Meurer	65	(65)
Günther Radusch	64	(65)
Rudolf Schönert	64	(64)
Heinz Rökker	63	(64)
Paul Zorner	59	(59)
Martin Becker	58	(58)
Gerhard Raht	58	(58)
Wilhelm Herget	57	(73)

Appendix 4

Recipients of the Knight's Cross with Oak Leaves, Swords and Diamonds

(Träger des Eichenlaubs mit Schwertern und Brillanten zum Ritterkreuz des eisernen Kreuzes)

The recipient's order in the overall number of recipients is shown in brackets. For example, Walter Nowotny was the sixth Luftwaffe Experte to receive the Diamonds but the eighth overall.

Recipient	Unit at time of award	Date of award
Oberst Werner Mölders (1)	JG 51	15 July 1941
Oberst Adolf Galland (2)	JG 26	28 January 1942
Major Gordon Gollob (3)	JG 77	30 August 1942
Oberleutnant Hans Joachim Marseille (4)	JG 27	3 September 1942
Oberleutnant Hermann Graf (5)	JG 52	16 September 1942
Hauptmann Walter Nowotny (8)	JG 54	19 October 1943
Oberstleutnant Helmut Lent (15)	NJG 3	31 July 1944
Oberleutnant Erich Hartmann (18)	JG 52	25 August 1944
Hauptmann Heinz-Wolfgang Schnaufer (21)	NJG 1	16 October 1944

Source: Gordon Williamson, *Knight's of the Iron Cross, A History 1939–45*, p. 142.

Recipients of the Knight's Cross with Oak Leaves and Swords

(Träger des Eichenlaubs mit Schwertern zum
Ritterkreuz des eisernen Kreuzes)

The recipient's order in the overall number of recipients is shown in brackets. For example, Heinz Bär was the fifth Luftwaffe *Experte* to receive the Swords but the seventh overall.

Recipient	Unit at time of award	Date of award
Oberstleutnant Adolf Galland (1)	JG 26	21 June 1941
Oberstleutnant Werner Mölders (2)	JG 51	22 June 1941
Hauptmann Walter Oesau (3)	JG 3	16 July 1941
Major Günther Lützow (4)	JG 3	11 October 1941
Hauptmann Heinz Bär (7)	JG 51	16 February 1942
Hauptmann Hans Philipp (8)	JG 54	12 March 1942
Hauptmann Herbert Ihlefeld (9)	JG 77	24 April 1942
Oberleutnant Max Ostermann (10)	JG 54	17 May 1942
Leutnant Hermann Graf (11)	JG 52	19 May 1942
Oberleutnant Hans Joachim Marseille (12)	JG 27	18 June 1942
Hauptmann Gordon Gollob (13)	JG 77	23 June 1942
Oberfeldwebel Leopold Steinbatz (14)	JG 52	23 June 1942
Hauptmann Joachim Müncheberg (19)	JG 51	9 September 1942
Major Wolfe-Dieter Wilcke (23)	JG 3	23 December 1942
Major Helmut Lent (32)	NJG 1	2 August 1943
Hauptmann Günther Rall (34)	JG 52	12 September 1943

Appendix 5: Recipients of the Oak Leaves and Swords

Recipient	Unit at time of award	Date of award
Hauptmann Walter Nowotny (37)	JG 54	22 September 1943
Major Heinrich Prinz zu Sayn-Wittgenstein (44)	NJG 2	23 January 1944
Oberstleutnant Egon Mayer (51)	NJG 2	2 March 1944
Hauptmann Gerhard Barkhorn (52)	JG 52	2 March 1944
Major Werner Streib (54)	NJG 1	11 March 1944
Oberstleutnant Josef Priller (73)	JG 26	2 July 1944
Oberleutnant Erich Hartmann (75)	JG 52	2 July 1944
Major Anton Hackl (78)	JG 11	9 July 1944
Oberstleutnant Johannes Steinhoff (82)	JG 77	28 July 1944
Hauptmann Heinz-Wolfgang Schnaufer (84)	NJG 1	30 July 1944
Major Kurt Bühligen (88)	JG 2	14 August 1944
Hauptmann Josef Wurmheller (108)	JG 2	24 October 1944
Oberleutnant Otto Kittel (113)	JG 54	25 November 1944
Major Erich Rudorffer (126)	JG 54	26 January 1945
Oberleutnant Ernst Wilhelm Reinert (130)	JG 27	1 February 1945
Major Werner Schroer (144)	JG 3	19 April 1945
Major Wilhelm Batz (145)	JG 52	21 April 1945

Source: Gordon Williamson, *Knight's of the Iron Cross, A History 1939–45*, pp. 143–6.

Appendix 6

Equivalent Ranks

Officers

Luftwaffe	Royal Air Force	US Air Force
Reichsmarschall	No equivalent	No equivalent
Generalfeldmarschall	Marshal of the Royal Air Force	General (5-star)
Generaloberst	Air Chief Marshal	General (4-star)
General der Flieger	Air Marshal	Lieutenant General (3-star)
Generalleutnant	Air Vice-Marshal	Major General (2-star)
Generalmajor	Air Commodore	Brigadier General (1-star)
Oberst	Group Captain	Colonel
Oberstleutnant	Wing Commander	Lieutenant Colonel
Major	Squadron Leader	Major
Hauptmann	Flight Lieutenant	Captain
Oberleutnant	Flying Officer	First Lieutenant
Leutnant	Pilot Officer	Second Lieutenant

Other Ranks (Approximations)

Luftwaffe	Royal Air Force	US Air Force
Stabsfeldwebel	Warrant Officer	Master Sergeant
Oberfeldwebel	Flight Sergeant	Master Sergeant
Feldwebel	Sergeant	Technical Sergeant
Unteroffizier	Corporal	Sergeant

Luftwaffe Hierarchy

Oberkommando der Luftwaffe:
> OKL – High Command of the Luftwaffe

Chef des Generalstabes der Luftwaffe:
> Chief of the General Staff of the Luftwaffe

Luftflotte: Air Fleet – commanded by a Generalfeldmarschall, Generaloberst or General der Flieger

Fliegerkorps: Air Corps – commanded by a Generalleutnant, General der Flieger or Generaloberst

Fliegerdivision: Air Division – commanded by an Oberst, Generalmajor or Generalleutnant

Geschwader: Wing – usually three or four *Gruppen* and equivalent to RAF Group. Commanded by a Major or an officer of higher rank

Gruppe: Group – three or occasionally four *Staffeln* and equivalent to RAF Wing. Commanded by a Hauptmann or officer of higher rank

Staffel: Squadron – usually ten to twelve aircraft and equivalent to RAF Squadron. Commanded by a Leutnant, Oberleutnant or Hauptmann

Schwarm: Formation of four aircraft made up of two *Rotten*

Kette: Unit of three fighters

Rotte: Two fighters working as a pair

Glossary

Ergänzungsgruppe: Training Group
Fliegerdivision: Air Division
Fliegerkorps: Air Corps
Geschwader: Air Wing
Gruppe: Air Group
Jagdgeschwader: Fighter Wing, abbreviated as JG
Jagdkorps: Fighter Air Corps
Jagdwaffe: the Luftwaffe's Fighter Force
Kampfgeschwader: Bomber Wing, abbreviated as KG
Lehrdivision: Testing Division
Luftgau: Administrative districts at Air Corps level.
Nachtjagdgeschwader: Night Fighter Wing, abbreviated as NJG
Nationalsozialistische Deutsche Arbeiter Partei: National Socialist German
  Workers' Party, otherwise known as the NSDAP or Nazi Party
Reichskommissariat für die Luftfahrt: Reich Commissioner of Aviation
Reichsluftfahrtministerium: RLM – Reich Aviation Ministry
Stab: Staff
Staffel: Squadron
Zerstörergeschwader: Destroyer Wing, abbreviated as ZG

Notes

1. Samuel W. Mitcham, *Eagles of the Third Reich*, p. 19.
2. Telford Taylor, *Sword & Swastika: Generals and Nazis in the Third Reich* (Simon & Shuster, NY, 1952), p. 248.
3. Bruce R. Pirnie, 'First Test for the War Machine', *WW II*, Vol 1, No. 5, January 1987, pp. 44–5.
4. Karl Drum, *The German Air Force in the Spanish Civil War* (USAF Historical Studies No. 150, Aerospace Studies Institute, Maxwell AFB, Montgomery, Alabama, 1965).
5. Mitcham, *Eagles of the Third Reich*, p. 29.
6. Ibid., p. 64
7. Mike Spick, *Luftwaffe Fighter Aces*, p. 32.
8. Mitcham, *Eagles of the Third Reich*, p. 70.
9. Brian Cull & Bruce Lander with Heinrich Weiss, *Twelve Days in May*, pp. 10–13.
10. Spick, *Luftwaffe Fighter Aces*, p. 41.
11. Tony Holmes, *Dogfight, The Greatest Air Duels of WW II*, 'Spitfire v Bf 109E', p. 60.
12. Spick, *Luftwaffe Fighter Aces*, p. 42.
13. Richard Hough & Denis Richards, *The Battle of Britain*, p. 359.
14. Alfred Price, *The Hardest Day*, pp. 183–6.
15. Alfred Price, *Battle of Britain Day*, p. 77.
16. Spick, *Luftwaffe Fighter Aces*, p. 94.
17. Christopher Shores and Brian Cull with Nicola Malizia, *Malta: The Hurricane Years 1940–41*, p. 158.
18. Ibid., p. 161.
19. Spick, *Luftwaffe Fighter Aces*, p. 75.
20. Ibid., p. 78.
21. Ibid.
22. The second-highest-scoring German fighter pilot of the First World War who was credited with sixty-two victories and was the nation's highest-scoring fighter pilot to have survived the war, Udet became the Luftwaffe's Director General of Equipment in 1939 but committed

suicide in November 1941 after Göring deflected Hitler's ire for the Luftwaffe's poor performance onto him.

23. John Weal, *Jagdgeschwader 27 'Afrika'*, p. 64).
24. Ibid., p. 68.
25. Ibid., p. 76.
26. Ibid., p. 4.
27. Matthew Cooper, *The German Air Force 1933–45* (Janes, London, 1981), p. 245.
28. John Weal, *Focke-Wulf FW 190 Aces of the Russian Front*, p. 12.
29. Earl F. Ziemke, *Stalingrad to Berlin: The German Defeat in the East* (US Dept of the Army, Washington DC, US Govt Printing Office, 1966), pp. 61 & 75.
30. Jerry Scutts, *Luftwaffe Night Fighter Units 1939–45* (Osprey Ltd, London, 1978), pp. 3–4.
31. David P. Williams, *Hunters of the Reich, Night Fighters*, p. 39.
32. Spick, *Luftwaffe Fighter Aces*, p. 175.
33. Ibid., pp. 42–3.
34. Holmes, *Dogfight*, 'P-47 Thunderbolt v Bf 109G/K' by Martin Bowman, p. 84.
35. Spick, *Luftwaffe Fighter Aces*, p. 161.
36. An excellent graphic showing a head-on attack against an American B-17 heavy bomber can be found in Mike Spick's *Luftwaffe Fighter Aces* p. 158.
37. Spick, *Luftwaffe Fighter Aces*, p. 162.
38. Mitcham, *Eagles of the Third Reich*, p. 236.
39. As things turned out, Hitler's demand for the Me 262 to be used exclusively as a fighter-bomber did not overly delay its introduction as a fighter.
40. Holmes, *Dogfight*, 'P-47 Thunderbolt v Bf 109G/K' by Martin Bowman, p. 115.
41. Spick, *Luftwaffe Fighter Aces*, p. 196.
42. This table of victories was put together using a number of sources but starting with Appendices 2 and 3 of Mike Spick's *Luftwaffe Fighter Aces* and then cross-referring with several other sources.

Bibliography

Aders, Gebhard, *History of the German Night Fighter Force 1917–45* (Jane's, London, 1979)

Bekker, Cajus, *The Luftwaffe War Diaries* (Macdonald, London, 1967)

Boiten, Theo, *Nachtjagd: The Night Fighter versus Bomber War over the Third Reich, 1939–45* (Crowood, Marlborough, 1997)

Boiten, Theo & Bowman, Martin, *Battles with the Luftwaffe* (Harper Collins, London, 2001)

Bowman, Martin, *P-51 Mustang vs FW 190, Europe 1943–45* (Osprey, Oxford, 2007)

Caldwell, Donald L., *JG 26: Top Guns of the Luftwaffe* (Ballantine, NY, 1992)

——, *Day Fighters in Defence of the Reich* (Frontline Books, Barnsley, 2011)

Cull, Brian, Lander, Bruce & Weiss, Heinrich, *Twelve days in May* (Grub Street, London, 1995)

Fernández-Sommerau, Marco, *Messerschmitt Bf 109 Recognition Manual* (Classic Publications, Hersham, 2004)

Forsyth, Robert, *Aces of the Legion Condor* (Osprey, Oxford, 2011)

——, *Jagdwaffe: Defending the Reich 1944/45* (Ian Allan, Hersham, 2006)

Hannig, Norbert, *Luftwaffe Fighter Ace: From the Eastern Front to the Defense of the Homeland* (Grub Street, London, 2004)

Holmes, Tony, *Dogfight: The Greatest Air Duels of World War II* (Osprey, Oxford, 2011)

——, *Spitfire vs Bf 109: Battle of Britain* (Osprey, Oxford, 2007)

Hough, Richard & Richards, Denis, *The Battle of Britain* (Guild Publishing, London, 1990)

Ishoven, Armand van, *Messerschmitt Bf 109 At War* (Promotional Reprint Company, Leicester, 1993)

James T. C. G., *The Battle of Britain* (Frank Cass, London, 2000)

Mitcham, Samuel W, *Eagles of the Third Reich* (Stackpole Books, PA, 1988)

Mombeek, Eric, *Defenders of the Reich – JG 1*, Vol. Two: *1943* (Classic Publications, Hersham, 2001)

——, *Defenders of the Reich – JG 1*, Vol. Three: *1944–45* (Classic Publications, Hersham, 2003)

Murray, Williamson, *Strategy for Defeat: The Luftwaffe 1939–45* (Eagle Editions, Royston, 2000)

Obermaier, Ernst, *Die Ritterkreuzträger der Luftwaffe 1939–45, Band 1: Jagdflieger* (Verlag Dieter Hoffmann, Mainz, 1989)

Parry, Simon W, *Intruders over Britain: Luftwaffe Night Fighter Offensive 1940–45* (Air Research Publications, London, 1992)

Price, Alfred, *Battle Over the Reich* (Ian Allan, London, 1973)

——, *Focke-Wulf FW 190 At War* (Ian Allan, London, 1977)

——, *The Hardest Day* (Arms & Armour, London, 1988)

——, *Battle of Britain Day* (Greenhill, London, 1999)

Scutts, Jerry, *Messerschmitt Bf 109: The Operational Record* (Airlife, Shrewsbury, 1996)

Shores, Christopher; Cull, Brian & Malizia, Nicola, *Malta: The Hurricane Years 1940–41* (Grub Street, London, 1987)

Spick, Mike, *Luftwaffe Fighter Aces* (Greenhill, London, 1996)

Tolliver, Colonel Raymond F. & Constable, Trevor J., *Horrido! Fighter Aces of the Luftwaffe* (Arthur Barker, London, 1968)

Weal, John, *Bf 109 Aces of the Russian Front* (Osprey, Oxford, 2001)

——, *Bf 109 Defence of the Reich Aces* (Osprey, Oxford, 2006)

——, *Focke-Wulf FW 190 Aces of the Russian Front* (Osprey, Oxford, 1995)

——, *Jagdgeschwader 27 'Afrika'* (Osprey, Oxford, 2003)

——, *Jagdgeschwader 51 'Mölders'* (Osprey, Oxford, 2006)

Williams, David P., *Night Fighters: Hunters of the Reich* (Spellmount, Stroud, 2011)

Williamson, Gordon, *Knights of the Iron Cross* (Blandford, Poole, 1987)

Index of Luftwaffe Personnel

This index provides a list of Luftwaffe personnel who are included in this book. Note that spellings can vary slightly from other sources. Due to the numerous changes that occurred throughout the war, ranks and units have not been included.